# The Permaculture Garden

# The Permaculture Garden

## A PRACTICAL APPROACH TO YEAR-ROUND HARVESTS

HUW RICHARDS

# CONTENTS

# INTRODUCTION

## "Permaculture is about seeking opportunities."

This was the phrase that greeted me every time I sat down to work on this book. Living at the top of the manuscript, it helped set the tone for a good writing session. Its purpose was to distill my writing intent into five words, cultivating the appropriate mindset for creating the following pages, with the goal of helping you seek your own abundant growing opportunities from the text, photographs, and diagrams.

Since I discovered permaculture at the age of 12, thanks to the *Permaculture Magazine* sitting on a shelf in a random cabin in mid-Wales, it has set the tone for the world that I want to live in: a world that is in partnership with nature, where we know our neighbor, and where there is hope.

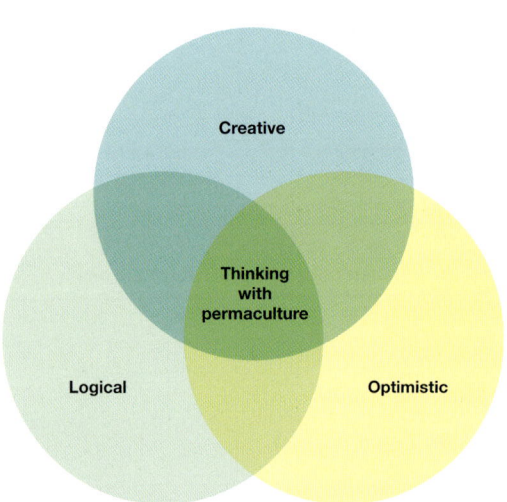

*The three styles of thinking involved in permaculture design and how they overlap.*

It's easy to feel that the world we find ourselves in offers little hope, particularly when watching the news or suffering the consequences of industrial farming. Modern agriculture is more a form of mining than farming, as it depletes our soils and aquatic life and ignores centuries of wisdom garnered from people working with their hands on the land. Driving a tractor for hours on end is not necessarily farming—it is just being a technician for patented tools designed by people who've probably never harvested their own potato or noted the first cuckoo of spring. The megacorporations are stuck in their own shrinking vacuum, trying to create ever more complex technological solutions to "save the world" that only drive us further away from the very thing we supposedly care about: nature. Technology is not the answer—it is often a distraction. It is a distraction from the hard truth that we have yet to accept on a societal level: We live in an epidemic of disconnection as a result of divorcing ourselves from nature.

Permaculture is about reconnecting and working hand in hand with nature. It is a design approach that is inspired by the patterns of the seasons, by the momentous diversity found within ecosystems, and by the indigenous knowledge of communities around the world.

What is permaculture to me? It is a harmonious blend of logical, creative, and optimistic thinking. Permaculture is the art of hope. And this starts in our gardens, where we get to create our own micro-ecosystem that provides an abundance of food for us and a home for nature. At the root of this abundance, quite literally, is the soil. The soil that we walk on is the foundation of our existence. It formed our past, it powers our present, and it shapes our future.

While the megacorporations continue to stray further away from what truly matters and continue to exacerbate the issues we are facing, the gardeners, growers, and regenerative farmers of this world know that shaping a future of hope starts with how we treat the soil.

The way we shape a positive future lies not in the technology we create but in the soil we regenerate. Permaculture offers the tools and opportunities to make this a reality.

## "Permaculture can make soil the solution. Or, as I like to put it, the 'soilution'."

I wrote this book to serve as a step toward creating a world that I want to live in, and I hope you can harvest inspiration from it as well as ideas and tips. But what I want you to know, speaking gardener to gardener, is that growing your own food is perhaps the greatest purpose someone can have. You get to nourish your mind, your body, your family, your neighbors, and the land around you.

Do not stop sowing, because to sow a seed is an act of love for our planet.

*This is my half-size permaculture allotment kitchen garden, nestled within my larger growing site.*

# What is permaculture?

# EXPLAINING PERMACULTURE

Permaculture, a portmanteau of "permanent" and "agriculture," is a responsible design approach inspired by natural patterns to create regenerative and resilient gardens, farms, and communities.

The Permaculture Association defines *permaculture* as "a design approach based on understandings of how nature works." Let's break this down to see how it applies to our gardens. There are three ethics of permaculture (see also p.28), which form the foundation of the permaculture philosophy and guide all its principles, practices, and designs:

- **Earth care**
- **People care**
- **Fair share**

There are also 12 design principles. Each serves a specific goal, contributing to the overarching aim of creating ecologically sound and economically viable systems. For more on these 12 design principles, see pages 14–25.

## WORKING WITH NATURE
These principles serve as a guide, a design toolkit, that can be applied to any situation from an edible balcony to a zero-waste city. They are not rules. Permaculture offers an environment of innovation and creativity, and these principles guide thought and action in harmony with natural systems rather than dictating specific practices. This ensures that permaculture remains a versatile, inclusive tool, applicable across environments and cultures and adaptable to the changing challenges and opportunities of our world.

A popular permaculture phrase is "whole systems thinking," a holistic design approach that looks at the interconnectedness of all elements within an ecosystem. In a permaculture kitchen garden, this starts with understanding the garden as being more than its plants. It's a complex web of relationships involving soil, water, plants, insects, animals, infrastructure, and even the gardener. Each element plays a crucial role in its health and productivity. The more you can bring the elements together, the more resilient and productive your garden becomes.

Permaculture is about working with nature; working against nature leads to more effort, expense, and damage. Understanding how to use nature to create efficient, productive food systems is the path to success. Permaculture is that path.

## PERMACULTURE, A BRIEF HISTORY

**1970s** Permaculture is founded by two Australians: Bill Mollison, a senior lecturer in Environmental Psychology, and David Holmgren, a student at the Tasmanian College of Advanced Education's Department of Environmental Design. They developed a garden together and published *Permaculture One* in 1978.

**1980s** Bill Mollison goes on international teaching tours, spreading the word. The global network began to form, including the UK's Permaculture Association.

**1990s** Permaculture sees an integration of other sustainable practices, such as agroforestry (tree-based agriculture systems), natural building, and renewable energy methods.

**2000s** Global awareness begins to grow of related techniques, such as Korean natural farming. The online permaculture community begins to form.

**2010s** Urban permaculture gains popularity, along with an emphasis on social permaculture, which focuses on building strong communities.

*A permaculture kitchen can offer great variety in an attractive, high-yielding space. This variety can include leaf shape and color, different habits and heights, and interesting structure (such as the leek flowers here).*

# WHY PERMACULTURE?

Permaculture is often seen as a hands-off approach—but all food systems need some degree of management. The goal of permaculture is smart rather than hard work. But, often you need both at the start of a project!

In general, the more time you put into a garden, the more yield you will achieve. This is important because perceived effort of different food systems often grossly misestimates actual effort. Food forest effort (see p.36) is often underestimated, whereas kitchen garden effort is often overestimated. Per square meter, a kitchen garden will require more of your time, but it will yield more than a food forest.

## ACHIEVING EFFICIENCY

The trick is to increase yield while reducing effort, and that is achieved through efficiency. This is where permaculture fits in. Applying permaculture principles, which will be covered in detail over the next few pages, helps you avoid unnecessary work while unveiling opportunities to increase production.

### Focus points for efficiency in a kitchen garden

**1. Save time** How can you reduce time without sacrificing yield quantity?
**2. Increase yield** How can you increase yield without requiring more time?

If you can combine the two focus points, you will reach peak efficiency.

## FINDING BALANCE

Peak efficiency in a kitchen garden is up to you to decide. To achieve it, every element of the garden needs to support the other elements in a balanced way. Peak efficiency is limited by time, seasonality, soil fertility, and knowledge. Time is often the gardener's greatest limiter, which is why designing a garden around your lifestyle is important to ensure there is balance.

The single most important step to having a working kitchen garden when time is limited is to plan carefully over the down season (winter) and be prepared to make quick decisions during the growing season. The 12 principles (see pp.14–25) will help in both long- and short-term decision-making.

Permaculture design is a skill, so the more time you invest in it, the better you will become. To master a skill, you must be persistent in practice. To best describe how permaculture design works, imagine being on a tennis court with your friend, playing a rally—only your friend is the garden, and the ball is information. This rally is not about winning points, it is about having a continuous flow of play. You and your garden share a continuous back-and-forth of information. This information can be run past the permaculture principles to help refine your technique, and the more you play, the better your technique becomes. The permaculture principles are versatile and applicable to a multitude of different situations.

Permaculture is a skill that requires both your head and your hands, the theory and the practice. These cannot be separated—they work as one. Next you will learn, starting with observation, all the principles you have at your disposal to design a highly efficient kitchen garden that nourishes your family and the land.

## SWEET-SPOT THEORY

The sweet-spot theory is a concept I have developed where every garden and its gardener have a point where an optimum point of synergy can be achieved. This is through a harmonious balance where the interplay of the two parties (garden and gardener) creates the most productive system for the least effort required. One step down from this optimum point would be the Goldilocks zone: the area in which the synergy naturally ebbs and flows due to the normal happenings of life but never deviates too far from the optimum. This deviation is usually avoided when strong goals are set.

*Permaculture creates not only bountiful growing spaces but beautiful ones, too. You can see purple sprouting broccoli (front), amaranth (right), chop suey greens behind with yellow flowers, and climbing beans (center), with dahlias and cosmos peppered throughout the planting.*

# THE 12 PRINCIPLES

The 12 principles exist to help you make informed decisions for long-term success when exploring designs and solutions. You do not need to use them all; instead, see them as points of query. The more you can combine, the more resilient and efficient the design becomes.

## 1 Observe and interact

"Observe and interact" is a foundational principle in permaculture that emphasizes the importance of close observation and active engagement with our environment.

Any aspect of permaculture design begins with observation. You need to take time to understand what is in front of you currently and see the specifics that add up to the whole. For example, if you have moved house and have a new garden that is currently a blank slate, you need to observe the specifics that are present: aspect, existing plants, water flow, and so on. By observing, you can work with nature to design your garden more effectively. For example, if you see a spot that gets a lot of sunlight, that's a great place to plant vegetables that need a lot of sun.

Sun position, average temperature, rainfall levels, land shape, and utility maps are all examples of useful data points for supporting design. Many free digital tools offer access to observed patterns that provide you with valuable information while saving you the time and effort of obtaining those results yourself (see p.280).

Permaculture design is often called "action learning," where there is a balance between observation and interaction. When an action is made, the results are observed, creating that back-and-forth of information I outlined on page 13 in the tennis example of mastering a skill.

### HUW'S TIP
Use the Google Maps timelapse function to see changes to your garden site since 1984. You could, for example, discover that there once was an outbuilding present, meaning that area of ground may have high soil compaction.

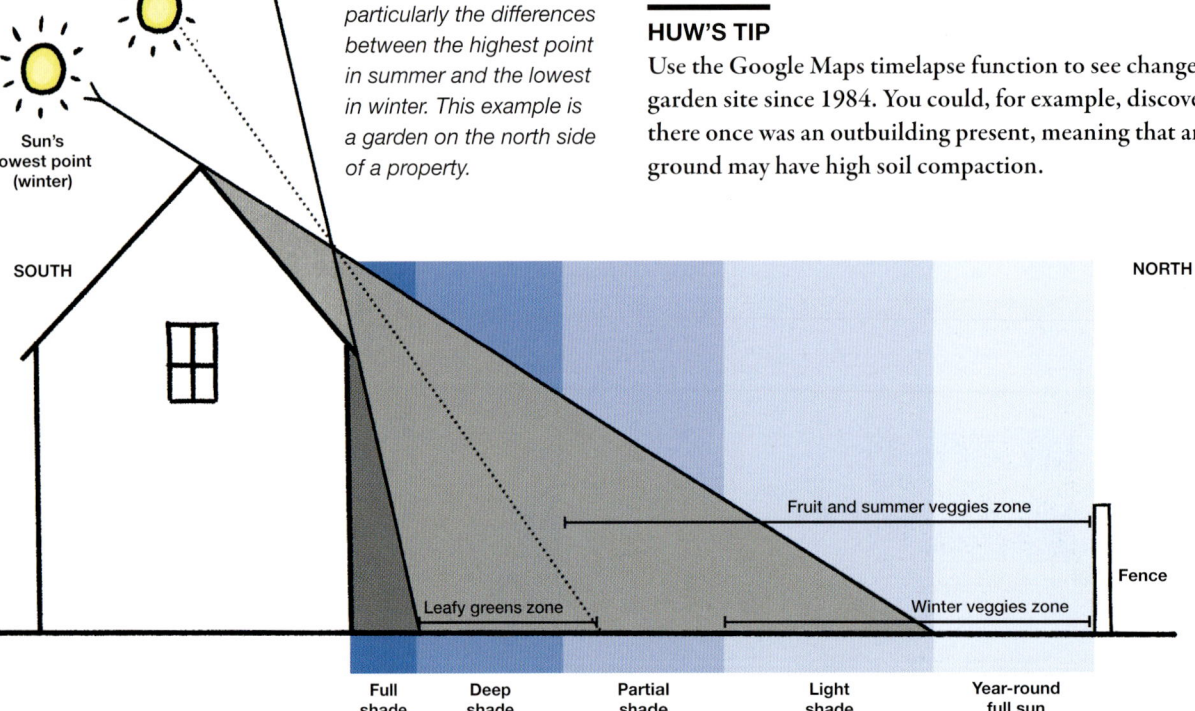

**Observing light levels**
*When creating a new garden, it's important to understand the light levels, particularly the differences between the highest point in summer and the lowest in winter. This example is a garden on the north side of a property.*

# ② Catch and store energy

Energy can be interpreted in many different ways. In its simplest form, a plant will catch and store energy from the sun. A rainwater-harvesting system on your roof is another example of catching and storing energy, water being that energy. When water is stored in a tank, it's like having a full battery that is ready to power any thirsty plants. It's similar with collecting leaves (catch) in the fall and composting them (store) to create leaf mold that can be added to your raised beds to retain moisture. Energy doesn't just have to come from nature. A passionate group of volunteers who feel invested in a project, perhaps a community garden, is another form of stored energy. Planting for beneficial insects allows you to capture the advantages of those insects (such as pollination), and if enough diversity is available, they will stay within your ecosystem. One of the key goals with permaculture is looking at how you maximize energy capture and storage in the landscape—or in this case, your garden. The more stored forms of energies, the more resilient the system becomes. In a kitchen garden, the key energies are sunlight, organic matter, nutrients, water, seeds, knowledge, and the gardener.

## Examples of storing energy

*There are many ways to store captured energy in a form in which it can be used in the future. The storage could be in a root vegetable or electricity stored in a battery. Here are a few examples of some of the "tanks" in a garden that store valuable energy that can be used at a later date.*

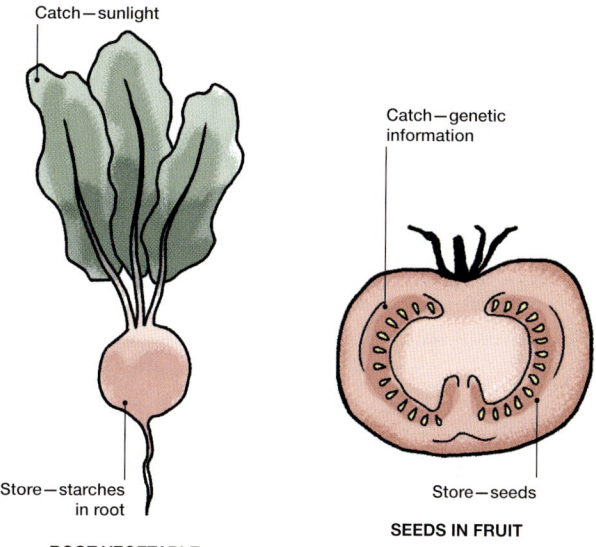

Catch—sunlight

Catch—genetic information

Store—starches in root

**ROOT VEGETABLE**

Store—seeds

**SEEDS IN FRUIT**

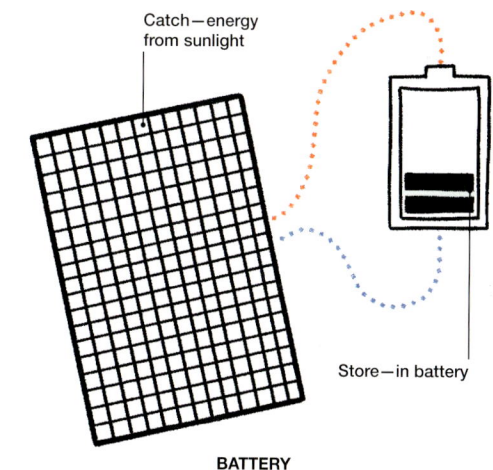

Catch—energy from sunlight

Store—in battery

**BATTERY**

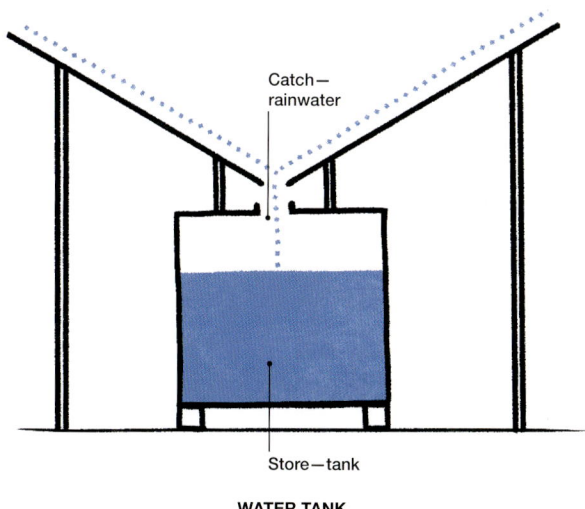

Catch—rainwater

Store—tank

**WATER TANK**

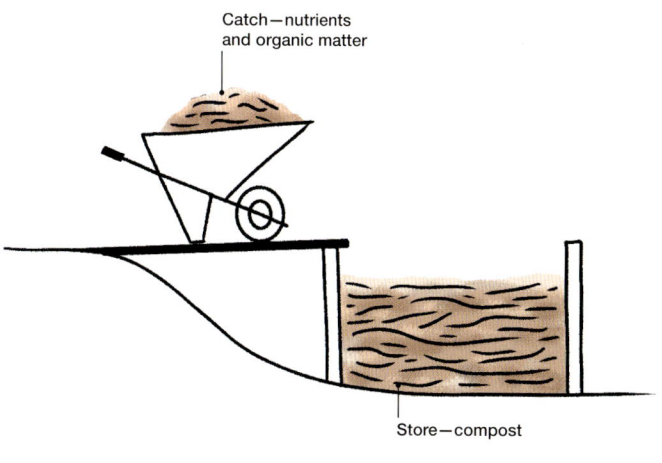

Catch—nutrients and organic matter

Store—compost

**COMPOST HEAP**

# ③ Obtain a yield

A *yield* is something that is produced, either as a primary goal or as a surplus. A primary goal would be growing tomato plants to produce tomatoes. The surplus yield is the organic material that can't be eaten but is "harvested" to place on the compost to turn into nutrients and organic matter for future crops. Arguably, the core goal of any kitchen garden is to obtain a yield. In agroforestry, which focuses on permaculture-inspired tree-based agriculture systems, there are five primary yields, also known as the five F's (even though only one starts with an F sound):

**1. Food** For people
**2. Fodder** Food for livestock
**3. Fuel** In the form of wood
**4. Fiber** For clothes and textiles
**5. Pharmaceutical** For natural medicine (for humans and livestock)

A wonderful quote by Bill Mollison helps put you, the designer, in a mindset of pure possibility—just swap the word *system* for *garden*: "The yield of a system is theoretically unlimited, or limited only by the information and imagination of the designer." This idea is vital because the underlying message is the importance of knowledge, which is something that only increases in time. The more knowledge you have, the more yield can be achieved.

### HUW'S TIP
There is often crossover between principles in permaculture. For example, seeds can be seen as both a form of stored energy and as a yield. As I've mentioned before, and to really drill it in, the more principles you can layer, the more resilient and productive your garden becomes.

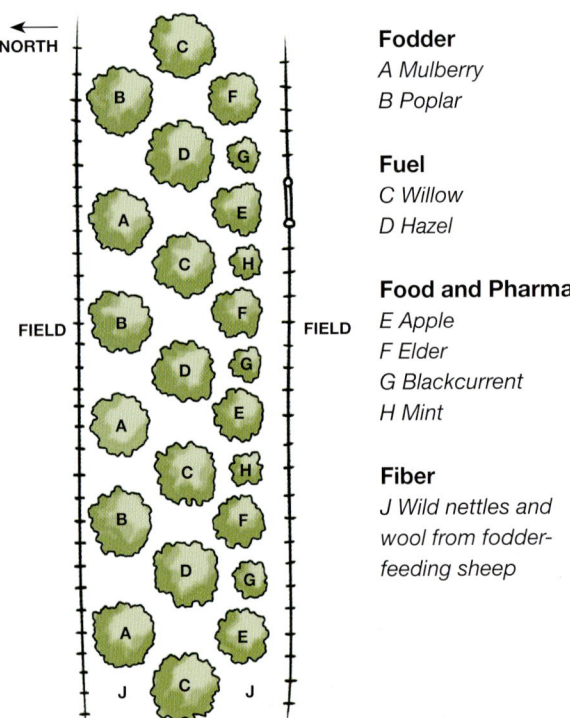

**Fodder**
*A Mulberry*
*B Poplar*

**Fuel**
*C Willow*
*D Hazel*

**Food and Pharma**
*E Apple*
*F Elder*
*G Blackcurrent*
*H Mint*

**Fiber**
*J Wild nettles and wool from fodder-feeding sheep*

### Yields from a linear forest garden
*This image shows a conceptual planting plan I developed for a linear food forest between two field boundaries. The selected plants all contribute toward the five primary yields that can be obtained from a forest garden.*

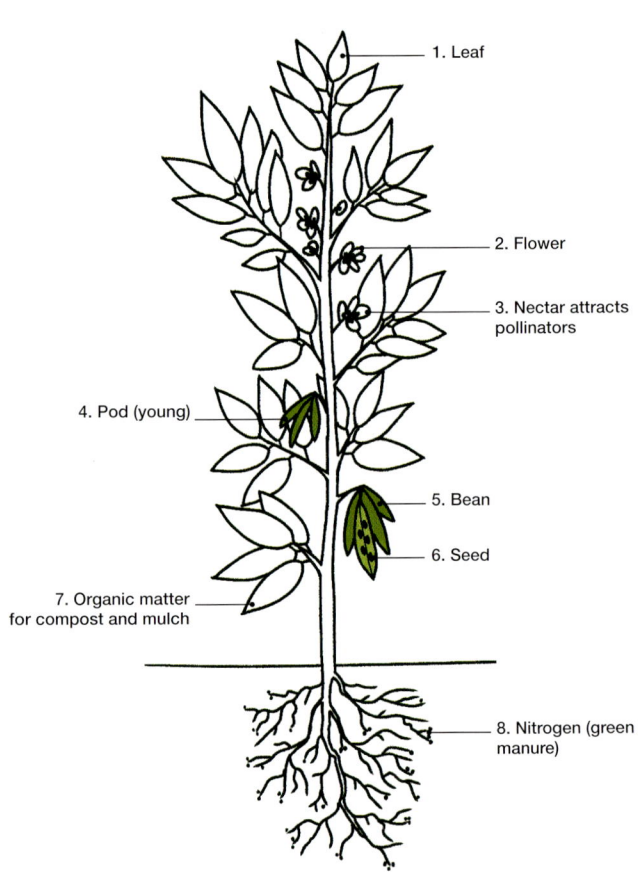

### Eight yields of a field bean
*The humble fava bean (broad beans and field beans) provides eight primary yields for a garden and gardener. In permaculture, one of the core skills is identifying every yield that a single plant or component can offer. This is closely related to the supporting principle of stacking functions discussed on page 27.*

**Making informed decisions**

*This is my decision-making framework when it comes to evaluating progress within my garden.*

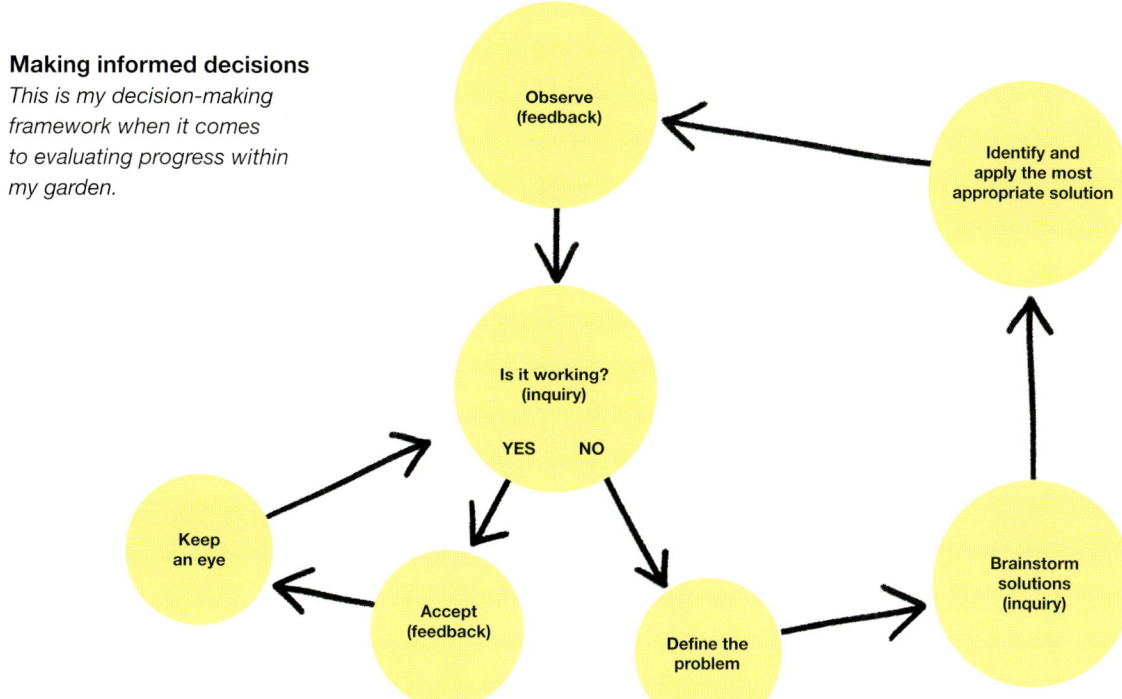

 **Apply self-regulation and accept feedback**

Self-regulation is about controlling our behavior, emotions, and thoughts in the pursuit of achieving long-term goals.

Often as gardeners, we have an exciting idea, and we explore that idea without fully considering less exciting potential side effects. Excitement is fantastic, but informed decisions are next to impossible when there is much emotion involved because bigger emotions are usually centered around the immediate and disregard the long-term implications.

Not everything you try in your garden will work perfectly the first time, which can be frustrating, but you learn far more from failure than you do from success. In permaculture, failure is still a step forward, contributing to your growing knowledge. If continuous failure occurs, it is a sign that perhaps it is worth taking a new approach—otherwise, there is a danger of falling prey to the "princess and the pea" effect where the focus is on addressing the symptom, not the cause.

Every spring, I used to experience major vole damage of my module seedlings. Peas were particularly susceptible, and after testing many different solutions, I decided rather than continuously fighting the voles, why not just prevent them outright by hanging gutters of sown peas from the polytunnel ceiling? Now, the majority of my module trays are placed on suspended shelves to keep them completely free from voles.

One of the best sources of feedback is other people. If you are growing crops for your family and find that, sadly, you are the only person who loves turnips, next year, you would grow fewer so you could provide an alternative, more valued yield.

*The simple act of hanging a wire mesh shelf in a polytunnel has eradicated all my vermin issues when it comes to raising healthy seedlings year round.*

**Plants as a resource**

*Here are the four key renewable plants I use for building fertility in my garden.*

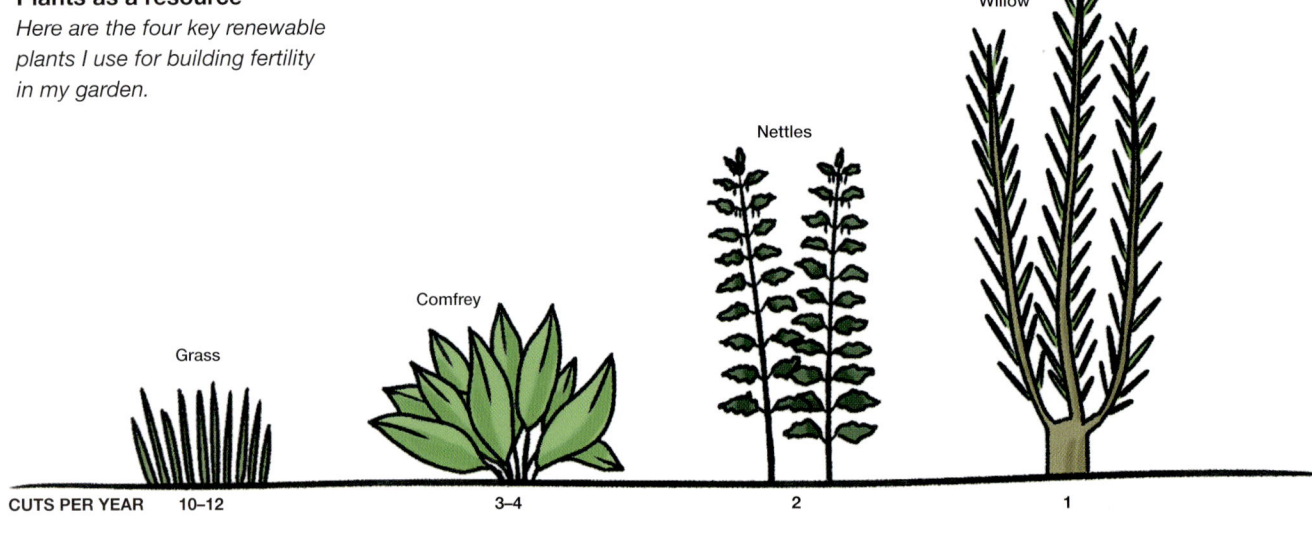

Willow

Nettles

Comfrey

Grass

| CUTS PER YEAR | 10–12 | 3–4 | 2 | 1 |

# Use and value renewable resources and services

A garden should make the most of the renewable resources and services available. Permaculture is about working in harmony with nature, after all, so you want to make the most of what is available to you.

Identify all the renewable resources in your garden and community and use this knowledge to help guide your approach. Grass is a renewable resource that you may have access to; you cut it, and it will grow back. Cut grass is a resource that can be used for mulching, making a liquid feed, and composting. If you have access to lots of grass, it makes sense to find as many ways as possible to use it in your garden. Other examples of renewable resources include wood chips from coppice; perennial leaves, such as comfrey; wool from sheep; sunlight; seaweed; and perennials.

An important consideration is the security of your sources—perhaps you have access to your own supply of grass clippings, but all your leaves come from a neighbor. Never place too much reliance on one single renewable resource that you don't directly have access to.

It's okay to use nonrenewable resources to establish a permaculture design if the long-term benefits outweigh the short-term negatives—so if you need a mini-digger to create a large wildlife pond, don't feel guilty! Renewable services cover natural processes and systems that can be used to benefit the garden. These services include the likes of pollinators, predators, nitrogen fixation, natural water filtration, and self-seeding crops.

**HUW'S TIP**

When designing a garden, enhance the positive impact of this principle by integrating it with the principles catch and store energy (see p.15) and produce no waste (see opposite).

*Comfrey is one of the most important renewable resources for a permaculture garden. Here, I'm making liquid concentrate (see pp.272–273).*

# ⑥ Produce no waste

Waste is a human construct. There is no waste in nature, only a constant flow of nutrients presented in different forms. As gardeners, we have the skill of being able to place a value on many types of waste that exist in modern society.

In some cases, waste can be treated as a renewable resource if there is a constant supply. Vegetable scraps from a restaurant, used coffee grounds from a café, pallets from the shopping center, and cardboard from the bike shop are all renewable

waste resources I have access to, provided those businesses keep trading. Some community growing projects take local waste to the next level by setting up a community compost project. They may have a more formal setup for collecting food and garden waste to produce compost that the community can access or to grow food that is then shared with the community in return.

Composting edible food is not a waste: The nutrients in the food are recycled back into the growing process to help grow future crops. There are ways to add value to waste, such as a chicken composting setup (see pp.78–79). Here, all surplus plant material is fed to chickens, which add their fertility (manure) and yield nutritious eggs. The end product of this waste plant material is still compost, but that "waste" has served more than one function.

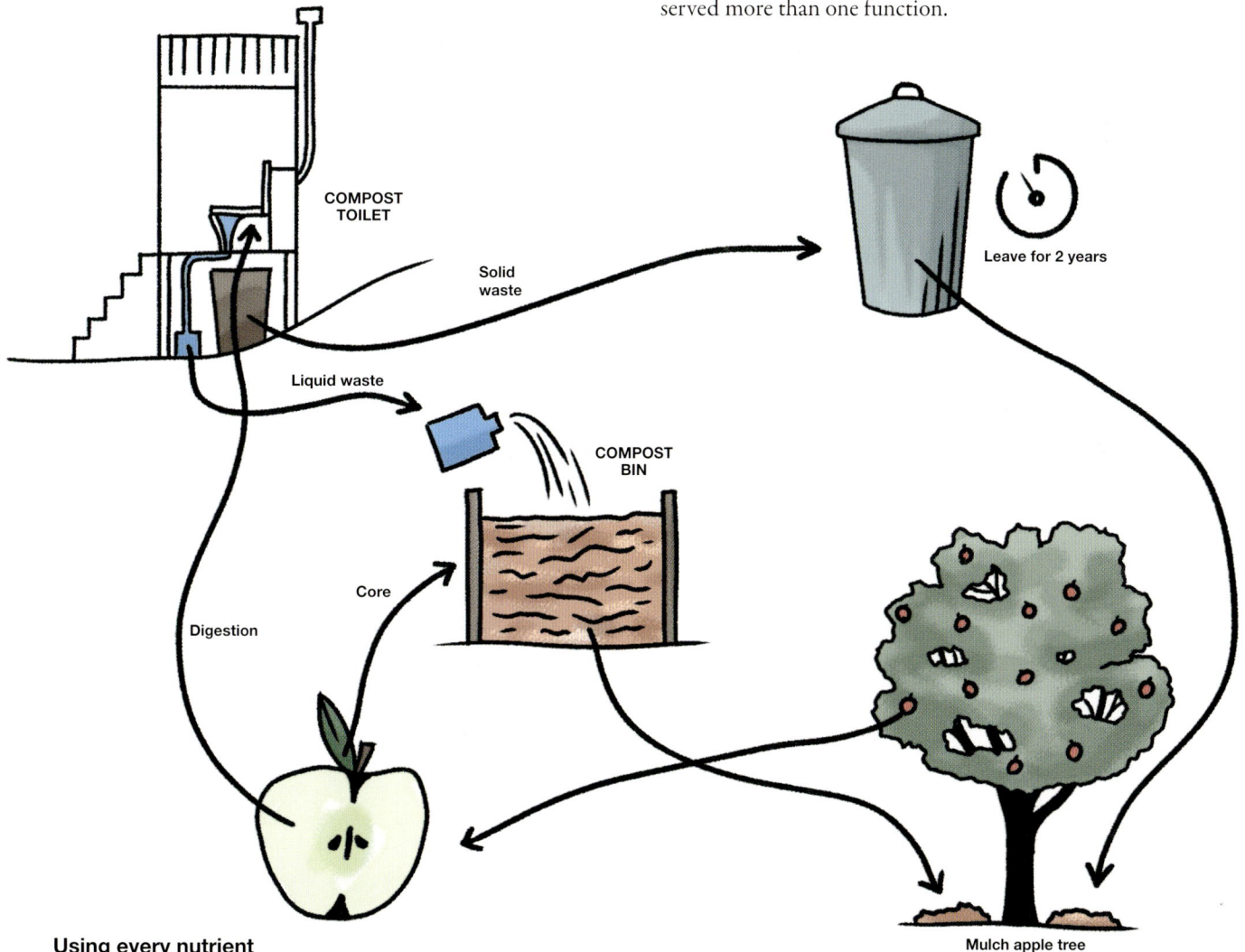

COMPOST TOILET

Solid waste

Liquid waste

COMPOST BIN

Core

Digestion

Leave for 2 years

Mulch apple tree

**Using every nutrient**
*This is an example flow of nutrients within a closed-loop cycle where every type of "waste" serves as an opportunity for building fertility.*

# ⑦ Design from pattern to details

Permaculture design advocates for looking at the big picture first, understanding all the patterns, and then working out the details by using that knowledge. The most influential pattern for planning a temperate kitchen garden is the four seasons. The seasons dictate the rough boundaries in which you get to play.

*This dahlia ('Night Silence') is just one example of the wonders of shape patterns within nature.*

I say *rough* because there are plenty of clever ways to gently manipulate seasons, such as by using hot beds and polytunnels.

One of the best tools for big-picture thinking is P. A. Yeomans' scale of permanence (see pp.40–41). The scale is the most accessible way to gain a holistic understanding of your site and is a great starting point for any garden design.

There are shape patterns everywhere in nature, such as waves, spirals, edges, webs, and branches. Each pattern can offer fascinating design points (see pp.38–39). A branch pattern is nature's efficient way of moving energy (sap of a tree, blood in our veins, and water on land). A permaculture garden may have a branching pathway network starting from the most used path (widest) to the least (narrowest).

Zoning (see pp.42–43) is another example of using patterns to take into account human energy to ensure a garden is as energy-efficient as possible. In simple terms, it involves putting the most intensive areas closest to the house and the least intensive farthest away.

The more you look, the more patterns can be found, from the lifecycle of a tomato plant to the layering habit of a strawberry plant. Pattern awareness and understanding are integral to permaculture design and decision-making.

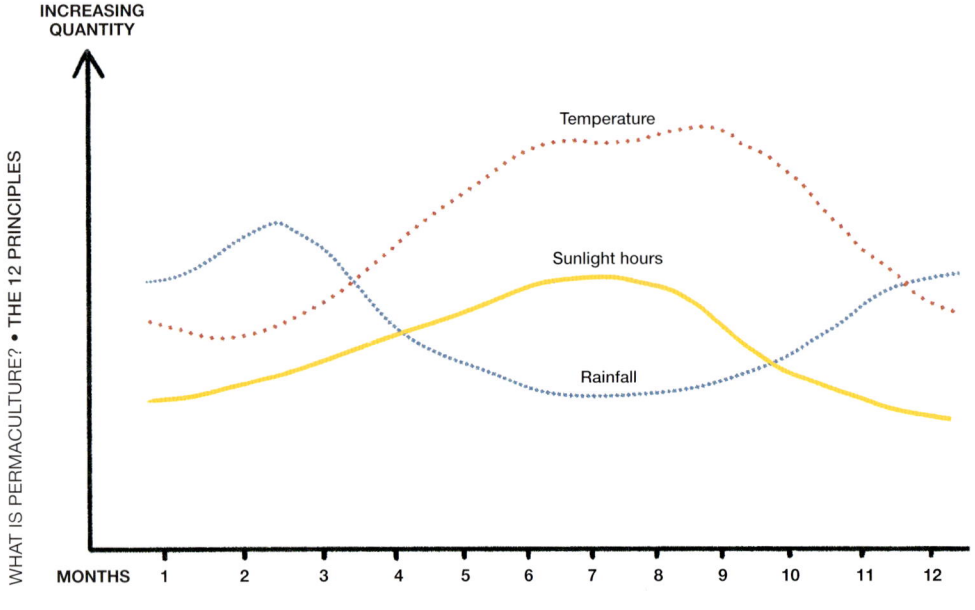

INCREASING QUANTITY

Temperature

Sunlight hours

Rainfall

MONTHS  1  2  3  4  5  6  7  8  9  10  11  12

**Starting from patterns**
*The average annual cycles of sunlight hours, temperature, and rainfall are the key metrics (pattern) that gardeners work with to create a plan (detail).*

**Block planting**
*Planting in blocks keeps plants separate.*

**Minimal polyculture**
*In this method, the plants are separated into smaller blocks.*

**Maximum polyculture**
*Here, crops are mixed together rather than in one area only. The amount of each crop is the same in each method, but those grown in polyculture are more resilient.*

 # Integrate rather than segregate

Nature is a complex web (pattern!) of relationships and interactions. More accurately, I like to think of nature as a limitless multidimensional web of Venn diagrams. You can picture it as human society, starting with individuals who make up families, which make up communities, which make up towns, which make up countries, which make up continents, and finally, make the world's society. Every single element, no matter how big or small, forms part of the whole and has near-infinite relationships, both subtle and strong.

But what does this all mean for a kitchen garden? In its simplest form, it is understanding that all the individual parts form a whole. The polytunnel, the beds, the rainwater harvesting system, the pathways, and the boundaries are all pieces of the same puzzle. Your task is to link these elements as best as possible to create an efficient garden.

My favorite implementation of integrate rather than segregate is the contrast between polyculture and monoculture. In a monoculture system, you have one (mono) crop growing in a large area, separated from other crops. Monocultures are at high risk of total crop failure from weather, pests, and diseases. A polyculture is a resilient system where you integrate many (poly) crops in one area. If one crop fails, the others can still provide. Polyculture is a design approach derived from observing the success of biodiversity in nature (see pp.228–255).

# ⑨ Use small and slow solutions

Many technologies and systems end up causing many more problems than they were originally intended to fix. Industrial agriculture is a perfect example. Yes, it meant that we could suddenly increase yield, but at what cost to the planet and, arguably, to human health? Yield in industrial agriculture is paid by weight, not by nutritional quality. Western society has an increasing problem with hidden hunger: malnourishment from eating the wrong kinds of food that are calorie-dense and nutritionally lacking.

Part of the problem is the mass global scale of our food system. Permaculture advocates for small and local solutions. Permaculture designs are considered, patient, informed, and, perhaps most crucially, willing to address mistakes. It's much easier to make a small adjustment than to do an entire redesign. When creating a garden, start slowly and build gradually. This is especially important when learning a new skill. If gardening is new to you, start with making a compost bin, followed by assembling a handful of beds, and see how the first season goes. This will help give you an idea of how much you can manage. Start small, make sure it can be kept in control, and then expand as you see fit.

**HUW'S TIP**

If you ever feel overwhelmed with too much to do, you can hibernate beds by growing a cover crop or covering beds with cardboard to prevent them from getting out of control.

*A watering can is an example of a small solution; after transplanting a few seedlings, it's simpler to use a watering can than to reel out the hose.*

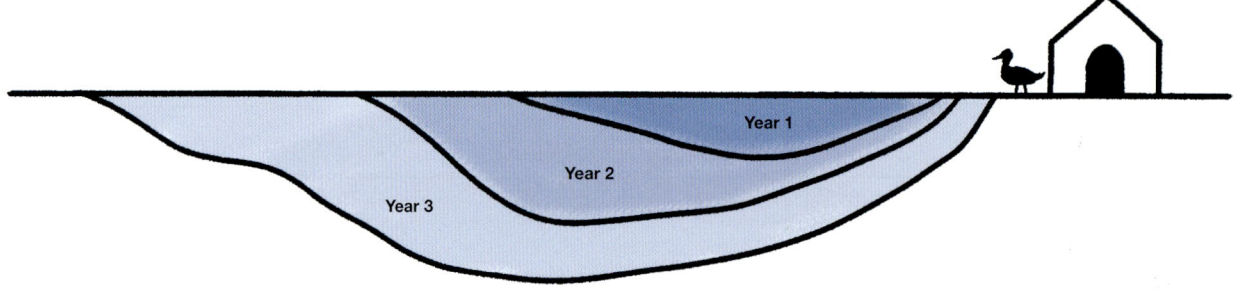

**Building gradually**
*A large project can be broken down into smaller, more manageable steps. Here, in a garden with no access for a digger, a duck pond is enlarged by digging manually, a little each year.*

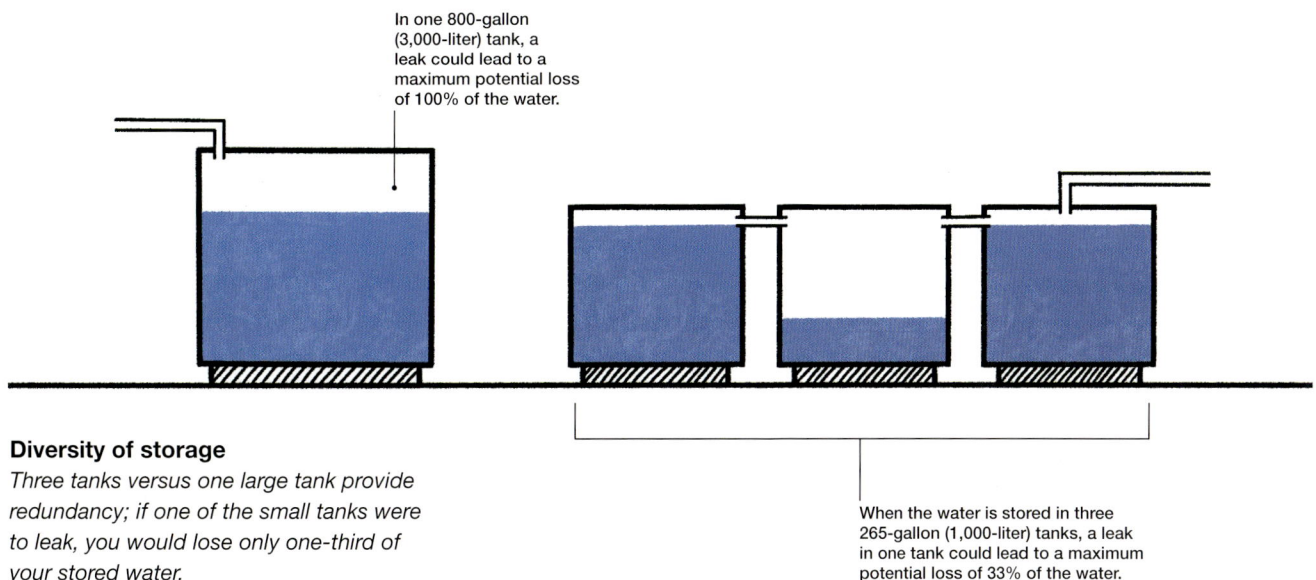

In one 800-gallon (3,000-liter) tank, a leak could lead to a maximum potential loss of 100% of the water.

**Diversity of storage**
*Three tanks versus one large tank provide redundancy; if one of the small tanks were to leak, you would lose only one-third of your stored water.*

When the water is stored in three 265-gallon (1,000-liter) tanks, a leak in one tank could lead to a maximum potential loss of 33% of the water.

## (10) Use and value diversity

One of the best descriptions I have heard of this principle is that it acts as an insurance policy. Polyculture is a perfect example of using and valuing diversity (see pp.228–255), but there are other garden-specific examples. One is to have a diversity of water storage: If one tank leaks, you don't lose your entire "stored battery" of water "energy." Another is to have a few different arborists who can drop off wood chips, so if one no longer can, you still have sources.

Growing a range of varieties of the same crop yields a diversity of flavors and characteristics. Tomatoes are a perfect example of this: There are hundreds of varieties, each offering something a little different in terms of flavor, shape, color, disease resistance, harvest timing, and so on (see p.205). Diversity is one of the core principles when recruiting an

army of beneficial insects to the garden. You need a diversity of habitats, plants, and food sources to encourage the beneficial insects to stay (see pp.260–261).

Most importantly, permaculture offers the gardener a diversity of different growing techniques to best suit their context. Strictly following only one style of gardening, such as no dig (see p.50), will stifle the creativity and out-of-the-box thinking that permaculture so passionately promotes and often results in missed opportunities or unnecessary effort or expense. My minimal disturbance gardening approach (see pp.51–53) is designed to address this as simply as possible.

## "Don't put all your eggs in one basket."

# Use edges and value the marginal

Edges, where two ecosystems meet, such as a forest and a field, are often richer in species, and more productive, than the individual ecosystems. In ecology, this highly diverse zone is known as the *ecotone*. Edges offer great opportunities for permaculture kitchen gardens: vertical growing, maximizing space by layering plant heights, natural windbreaks, microclimates, habitat for beneficial insects, and the efficient movement of energy and resources. With careful planning, the more edges you can incorporate in your garden, the more productive and resilient it becomes. By designing your garden to include a variety of edge environments, you create a rich patchwork of microclimates and microhabitats. This supports a wider range of planting opportunities and fosters robust ecosystems that can better withstand pests and diseases.

Valuing the marginal is about taking notice of ideas or practices that are not mainstream and may offer innovative solutions to problems. The majority of designs and concepts I create for my kitchen garden focus on integrating as many functions as possible and are born from a fusion of both mainstream and marginal methods and practices. Valuing the marginal extends to community, too, ensuring every voice is heard and promoting open-mindedness and tolerance. Fostering an environment where conversation can be free of judgment and allow diversity of thought is essential for a functioning society. One of my favorite sayings is that we were given two ears and one mouth for a reason—and permaculture is all about active listening and creating solutions together that are both respectful and understanding.

## Making the most of the edges

*This planting along contour lines of two fields on either side of a river is an example of maximizing the "edge" and increasing the ecotone, resulting in greater biodiversity and microclimates to work with, not to mention additional shelter from the elements.*

Each black line parallel to the river represents a different edge habitat created

Land beside the river may flood, so it is planted with trees and shrubs, which protect the bank and decrease the risk of flooding

Cereals

SOUTH

NORTH

Wild area

Grazing pasture

Oak

Willow coppice

River

Poplar

Hazel coppice

Fruit trees

# Creatively use and respond to change

This principle focuses on establishing long-term resilience by embracing current challenges and anticipating future changes. These could be changes in society, fluctuation in prices, alteration in weather patterns, or even personal life changes. Changes that are out of our control are inevitable, and it is how we respond to change that ensures resilience. Applying self-regulation and accepting feedback is the first step, because acknowledging change is always better than avoiding it. Then, if a response is required, apply small and slow solutions to adapt to the change in a sustainable way.

In a kitchen garden, understanding each season in detail allows us to harness the natural changes to make sure we know the most productive use of our energy at a given point in time.

Always endeavor to view change through the lens of opportunity. Change often sparks outcomes that improve what already existed. This mindset is essential not only for gardening but for any part of life.

## HUW'S TIP
Collaborating with a group/community of like-minded individuals who share similar goals is a high-impact method of creating solutions for responding to change. This is due to the diversity of experience and knowledge each individual offers (which links to the use and value diversity principle, p.23).

### Being flexible when things change
*After a huge increase in the price of compost, this is my response over a two-year period to producing fertility while removing the need to buy compost.*

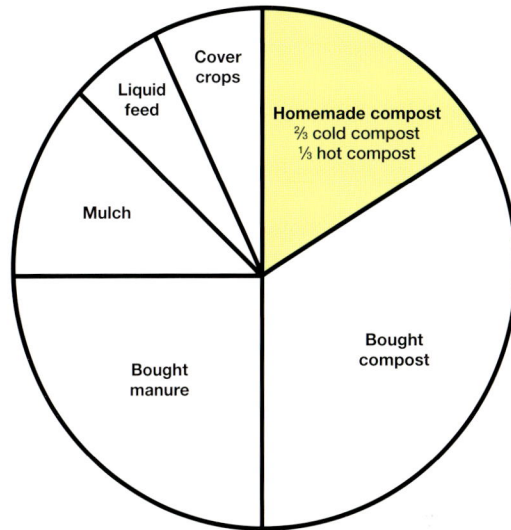

**2022 FERTILITY-BUILDING INPUTS**

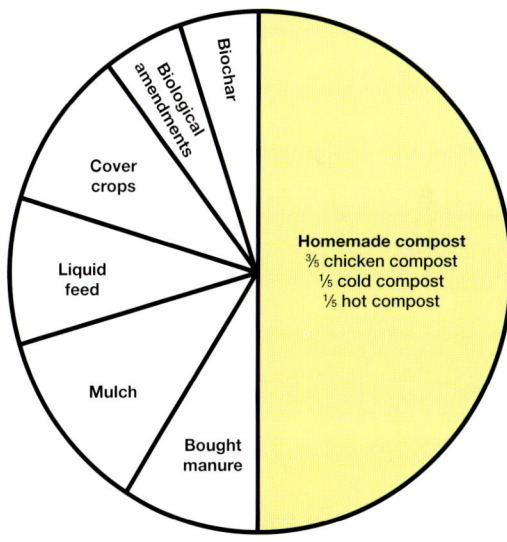

**2024 FERTILITY-BUILDING INPUTS**

*Increasing the use of chicken compost (see pp.78–79) has been the most significant contribution to reducing my reliance on bought compost.*

# BUILDING ON THE PRINCIPLES

Two more suggestions encourage you to think about your garden methods and to get creative in your planning and efficiency. The first is to spark ideas by thinking "What if?" when designing your garden; the second is to stack functions within the garden to aid productivity.

## WHAT IF?

This technique, inspired by Rob Hopkins's philosophy in his book *From What Is to What If?*, harnesses the power of imagination to support all aspects of permaculture design. When coming up with solutions or ideas, run them through a "what if?" brainstorm. Picture it as playing devil's advocate. The goal is to cover as many different perspectives as possible before undertaking the physical change in order to increase long-term success and reduce any oversights.

**Five key benefits of using "what if?"**
**1. No garden consequence** It allows you to creatively explore ideas and designs without doing the physical work or making potential mistakes.
**2. Avoids bias toward familiar solutions** It can prevent us from becoming too attached to our first idea or solution, encouraging us to explore alternatives.
**3. Risk management** "What if?" is essential in risk assessment and allows you to think through and minimize problems as much as possible.
**4. Encourages critical thinking** It enables you to form a strategy based on the long term, taking into account your current context, and strategize for various outcomes or evolving needs from the garden.
**5. Decision validation** If multiple "what if?" scenarios are explored and the decision still seems sound, it can reinforce confidence in that choice.

Here are some good starting points: What if I don't buy compost this year? What if I am growing too many greens? What if I had only half the time to garden each week? What if there is no rain in the spring? What if I could make some income from my garden?

### HUW'S TIP
"What if?" can be used in any situation and in any location. Bored during your commute? Standing in line for coffee? Waiting for the in-laws to leave? Brighten your mood by focusing on your exciting permaculture garden ideas instead.

## NATIVE VS NON-NATIVE

Native plants are those of indigenous origin to a geographical area. Some purists believe that one should never include non-native crops in a garden, but (in the spirit and open-mindedness of the "what if?" question), if I took that approach, I would have to stop growing Jerusalem artichokes, apples, tomatoes, sweet corn, cucumbers, beets, onions, garlic, and potatoes, to name a few.

There are so many crops and varieties that offer characteristics and benefits that native plants may not provide, which is why I have no problem growing crops that originated from other geographical regions. Provided that a crop is noninvasive and can be grown successfully with little additional effort, it is welcomed in a permaculture kitchen garden. This range not only widens the flavor and nutritional palette of a garden but also increases its diversity and resilience.

Non-native perennials pose a slightly greater challenge, as unlike annuals, which mostly grow during the frost-free period, perennials have to weather every season for years. Using plant hardiness ratings in relation to your hardiness zone (see resources, pp.32–33) is the best way to check whether a plant is suitable and will thrive, as well as speaking to local gardeners. For more extreme climates, growing carefully selected perennials in a polytunnel can create incredible results.

## STACKING FUNCTIONS

Looking beyond the single utility of an element, stacking functions is a theme in permaculture. For example, a polytunnel is not just there to help grow warm weather crops in summer. It helps you start seedlings earlier in the season, acts as a garden office, provides a dry area for storage, enables you to enjoy winter salads, provides shelter from wind, can house chickens over winter, and isolates crops for seed saving, among many other additional benefits.

Stacking functions enhances the principle of integrate rather than segregate (see p.21) and mirrors the ethos of mimicking natural ecosystems, where everything is interconnected and multifunctional. Integrate rather than segregate creates breadth, and stacking functions creates depth. I believe that permaculture design can be distilled down to these two methods of thinking.

### The object exercise

The object exercise is one of my favorite ways of practicing creative/lateral thinking about different functions:
1. Find a random object in your house (a book, envelope, doorstop, pillow, etc.).
2. Set a timer for 2 minutes.
3. In those 2 minutes, use your experience and out-of-the box thinking to list as many uses as possible for this object.
4. Review your list and then leave it for at least a day.
5. Repeat steps 1–3 to see what your subconscious has come up with in the meantime.

You can practice this exercise whenever. Feel free to also run the exercise by using elements within your garden: the polytunnel, grass clippings, a pair of pruners. The more you practice, the more easily you will be able to spot opportunities to increase the efficiency of your garden.

This is an example of what I came up with for a cardboard box:

### Garden ideas for using cardboard
1. Brown material for the compost bin
2. Base layer for starting a no-dig bed
3. Covering empty beds over winter
4. Temporary potting bench
5. Tear up to use for starting a fire
6. Place over tender plants to protect from light frosts
7. Have a few layers of cardboard and use as knee pads
8. Overnight slug trap (by placing on the soil)
9. Sketch rough garden plans on
10. Temporary harvest basket

### Other ideas for using cardboard
1. Tear piece to stabilize a wobbly chair
2. Cut into placemats
3. Attach to shed walls to insulate
4. Cut up and glue together to build models
5. Use a piece to fan a breeze in my face during hot weather
6. Place over a bowl of food to stop flies
7. Fold up and wedge a door open
8. Cut into shapes and paint for decorations
9. Sheets for a flower press
10. Draw on to make your own chess board

*One use for cardboard: as a weed suppressant over the winter months.*

# GOALS

A goal is a desired result, and it acts as a filter to help with decision-making: does action X help achieve goal Y? A gardener can have numerous types of goals to guide them towards achieving what they want from their space.

## FOUNDATIONAL GOALS

What are the goals of a permaculture kitchen garden? I have shared the 12 principles of permaculture (see pp.14–25); these are underpinned by three core ethics that I mentioned at the start of this chapter, which form the foundational goals for any permaculture projects.

- **Earth care** To look after and positively contribute to the soil and local ecosystem
- **People care** To nourish people and the community
- **Fair share** To share knowledge and surplus resources with others

## FINITE AND INFINITE GOALS

These are two categories of personal goals you can set for your garden. Finite goals are objectives that are clearly defined, quantifiable, and have a specific timeframe. They usually focus on achievable targets that can be accomplished within a set duration. For example:

- Aim to harvest 800lb (365kg) of food in the next 12 months.
- Grow five new crops this season that I've never tried before to test their characteristics.
- Produce enough homemade compost to mulch 80 percent of my raised beds in autumn.

Infinite goals, however, are ongoing. They are not constrained by time limits or distinct objectives, rather they focus on setting behaviors and habits that lead to compounding long-term success, such as:

- Eat something from the garden daily.
- For the garden to be my escape from this busy world.
- Prioritize growing the tastiest crops I possibly can.

The more detailed your goals are, the more likely you are to understand them. Set your goals, follow their steps, and conduct an annual review at the end of the growing season to see how close you were to achieving them. If you wish you can make changes or additions for the next year.

## THE INVERSE GOAL

Another useful thought exercise to help bring clarity to ideas and sketch out a journey to a goal is to create an inverse goal. This is where you think about how you would achieve the opposite of the solution you are trying to create. By understanding what not to do, you can more clearly define what should be done to achieve the goal, thus sharpening your focus and objectives. Setting an inverse goal also opens the space for lateral thinking: by considering the inverse of your desired outcome, you might uncover unconventional approaches or solutions that you wouldn't have otherwise considered. Value the marginal!

**Goal** I want a garden that brings me joy every time I visit.

**Inverse goal** I want my garden to be a constant source of dread every time I even think of it.

To achieve the inverse goal I need to:

- Make sure that the garden is messy and disorganized.
- Grow plants and crops that I don't care much about.
- Have no plan or vision to follow so I have no clue where I am heading.
- Produce terrible yields that make me question if it's worth it.
- Have no diversity so everything is the same and boring.

From this exercise we can decipher what we should actually do to have a garden that brings joy with every visit:

*Measuring the total yield of your garden is a fun way to track impact, from gluts (cucumbers, above) to a quick harvest for dinner. Remember that small harvests little-and-often add up quickly, too.*

- Ensure the garden is easy to maintain.
- Grow plants and crops that excite me.
- Have a strong understanding behind why I garden and what I want from it.
- Ensure that there is always at least something to harvest for every visit.
- Create little corners of interest, have different growing areas, and add pops of color and texture throughout.

# Patterns
# and design

---

# CLIMATE

The first pattern to understand when it comes to creating a garden is the climate—the weather conditions of a specific area over a long period. It has the greatest influence on what will (and won't) thrive in your garden.

## TEMPERATE CLIMATE

Climate works like a spectrum between two extremes: temperatures and rainfall level. The temperate climate, which experiences distinct differences in all four seasons, sits between the subpolar and subtropical regions of Earth in both the northern and southern hemispheres. The simplified world map here highlights the temperate regions of our planet. I have written this book for this zone, and while there are warmer and cooler areas within the temperate zone, much of the information can be easily adapted.

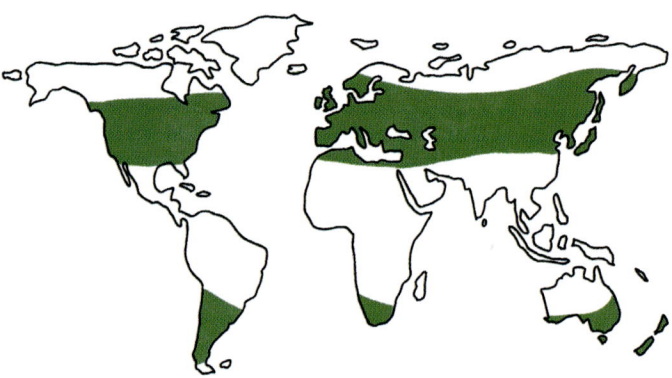

**World map of temperate climates**
*Areas in green represent temperate zones.*

## TEMPERATURES: HARDINESS ZONES

Hardiness zones are a very useful pattern for adding further detail to understand your climate. Each zone is defined by the lowest average annual extreme temperature—the lower the zone number, the colder the winter. Some plants are only hardy down to a specific temperature, and any colder temperatures will severely damage or kill the plant. This book is primarily geared toward zones 6–9, covering the

whole of the UK and much of the USA, and much of the information can be adapted for even colder zones. This table shows the most relevant hardiness zones as defined by the US Department of Agriculture (USDA).

### Minimum temperature

| Zone | From | To |
| --- | --- | --- |
| 4 | -30°F (-35°C) | -20°F (-29°C) |
| 5 | -20°F (-29°C) | -10°F (-23°C) |
| 6 | -10°F (-23°C) | 0°F (-18°C) |
| 7 | 0°F (-18°C) | 10°F (-12°C) |
| 8 | 10°F (-12°C) | 20°F (-7°C) |
| 9 | 20°F (-7°C) | 30°F (-1°C) |
| 10 | 30°F (-1°C) | 40°F (4°C) |

### The issue with hardiness zones

An easy rule of thumb is that hardiness zones are generally for perennials, while frost dates (see opposite) are for annuals. For growing annual crops, with the exception of overwintering, a hardiness zone makes no difference to what can be grown over summer. For example, I am in zone 8, but with my cool summers, it means growing tomatoes outside doesn't always succeed, but I know of gardeners in zone 5 who have warmer, brighter summers and grow incredible tomato crops outdoors every year.

### Frost dates

The dates of your last frost date in spring and first frost date in fall define the growing window. There are many useful online resources that share average last and first frost dates for specific regions; I encourage you to use these to find your average window. Remember, we are working with nature, so I like to put in a two-week buffer zone to work around; this is explained in detail on page 183.

**Altitude**

The higher the altitude, the cooler the temperature. In general, for every 3,300ft (1,000m) above sea level, the temperature drops by about 11.7°F (6.5°C). This means that a village in a valley could be in zone 7, but a farm on the mountainside above the village could be in zone 6. To see what is possible in a high-altitude environment, look at the incredible work by Sepp Holzer, who farms at 4,900ft (1,500m) above sea level in the Austrian Alps.

## RAINFALL LEVELS

The rainfall patterns of each month are an important consideration for setting up water storage as well as knowing what is the best watering infrastructure for your garden.

I personally think that mulching is the best investment for this, but various hoses and microdrip systems will be very useful, especially for undercover growing.

## LOCAL KNOWLEDGE

Using the general pieces of climatic information discussed here will help create a strong foundation on which to start designing a permaculture garden, but no book or resource will beat the lived knowledge of other growers in your area. You can learn firsthand about their experience with your climate, what plants thrive, and what techniques they follow to expand the range of crops they can successfully grow.

## CHANGING CLIMATES

The more closely you work with your climate, the more successful your garden becomes. While we are experiencing increasingly extreme weather conditions, a permaculture garden is designed to be incredibly resilient. An emphasis on growing perennial crops (below) and building healthy soil are the two core areas that build resilience.

# NATURAL PATTERNS

Key patterns in nature offer knowledge and context to permaculture design. Some are great starting points for aesthetic design, while others teach us vital growing stages and processes in nature to see and use in our own garden.

## LIFE AND DEATH

The pattern of life and death reminds us of the cyclical nature of existence, where every end is a new beginning. What are we at the end of the day? We are nutrients. When something dies, it decomposes. This is nature's recycling process, offering up now-available nutrients to benefit other forms of life.

A compost bin is the garden's recycling process, forming a bank of nutrients that can be transported by the gardener to benefit the next generation of crops. This pattern is simple: There is no life without death and no death without life.

## SUCCESSION

Succession is another pattern that can only be observed over time. In the simplest form, nature, when left alone, will mature into a state of permanence where there is an equilibrium within that ecosystem. An example of natural succession can be seen in a grassy field if it's left unplowed or ungrazed; it becomes scrubland and eventually a woodland, which is that land's natural state of permanence. Only external factors, such as changing atmospheric conditions or human intervention, will challenge that permanent state on a large scale.

As gardeners, what can we learn from succession? Any piece of land you have, be it a field or backyard, wants to return to that permanent state. You only need to visit an abandoned allotment plot to see how quickly this process starts. The first year the soil would be covered in annual grasses and weeds, then nettles and brambles would quickly appear, followed by fast-growing shrubs, like buddleja and willows. A permanent state is dominated by perennial plants; there are very few annuals in a woodland (unless disturbance has occurred due perhaps to a deer wallow, a snuffling boar, or a fallen tree.

An annual vegetable garden will thrive only if the gardener can ensure that succession is kept on pause. The application of minimal disturbance gardening techniques (see pp.50–53) will ensure that the soil remains suitable for annuals.

Here is the succession process split into the plant types that characterize its three core stages.

### Annuals

These fast-growing and nutrient-hungry plants are the first to appear in disturbed ground and are nature's bandage to ensure that any bare ground is covered with living plants. Examples include thistles, chickweed, and some grasses.

### Short-lived perennials

These will soon start to replace the annuals. Depending on the light and moisture levels, nettles and docks are two common examples of short-lived perennials, as well as certain grasses. There will be mostly permanent living cover year-round within one or two growing seasons.

### Long-term perennials

Gradually shrubs and trees will emerge, and over time taller trees will fill in the canopy, causing shade and limiting growth underneath. When one of these trees eventually falls, a gap appears, light comes through the canopy, and the whole process starts again.

## TO WEED OR NOT TO WEED?

A weed in a garden is the first visual step in natural succession (see opposite). Any gardener knows that a bed left bare for a few months will soon become a thick mat of weeds.

Now, there is much debate about what a weed actually is. A weed is a plant that is growing in the wrong place. It is context-specific. In a kitchen garden, this tends to be thistles, grasses, nettles, dandelions, and so on that are the first to appear in our annual beds. A self-sown tomato among your carrots could be a weed, while nettle in a hedgerow is not a weed. In fact, in this situation, a nettle is a highly beneficial plant that supports a vast array of wildlife.

Growing your own food, where the majority of the flavor and bulk comes from annual crops, is about prioritization. I would always prefer to have peas instead of a thistle. There is plenty of opportunity for these "weeds" to grow elsewhere around your garden. Weeding out the unwanted can also present opportunity: One of the best natural liquid feeds you can make for your crops is a plant soak from a mix of different garden weeds (see p.272), or you may be able to forage food from plants considered to be weeds (such as nettles, left).

## BIENNIALS

Biennial plants are generally found in temperate climates and have a two-year life cycle. Their first year is spent on growing leaves and storing energy for the second year, when the plant then flowers and sets seed. A foxglove is a perfect example. Many crops grown in a garden are biennial but treated like annuals; carrots, kale, leeks, bulb fennel, beets, and celeriac (right) are a few examples. We eat these in their vegetative (leaf) or energy storage (root) state. This is because both leaves and roots are at their best in the first year and diminish in quality in the second year, when all the energy is focused on flowering and forming seeds. There are a few crops, such as purple sprouting broccoli, where this flowering stage provides a harvest, but in this book, for simplicity, I will be treating all biennials as annuals.

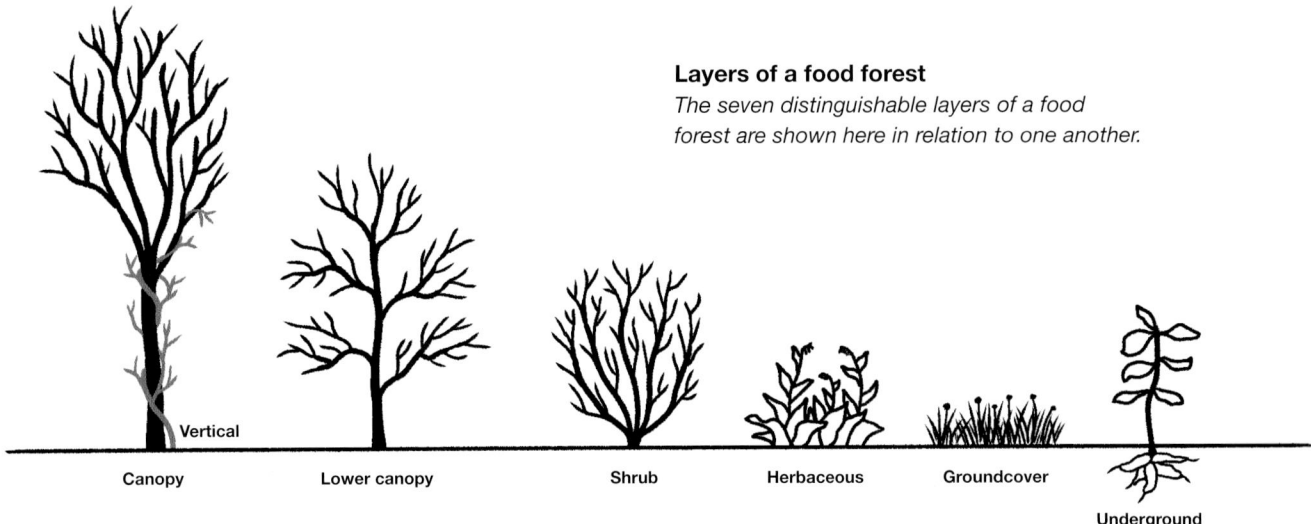

**Layers of a food forest**
*The seven distinguishable layers of a food forest are shown here in relation to one another.*

Vertical

Canopy    Lower canopy    Shrub    Herbaceous    Groundcover

Underground

## FOOD FORESTS

The layers of a forest form one of the most common patterns applied in permaculture design. Food forests are carefully planned designs that take into account the seven layers found naturally in a forest. Their goal is to create an abundant low-maintenance food system that is harvested by using a foraging approach. Food forests can also come under the agroforestry umbrella as a technique that combines food production with trees of various scales.

While food forests are excellent for some edible food, wildlife is what truly benefits in a temperate climate where the productivity of food forests is often over-romanticized. Poorer light levels and a much shorter growing season limit the food that can be produced.

However, the simplification of the layers of a food forest presents a huge opportunity for gardeners to create low-maintenance growing areas that still produce a respectable crop. Food forests are popular within the permaculture community, and you will see some examples later in the book (see pp.236–241) of layers inspired by this growing approach.

### The seven layers of a food forest

UK permaculture pioneer Robert Hart created the seven layers of a food forest, which were inspired by his years of observations from nature as well as his own forest garden. Here are the seven layers scaled to a kitchen garden, including an example plant:

**1.** Canopy (large fruit tree)
**2.** Lower canopy (dwarf fruit tree)
**3.** Shrub (currants)
**4.** Herbaceous (comfrey)
**5.** Groundcover (strawberry)
**6.** Underground (potatoes)
**7.** Vertical (grapes)

Instead of implementing all seven layers, it's possible to focus on two or three in any given area. Many combinations are possible, such as canopy and herbaceous, shrub and groundcover, or groundcover and vertical.

### An ancient technique

Versions of forest gardening can be found in Indigenous communities worldwide. On the slopes of Mount Kilimanjaro, the Chagga people have been practicing a multilayered agroforestry system (Chagga home gardens) for more than 2,000 years. Under the canopy of local tree species, they grow coffee, bananas, vegetables, and other crops. The gardens are incredibly biodiverse and have been working in harmony with nature for centuries but sadly are under threat. The farming of modern coffee varieties that demand less shade is leading to the removal of trees—igniting a slippery slope to monoculture.

## THE FIVE FS OF A FOOD FOREST

There are five core yields (see p.16) that can be obtained from a food forest that all begin with the "f" sound: food (for us), fodder (animal feed), fuel (firewood), fiber (clothes), and pharmaceutical (medicines).

### HUW'S TIP

You can apply the "layer" pattern when growing annual crops, too. Growing tall kale? Sow some lettuce underneath. Have a trellis of runner beans? Transplant parsley at the base.

*This image from my kitchen garden demonstrates the many layers of growth just among annual plants.*

# TEN GEOMETRIC PATTERNS FOR DESIGN

Nature provides many geometric patterns that can inspire us to form beautiful kitchen gardens. Patterns can be regular or irregular and applied in a literal sense (a branching pathway) or a metaphorical one (bubbles to organize areas).

Use these ten patterns as a starting point when creating designs, finding solutions, or even observing the natural world around you. There are also many other types of patterns in nature, such as lobes, radial, and scatter.

**HUW'S TIP**

If you are starting with a blank canvas, geometric patterns are a wonderful opportunity to design the layout of a garden. Could your annual growing space be divided into bubbles, with each bubble boundary being a linear food forest (see pp.240–241)?

**Spirals**
*These are found from the seed head of a sunflower to the shape of galaxies.*

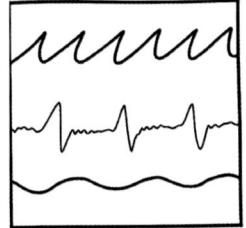

**Waves**
*From invisible sound waves, to the shape of massive sand dunes, waves recur in nature.*

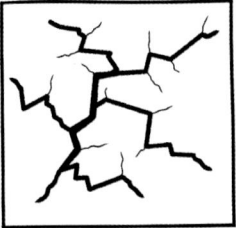

**Cracks**
*This pattern ranges from cracks of dry mud to huge canyons in North America.*

**Fractals**
*This repeating pattern is often seen from a pine cone or fern to a romanesco broccoli.*

**Fractal branching**
*From snowflakes to river tributaries or tree growth, this occurs at all scales (opposite).*

**Meanders**
*This describes the way ivy climbs up a tree as well as the twists and turns of a river.*

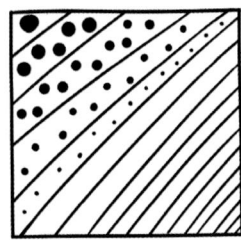

**Spots and stripes**
*Mole hills dotted across the field and the stripes of a zebra form two contrasting examples.*

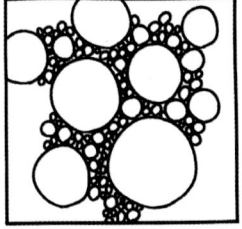

**Bubbles**
*From the foam of a spittlebug to the bubbling of lava, this is an irregular pattern.*

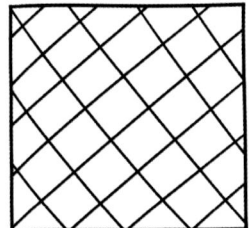

**Tessellations**
*Regular shapes are found from the honeycomb of bees to scales of a fish.*

**Webs**
*These can be literal, such as a spider's web, or metaphorical, such as the World Wide Web.*

## BRANCHING

The branching pattern in nature is my favorite of all the patterns. It's a fractal-type pattern where the same pattern characteristic is repeated at progressively smaller or bigger scales. Branches can be found almost anywhere: blood vessels, trees, leaf veins, cracks of ice, lightning, rivers, road networks, and root systems of plants.

Branching is a useful pattern for thinking about the flow of energy and movement in the garden. The main stem is the most-trodden path, with branching paths taking you to different areas. The paths open out from the entrance, ensuring that as you enter the garden, you can walk onward and outward rather than going back upon yourself. This offers maximum efficiency.

*Here, the main path leads from the entrance to the polytunnel, with easy access to the compost heaps. Side paths branch off to the main raised beds, with smaller paths running between the beds.*

# SCALE OF PERMANENCE

This is a hierarchical framework to assist in the planning and management of land. It's a helpful way to prioritize aspects of land planning based on their rate of change and degree of permanence.

The scale of permanence was developed by Australian engineer P. A. Yeomans to encourage farmers and land planners to make decisions that work with the natural attributes of the land rather than against them. It helps with strategic decisions about where to invest effort and resources for the greatest long-term multilayered benefits.

## "Remember, half of the word *permaculture* is derived from the word *permanent*."

The scale typically includes the following elements, listed from most to least permanent:

**1. Climate** The macro patterns of weather over time, which dictate your specific growing season.

**2. Landshape** The topography of the land, which can be modified, but at a high energy/cost, and will impact the surroundings too (such as water flow).

**3. Water** This includes the water supply, water bodies, and water movement across the land, which can be managed and designed for optimal use.

**4. Roads and access** These are relatively permanent once constructed and significantly influence land-use patterns and water movement.

**5. Trees and perennials** Woody vegetation and perennials that have long life-spans.

**6. Buildings** Structures are somewhat permanent but are also subject to change as needs evolve.

**7. Boundaries** Less permanent than buildings and often moved or changed as land use changes.

**8. Soil** While it seems permanent, soil structure and fertility can be improved or degraded relatively quickly through management practices.

**9. Economic factors** Markets, labor, and capital are very dynamic and can change from season to season.

## APPLYING THE SCALE OF PERMANENCE

Here's how you might adapt and apply the scale of permanence to aid design and decision-making in your kitchen garden, especially if you're starting from scratch:

### Climate
Understand the climate in your area, including temperature ranges, rainfall patterns, season lengths, frost dates, and so on (see pp.32–33). Design your garden to work with these conditions by choosing appropriate plant varieties and using microclimate modifications, such as undercover structures or windbreaks.

### Landshape
Observe the topography of your garden space. Are there slopes that will affect water runoff? How might the movement of resources be affected by height? It is easier to bring heavy compost downhill rather than carting it uphill.

### Water
Water is a key element. Design your kitchen garden with a water-efficient layout, considering tap access, drip irrigation, rainwater harvesting, and mulching to reduce evaporation.

### Roads and access
Plan for paths and access points in your garden that are both functional and aesthetically pleasing. Permanent paths ensure that you can reach all parts of the garden without damaging plants or soil structure.

### Trees and perennials
Incorporate fruit trees, perennial vegetables, and herbs into your garden design. These should be placed thoughtfully since, unlike annual crops, they will not be grown in different locations each year. Smaller perennials are much easier to move than larger ones. Consider how larger perennials will impact light levels nearby.

## Buildings

If your kitchen garden includes or is near structures like a greenhouse, shed, or even your home, consider how these affect sunlight, wind, and water flow. If you are placing a new structure, what opportunities or drawbacks will it bring?

## Boundaries

How is your boundary defined between your garden and the neighbors' space? Do you have fences/boundaries/hedges within your garden that further divide it up into different sections? Will you perhaps create a rabbit-proof area or use temporary fencing to move poultry through the season?

## Soil

In permaculture, soil health is paramount. Build rich, healthy soil through mulching and have living plants in the ground for as long as possible. What can you do to improve the soil as well as protect it from damage?

## Economic factors

Although a kitchen garden may not be an economic enterprise, there are still economic considerations, such as the cost of seeds, plants, materials, and time. This should align with your budget and garden goals (see pp.28–29).

### HUW'S TIP

**Climate, landshape, and water are your limiting factors (or factors of opportunity). By taking time to understand as much about these three categories as possible, such as prevailing wind direction, your decisions will naturally complement the geography of your area. Work with nature.**

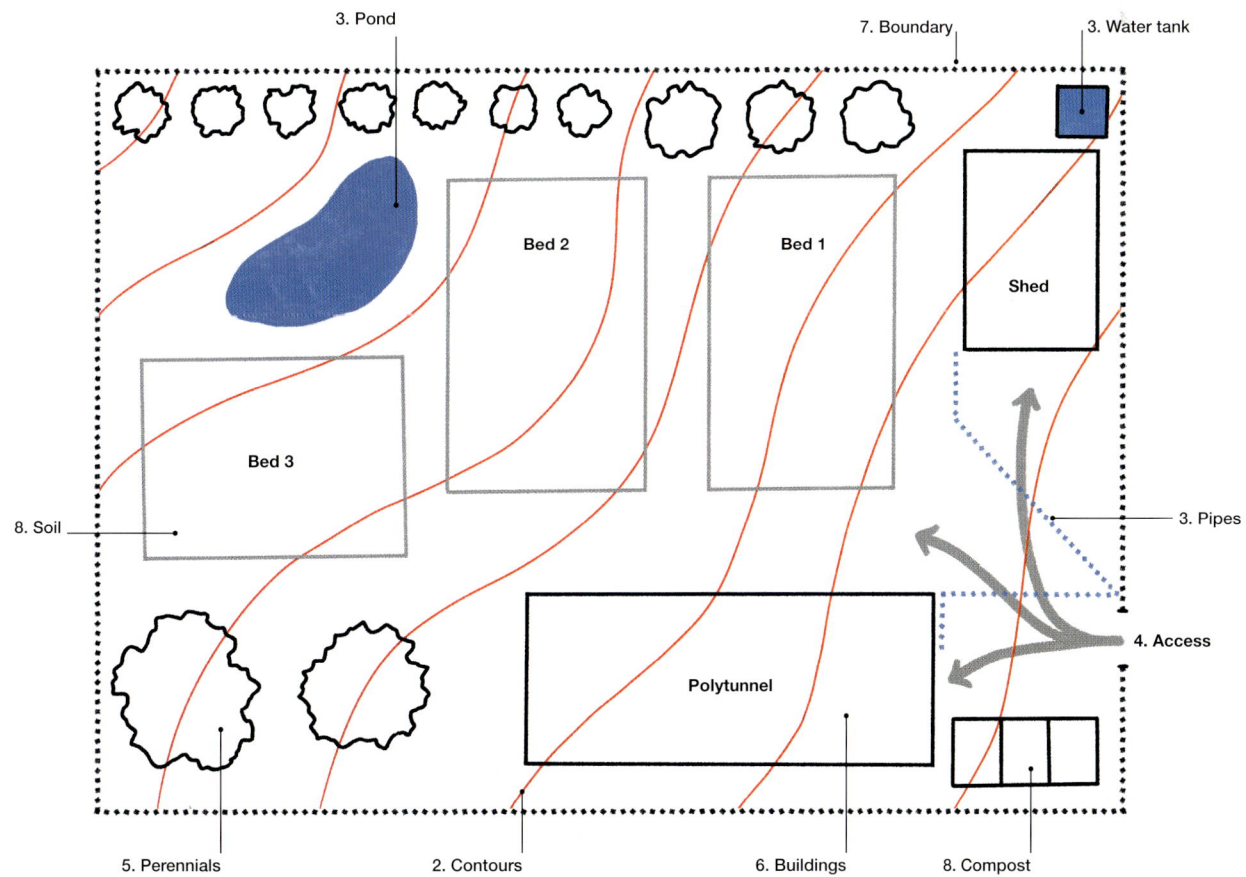

### The scale of permanence in a garden

*This simple line diagram of an allotment plot in climate zone 8 highlights the key elements on the scale of permanence.*

# ZONING

A zone is a conceptual boundary to help you to maximize the efficiency of your garden or homestead. Zones can be applied regardless of the size of your plot.

The goal is that the elements that require the most attention are closest to your house (or entrance). As the need for attention of specific elements decreases, their distance from the house (or entrance) increases.

I have created an example of how these zones would apply to a suburban back garden. Regardless of what scale your site is, when designing the space, you can use these zones to help inform the most suitable locations for each element. For particularly small gardens, you may have only zone 1 and zone 2, with zone 2 also integrating some perennials from zone 3.

### Zone 0 (Your home/entrance)
Your home is zone 0. This is where the majority of your yields will end up. Zone 0 could also be classed as the main entrance to your site if the site is not connected to your home.

### Zone 1 (Intensive)
This is immediately adjacent to your house (or entrance) and used daily. It is where your most commonly harvested crops, such as herbs and salads, exist. Your primary composting setup is here, and perhaps an outdoor kitchen. If you keep chickens for composting, then this would lead to their coop for egg collecting and feeding. The boundary between zone 1 and zone 2 is an excellent place for tool storage for larger sites and homesteads, or between zone 0 and zone 1 for smaller gardens.

### Zone 2 (Semi-intensive)
The staple annual kitchen garden crops are grown here and will need a few visits a week. A polytunnel would also be here, as well as rainwater storage tanks. The outer areas of this zone would be perfect for pollinator and cut flower plantings.

### Zone 3 (Extensive)
Here, you would find the perennial vegetables, soft fruits, field-scale crops, and orchard. It is also a common place for more extensive poultry as well as larger livestock. Place their shelters/feed troughs on the zone 2/3 border to reduce travel time when checking up on them.

### Zone 4 (Semi-managed)
This is ideal for occasional pasture use, beehives, foraging for wild food, sustainable timber production, and ponds/natural swimming pools. The zone also suits a food forest as well as being a perfect spot to set up a tent for any outdoor camping.

### Zone 5 (Unmanaged/wild)
A hands-off zone where you let nature do its thing. You may have to occasionally manage the edge between zone 4 and 5 to prevent natural creeping, but otherwise you just let nature run its course. For smaller projects, zone 5 could simply be a thick hedge.

*In this zone 1 area, I'm putting tools away at the end of a gardening session as I leave through the gate.*

## Zoning for efficiency

*Using zones can help you plan your garden: Things that need frequent attention should be closer to your house, and those that need less attention are farther away.*

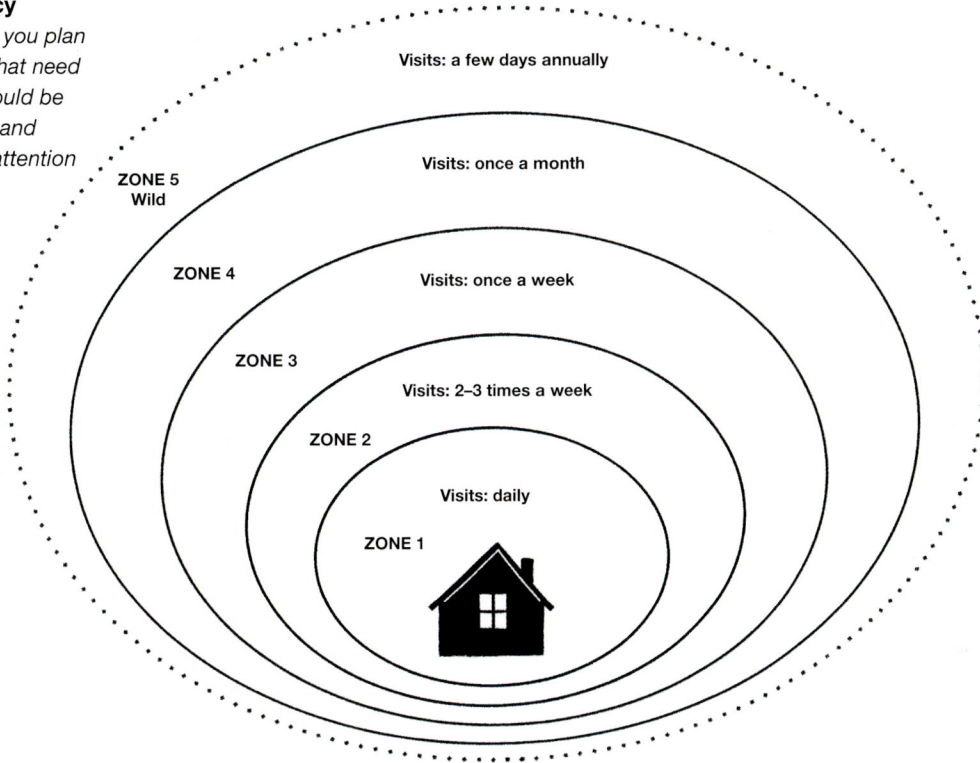

Visits: a few days annually

**ZONE 5 Wild**

Visits: once a month

**ZONE 4**

Visits: once a week

**ZONE 3**

Visits: 2–3 times a week

**ZONE 2**

Visits: daily

**ZONE 1**

## BEING FLEXIBLE WITH ZONES

The zones don't need to follow a strict ripple pattern—zone 4 could have a lobe that extends into zone 2, or you could have an island of zone 5 in the midst of zone 3 (below) for additional biodiversity benefits.

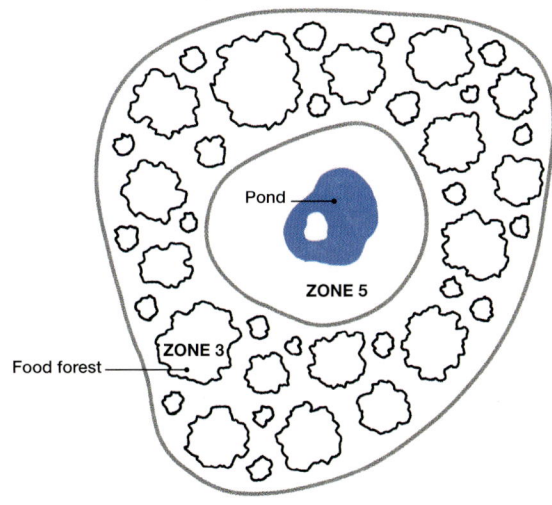

Pond

**ZONE 5**

**ZONE 3**

Food forest

*This foraging hedgerow, where I'm harvesting rosehips, is in zone 4.*

# Soil health
# and compost

# SOIL HEALTH EXPLAINED

It's all too easy to get caught up in the never-ending complexity of soil science, but I have some good news for you: There's no need to become a soil scientist to get fantastic results from your garden.

I am pleased to see soil health becoming a more prominent talking point in the horticultural world. I am less pleased that it is starting to confuse and paralyze gardeners with excessive out-of-context information that really doesn't make a bit of difference in a kitchen garden. This book will give you everything you need to know to nail the basics—because that's all you need!

### SOIL HEALTH IN A NUTSHELL

A healthy soil is made up of three factors: physical, biological, and chemical. These factors need to coexist in a somewhat balanced manner.

### Physical

The structure of the soil is influenced by the shape and arrangement of particles of clay, sand, silt, and organic matter.

## THE PARETO PRINCIPLE (80/20 RULE)

The Pareto principle states that for many outcomes, roughly 80 percent of consequences come from 20 percent of effort. To put it another way, 80 percent of output comes from 20 percent of input. This is true when applied to soil health: You only need to know a fraction of what makes a healthy soil to get an abundance of food.

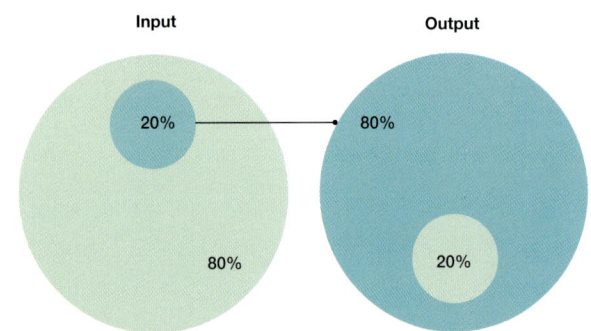

Input    Output

20%    80%

80%    20%

## "Your job as the gardener is to facilitate the right soil conditions to let nature work its magic."

The soil could be hard and compacted or crumbly and fluffy in texture. It could be dark in color or light.

### Biological

The biological element of the soil is all the living beings, both observable (such as worms) and microscopic (such as bacteria). They are essential for recycling and decomposing organic material as well as forming a natural immune system to protect plants and soil life from pests and diseases.

### Chemical

The chemical element is the nutrients and minerals. As mentioned in "Life and death" (see p.34), living organisms are essential for making nutrients available to plants. Nutrients and minerals enter and exist in the soil from the weathering of rocks and the breaking down of plant material.

### Organic matter in soil

For growing annuals, you want your soil to be crumbly in texture, dark in color, and full of life and to contain plenty of organic matter. Organic matter results from the decomposition of mostly biological elements (plants, animals, etc.) into carbon-rich organic compounds. Compost is a perfect example of organic matter. On the following pages, there are simple soil tests that you can use to better understand what soil you have. The good news is that the poorest soils can be easily improved, and gardeners can influence all three key elements of soil.

*A good indicator of healthy soil is strong, dense root systems on your crops, such as on this celery plant.*

Physical, biological, and chemical aspects of the soil can all be improved by adding organic matter and avoiding excessive damage. This is how simple having healthy soil can be!

Perennial herbs, flowers, soft fruits, and tree fruits enjoy a healthy thriving soil but still grow well in subpar soil, provided there is no waterlogging and some organic matter is present. The exception is perennial vegetables, which enjoy high levels of organic matter, particularly tubers, such as oca and yacon.

## PLANTS FEED THE SOIL

One of the amazing things about plants is that they contribute to improving soil health. Plants release substances through their roots called root exudates, which are organic compounds that are enjoyed by soil microbes (microorganisms). Root exudates create a place for beneficial bacteria to coat and protect the roots from pathogens while also making soil nutrients available via the roots.

# TESTING YOUR SOIL

It's a good idea to have a basic understanding of your soil when you're starting out. The simple tests here give an overview of how good your soil is structurally and biologically. You can repeat these in future years to track soil improvement.

## SQUEEZE TEST

The squeeze test helps identify the structure of your soil. The goal is a loam: a balance between sand, silt, and clay. Conduct a squeeze tests two or three days after heavy rainfall for the most accurate results. When squeezed, a chunk of loamy soil should maintain its shape but break apart if poked. Overly coarse soils (which have a high sand content and do not hold water well) will not hold a structure after squeezing, while overly fine soils (which have a high clay content and are not able to drain water well) will not break if poked and will be sticky to the touch. You are after the Goldilocks state: not too coarse, not too fine. Fear not if your soil is one of the extremes—adding organic matter will create more of a balance.

*A loamy soil keeps its shape when squeezed but crumbles when pushed.*

## SOIL PH

This is a measure of how acidic or alkaline the soil is. In the vast majority of cases, soil pH isn't a concern. If you are curious about soil pH (soil that is too acidic or too alkaline will significantly affect crop yields), then use a simple soil pH testing kit (left). If your soil pH is between 6 and 7, nothing needs to be done. If it's outside this range, some treatment may be necessary. Again, adding compost can often remedy out-of-balance soils. For extreme cases, add lime to soil to reduce acidity and sulfur to reduce alkalinity.

## COMPACTION TEST

Compacted soils have poor drainage and poor structure and cause poor root growth; overall, they have a negative impact on productivity and plant health. Compaction is caused by excessive weight on the soil and can be exacerbated in saturated soil. There is a very simple compaction test involving a straight piece of wire (such as from a coat hanger). In spring or fall, push the wire into the ground and stop when it starts to bend—measure this length. If it is under 8in (20cm), your soil is compacted. The aim is a depth of at least 12in (30cm) before the wire starts bending. Compacted soils are rectified by using a broadfork to gently break up the soil to immediately improve aeration and drainage. Increasing the volume of organic matter over time also helps.

Clay soils are far more prone to compaction due to their small particle size and high water content. Avoid walking on any growing spaces on clay soils, particularly in wet weather.

*When using a broadfork on compacted soil, you can stand in the bed as you work backward.*

## EARTHWORM COUNT

Earthworms are a great indicator of general soil health because their food source is organic matter and microorganisms. If you have loads of earthworms, they are there for a reason. They also do an excellent job at recycling nutrients, improving aeration, and improving soil structure.

To establish how many earthworms your soil has, on a warm spring or fall day after it has rained in the last three or four days, dig a section of soil about 12in (30cm) deep, wide, and long and place it on a large sheet or piece of cardboard. Count out all the earthworms in the sample and make a note. Repeat this at least three or four times within an area of 10–16ft (3–5m) to figure out an approximate average worm count. The goal to aim for is 10 per sample.

*When counting worms in your garden, aim to survey 8–10 areas to gain a rough overview.*

# MINIMAL DISTURBANCE

In my garden, I want a balanced, practical growing approach that equally prioritizes nutritious food production and long-term soil health. I like to view my approach to growing as "minimal-disturbance" gardening.

## NO-DIG GARDENING

One of the most popular movements in the gardening world in recent years has been the rise of no-dig gardening, thanks to the fantastic work of Charles Dowding. The idea of gardening without digging has been around since at least the 1940s. Gardeners and authors Albert Guest and Frederic Charles King released no-dig books in this decade.

No dig has a very important goal: to cause as little disturbance to the soil as possible. However, I have observed a growing dogmatism surrounding the method. Most of this comes from an obsession with soil health and a lack of empathy toward challenges many gardeners face, such as financial limitations.

### Drawbacks of no dig

Let's cover the soil health side first. Most crops in a kitchen garden are annuals or biennials. Putting my permaculture hat on: Where do you find annuals in nature? The answer is, newly disturbed ground. But why? Annuals are fast-growing and nutrient-hungry and are nature's way of ensuring that any bare ground is covered with living plants. Soil microbes, such as bacteria (and fungi, even though they are far less important for annuals), break down nutrients into plant-available form. These plant-ready nutrients are released when soil microbes die, such as when soil is disturbed. This high nutrient concentration complements the hunger of annuals.

Setting up productive no-dig beds of mounded soil to protect crops from waterlogging requires a significant amount of compost, which, if you haven't managed to make a large volume yourself, will be expensive to purchase. You also then need to add compost annually to maintain fertility.

By using other methods of adding organic matter to your soil, as discussed in this chapter, you can enjoy the benefits of no dig while saving money and time by working with the resources you have. I'm not saying to revert to double digging, but I am saying that a little disturbance isn't a bad thing.

## WHAT COUNTS AS MINIMAL DISTURBANCE?

Gardening is about balance. As gardeners, we all have different things we need to balance: time, energy, finances, and goals. My goal is to make growing food as accessible and practical as possible for as many people as possible. The only way to achieve that is to understand that there are multiple gardening methods that exist and that they all offer opportunities and drawbacks. Don't have enough money for compost, but need to plant? Then look at trench composting (see pp.70–71). No-dig beds a little compacted over many years due to excessive rainfall? Then gently broadfork them at the start of the season. Want to create a new bed from scratch with as little compost as possible? Take off the turf, fluff the soil, and combine organic matter. Want to protect bare ground over winter? Look at growing cover crops (see pp.74–76).

For me, minimal disturbance gardening offers flexibility, as well as the fact that minimal is far more achievable than "no." It is up to you to decide what is minimal in relation to your situation. Nobody knows your garden, challenges, and opportunities as well as you do, so don't feel guilty if it seems necessary to pick up the spade or fork. Plus, the fact that you are growing your own food to nourish yourself and your family is infinitely more important than the gardening methods you choose.

Any soil disturbance I do is strategic and thoughtful and takes in multiple consideration points. Perhaps the best description is "commonsense gardening."

*I am mulching a raised bed with homemade compost in the late fall before covering it with a protective mulch of leaves and grass clippings.*

## FIVE PRINCIPLES OF MINIMAL DISTURBANCE

Like the permaculture principles (see pp.14–25), these five principles are not to be viewed as rules. Being confined to too many rules suffocates the creativity mindset required for achieving your goals.

### 1. Assess before action

When you're undertaking a specific garden task that may require soil disturbance, assess all the options, consider which will be most suitable and beneficial, then act accordingly.

### 2. Ecosystem emphasis

View the garden as a complete ecosystem rather than from a soil-centric view. An emphasis is placed on encouraging biodiversity and bioabundance of microbes, invertebrates, and other living organisms in your garden. This is achieved by habitat creation (shelter and food sources), carbon in the soil, and application of homemade biological amendments (liquid and compost-based).

### 3. Responsible resourcing

Use local and sustainable resources to save money and improve yields—for example, vegetable scraps from restaurants, fall leaves from neighbors, or cardboard from nearby shops. Economic responsibility in tune with your household budget is also vital—for example, you may choose to buy non-organic seeds so that you can save money that can be better used elsewhere.

### 4. Dynamic crop polyculture

Use a wide variety of planting techniques if possible to ensure a thriving dynamic polyculture (see pp.228–255). These include succession planting, interplanting, relay cropping, and growing staples in more than one block (see pp.244–247). Having multiple types of plants growing over the season will naturally create a productive, resilient garden.

### 5. Continuous cover

Whenever possible, avoid bare soil: It is an invitation for soil erosion, weed issues, and poorer soil biology. The simplest trouble-free way to prevent bare soil over winter is by mulching with a layer of compost. You can also use such methods as succession planting, cover crops, and covering the ground over the winter with breathable material, so there is as little soil exposed to the elements as possible.

*For establishing a new site, local waste resources, such as these wood shreddings, help fast-track building healthy, carbon-rich soil.*

*Garden health needs diversity—of plants, layers, insects, soil microorganisms, growing areas, and growing techniques.*

The permaculture principle use and value of diversity is a fantastic reminder that there is a plethora of different gardening methods available to us to try and choose from to achieve our core growing goals. Diversity leads to resilience, and to create resilient diversity, there must be space for flexibility. The more flexibility we have, the more likely we are to achieve our goals. Flexibility is one of permaculture's greatest strengths because it acknowledges that you need to adapt to different environments, create customizable or bespoke solutions, be responsive to change, have a holistic outlook, and that you are on a constant learning journey.

## MY CORE ATTITUDES

These attitudes are always in the back of my mind when I'm gardening and help keep me on track:

**Be observant** Observation harvests information, which matures into knowledge.
**Be curious** Always ask questions and always seek new learning.

# COMPOST

Compost results from decomposition of organic materials into organic matter. It's rich in nutrients, microbes, and carbon. Here, I cover its basic components and compost for seeds and seedlings. For more on compost-making techniques, and alternatives, see pages 58–61.

## THE BASICS

You can have a highly productive perennial garden without compost, but for annuals, compost is a must—even if it's just for raising seedlings. In its simplest form, compost can be seen as a fertilizer because it is a substance that is added to soil to increase fertility. Its high carbon content creates a pro-microbe environment and greater water-holding capacity in the soil. To make compost, you need two types of ingredients, known as the "greens" and "browns." Greens are materials that are high in nitrogen, and browns are high in carbon. You need a volume of around 2:1 or 1:1 greens and browns for good compost. Too many browns, and the materials will take forever to decompose and be lower in nutrients; too many greens, and you will end up with a smelly sludge. Most plants aren't fussy about what compost they grow in as long as it is created with a balance of greens and browns. If you are starting out, an easy approach is for every bucket or two of green material, add a bucket of browns.

*This is a handful of beautiful homemade compost ready for action.*

### Green materials

- Used coffee grounds and plastic-free tea bags
- Weeds without seed heads
- Grass clippings (unsprayed)
- Fruit and vegetable scraps
- Horse, cow, rabbit, and chicken manure
- Freshly cut plant material
- Seaweed (leave out in the rain to wash off excess salt)
- Spent brewery grain (from a local brewery)
- Green leaves from herbaceous plants
- Wool (from packaging)

### Brown materials

- Cardboard, newspaper, and shredded paper (vegetable-based ink and nonglossy)
- Dust from vacuuming and dryer lint
- Ramial chipped wood (see pp.66–67)
- Sawdust (from untreated wood)
- Autumn leaves (shredded by a lawnmower, if possible)
- Hay and straw
- Fall and winter woody prunings
- Fallen pine needles
- Wood ash
- Tissues and paper towels
- Spent potting mix (from this season's pots)

### Combined materials

If you can get a pre-combined compost material, such as used animal bedding, which has an ideal blend of greens and browns, you have a winner! More details on this is given in the hot-beds section later in this chapter (see pp.60–61).

### SEED SOWING STARTING MIX

When starting seedlings, the type of growing medium is more important, as you want to prevent your crop seedlings from competing with weed seedlings. If purchasing potting mix for this process, opt for quality peat-free multipurpose potting mix (see suppliers for my recommendations, p.281). This is because it is going to be completely weed-free.

To make your own seed-starting mix, use 1 part sieved homemade compost to 2 parts sieved leaf mold (see p.58) or decomposed wood chips. Use compost made from hot composting (see pp.60–61) because the heat kills off the weed seeds. You can make a large batch of seed compost over winter in preparation for spring. Store it in used mulch bags or a builders' bag and keep it out of the rain. If you don't have much undercover space, a tarpaulin will work.

*A bucketful of green, nitrogen-rich plant material is added to the compost after a weeding session.*

### POTTING MIX

Raising healthy seedlings really isn't as complex as so many other books and gardening sites make it out to be. Potting mix for growing seedlings can be made by using 1 part compost, 1 part garden soil, and 1 part leaf mold. There will be some weeds, but because your seedlings are maturing, the weeds will be much easier to manage. Alternatively, use the same peat-free multipurpose growing mix for potting too.

---

### HUW'S TIP

To echo many other areas of the permaculture garden, diversity is key for healthy compost: Add as many different ingredients as you can to your compost bins.

# THE PROBLEMS WITH COMPOST

There are two big issues with compost. The first is the rising cost of bought compost. The second, if you're making your own compost, is sourcing enough material to cover your needs.

One of the core goals for a permaculture kitchen garden is to get to a stage where you have full control over its fertility. In other words, your garden isn't dependent on your purchasing compost and other amendments, and all nutrition can be sourced from your garden, home, and/or free resources from your local community.

**A LIST OF ACHIEVABLE SOLUTIONS**

The solutions offered here all directly contribute to increasing the soil organic matter of your growing spaces (focused on annual crop production). Use this list as a starting point to help identify what is possible for your given situation. An asterisk indicates methods that are suitable for gardens with high slug concentrations.

- Leaf mold (see p.58)*
- Compost bin (see p.58)*
- Pathway composting (see p.58)
- Mulching (see p.62)
- Green manures (see pp.74–76)*
- Hot compost and hot beds (see pp.60–61)*
- Trench and pocket composting (see pp.70–71)*
- Chop and drop (see p.62)
- Worm compost (see pp.64–65)*
- Ramial chipped wood (see pp.66–67)
- Organic matter incorporation (see p.72) *
- Biochar (see pp.68–69)*
- Leave the roots behind when you harvest (see p.74)*

## "When it comes to gardening, there is no such thing as too much homemade compost."

There are also many ways to reduce compost requirements in your garden, which are covered at the end of this chapter (see pp.80–81). By focusing on increasing your soil organic matter levels while also implementing ways to reduce the dependence on finished compost, you will quickly move your garden toward a state of high resilience. These solutions show how many opportunities you have to grow an abundance of food!

## SLUGS

With their love for the tender young growth of many annual crops, slugs are one of the key reasons why compost is the preferred method of applying nutrition and organic matter to annual crops. Other soil-improving methods, such as mulching, can create habitats where slugs will hide under the material, whereas this is not possible if there is only a layer of compost on the ground. There is good news—numerous ways to reduce slug pressures in a permaculture garden exist (see pp.262–263), but for a brand-new garden, it's best to be cautious.

*A series of compost bins means you can have compost at staggered stages of decomposition. As one bin of compost gets used up, another should be ready before too long.*

# COLD COMPOST

Cold composting, or slow composting, is the easiest way to make compost at home. You can follow a fill-as-you-go approach, and once a bin is full, it will generate high-quality compost for the next growing season.

## SIMPLE COMPOST

A cold compost bin should be at least 35 cubic feet (1 cubic meter) in size so it has enough space to create a "core"—this is well insulated by the rest of the material and is the point of peak decomposition activity. As compost materials become available, you add them to the compost bin. Once the bin is full, cap the pile with some layers of cardboard and leave it for 6–12 months. You don't need to mix the materials in cold compost bins, but mixing the ingredients every eight weeks or so will help speed up the process. Chopping up the greens and browns into smaller pieces will also significantly speed up decomposition. Homemade microbial amendments, such as LAB (see p.273), also help.

## COMPOST PATHWAYS

An alternative cold compost method that is perfect for small spaces is compost pathways. These are inspired by Liz Zorab's wood-chip paths where, after two years, she would scoop the old composted wood chips from the path and mulch the raised beds on either side. Compost pathways take the process a step further: You add a base layer of cardboard or wood chips and then treat the path like a linear cold compost bin, adding a mix of green and brown materials. You can still use this path for access. Once the material is around 8–12in (20–30cm) deep, stop adding to it, mix it every few weeks, and you will have a path of rich compost a few months later. This can be used to mulch raised beds or to add to the base of holes when transplanting.

## LEAF MOLD

Create a 35-cubic-foot (1-cubic-metre) compost bin—for example, by strapping four pallets together to form a box—and fill it with leaves in the fall. If you can, shred the leaves

"**Compost pathways are an excellent option for polytunnels over winter, ready for tomato-planting season.**"

first by using a lawnmower or similar to avoid waiting an extra year for the leaves to break down. Mix the leaves twice, once in the spring and again in the fall, and you will have beautiful leaf mold ready to use in the spring the following year. If you create two leaf mold bins, you can use them in turn for a steady supply each spring.

## WOOD CHIPS

For cold compost of wood chips, have a pile of wood chips of at least 35 cubic feet (1 cubic meter) and leave the wood chips to break down over a three-year period. Turn every six months and water the pile if the core becomes dry. It is a long process but well worth the wait.

Again, as with leaf mold, you can create a new pile of wood chips to decompose on an annual basis, and after three years, you will have an annual supply. For other uses for wood chips, see pages 66–67.

*This before and after shows a compost pathway (top left and immediate right) within a six-month window. A layer of grass clippings is added to a cold compost heap made from willow (far right).*

# HOT COMPOST AND HOT BEDS

Unlike cold composting, where you gradually fill the bin, when hot composting you need all the material at the start. For small gardens, a hot bed can maximize productivity by providing compost and food in the same footprint.

## HOW TO MAKE HOT COMPOST

Hot composting requires a volume of material to heat up (at least 35 cubic feet/1 cubic meter), meaning you will need to keep your green and brown materials separate before you build the pile. Provided you have about 35 cubic feet of material, making hot compost is easy. You need a roughly 50:50 split of green and brown materials, all cut up or shredded into smaller pieces. For example, cardboard should be shredded into strips.

On the ground or in a compost bay, combine the materials, alternating between greens and browns and giving the pile a thorough mix every so often. You also want to water the ingredients well as you make the pile—if it's too dry, there won't be enough heat. Once all the ingredients have been added, insert a compost thermometer and place a tarpaulin or similar over the top of the pile. Whenever the temperature starts to fall, turn it, ensuring the outer materials go into the core of the pile. Hot compost is ready in about eight weeks.

## HOT BEDS

Hot beds, which I learned how to use from expert Jack First, are best described as a hot compost pile with some growing medium and a cold frame on top (see pp.274–275 for construction). They are one of the most productive gardening methods. Not only do they provide a large volume of fantastic quality compost at the end of the season; they allow you to start growing outside much earlier than usual, as they create a frost-free environment. The heat generated from the natural decomposition process of the material leads to rapid germination and growth of crops planted on top. The cold frame acts as a mini-greenhouse to keep the heat in, meaning that on frosty nights, your seedlings are kept warm.

Hot beds are so effective at generating heat that you can sow crops three months before your last average frost date and before pests become active. Getting seeds sown early allows them to capitalize on lengthening daylight hours too. Hot beds also offer opportunities for succession planting, such as squash or tomatoes, after the hot beds are cleared of their first crop in May.

It is worth noting that hot beds are made in the late winter when there is little else to do in the garden, opening up time to collect the materials you need if you don't have immediate access to them—for example, gathering a few big bags of seaweed or used horse bedding (see opposite).

*A hot bed can keep a family self-sufficient in salad during the whole hungry gap.*

*The lights on a cold frame keep in warmth for this freshly sown hot bed in late winter.*

A hot bed should have a footprint of at least 16 sq ft (1.5 sq m), and the cold frame needs to be 13 sq ft (1.2 sq m). The depth of material used in a hot bed determines roughly how long you will enjoy consistent heat:

| | |
|---|---|
| 32–36in (80–90cm): 3 months |
| 24–28in (60–70cm): 2 months |
| 14–18in (35–45cm): 1 month (ideal for a polytunnel in the early spring for getting your first core seed sowings off to a great start) |

### Materials for a hot bed

Used horse bedding is the traditional material for hot beds. If you can find a local equestrian center that will accept a donation for a delivery of manure, this is ideal. Check first whether the bedding is suitable—some may contain a broad-leaf fungicide known as aminopyralid, which significantly impacts numerous garden crops, causing stunted growth and curled leaves, and so is best avoided. There are some other options available. The first is ramial chipped wood (see pp.66–67), which I used for one of my hot beds. The layer was 36in (90cm) deep and generated continuous heat for around four months. The second is seaweed and leaves, about 50:50 of each, and thoroughly mixed. I did not chop up the seaweed. You can also use grass clippings and fall leaves.

### Seedling germination

You can fit six or seven rows of crops inside a hot bed cold frame, or inner frame, spaced at around 7in (17–18cm) apart. The table (above right) shows what is suitable for early hot bed sowing and the approximate time to harvest after sowing.

| Crop | Weeks to first harvest |
|---|---|
| Radishes | 4 |
| Pea shoots | 2 |
| Leafy salads (lettuce, mustards, etc) | 5–6 |
| Spring onions | 12 |
| Carrots | 10 |
| Turnips | 6 |
| Bok choy | 8 |
| Beets | 8 |

Hot beds offer an opportunity to germinate tender seedlings without needing electrical heat mats. Use pots or thin module trays and place them between the rows in a hot bed to use bottom heat for germination.

*You'll be surprised by how quickly seeds will germinate and grow in a hot bed.*

### Ventilation

For the first few weeks of a hot bed's life, you won't need to water it, as the cold frame will create a self-watering type system, and there will be plenty of moisture available from the building process. However, on warmer and sunnier days, do ventilate your cold frame for a few hours to ensure good air circulation. Start to water your hot bed whenever the top 2in (5cm) feels dry to the touch.

### Dismantling

At the end of the year, remove the old plant matter. You can leave the hot bed in situ as a temporary compost heap. Open up one of the sides to collect compost for mulching your beds from late fall to early spring. Save some of the compost in bags, ready to be the growing medium for the next hot bed.

# MULCH

Mulch is a layer of material that is applied on the surface of the ground. Its primary purposes are to reduce evaporation of water, suppress weed seeds, and, if it is an organic material, feed the soil.

Organic materials used for mulch include many things you would naturally compost: grass clippings, straw, leaves, cardboard, wool, wood chips, plant matter, and seaweed. Compost itself can also be used as a mulch, as it is for no-dig gardening, and is the most appropriate mulch material for areas that have slug issues. There are also non-compostable mulches, such as landscape fabric and black plastic; both have natural starch-based versions available to purchase. Natural fabrics are ideal as mulch when planting large areas of perennials to keep weeds down while plants establish.

### MULCHING PERENNIALS
A rule I follow is that every single perennial in my garden should have at least one mulch a year, usually at the beginning of the spring and at least 2in (5cm) thick. Because perennials tend to suffer far less from slug issues than annuals, I mulch with whatever available organic material I have. Any mulching of stemmed perennials, such as apple trees and red currants, should be up to but not touching the stem to allow good airflow. I leave a 1–2in (3–5cm) gap between the stem and the mulch. If you place two to three layers of cardboard down before the mulch material, your plants will be kept weed-free for the majority of the growing season.

### MULCHING ANNUALS
For annual crops, the annual minimum mulch is 1in (2–3cm) of compost. Occasionally I will do some light mulches of ½–¾in (1–2cm) of grass clippings during the growing season. Annual beds respond well to a 1–2in (3–5cm) mulch of seaweed, semi-composted manure, or chopped-up plant material in the fall, which will decompose by the next spring.

### MULCHING CONTAINERS
Containers can also be mulched. In fact, mulching containers should be prioritized over mulching beds because pots and containers dry out much faster, and keeping them mulched will save a lot of water and a lot of your time watering.

## CHOP AND DROP

This popular permaculture technique is as much about soil building as it is about efficiency. Rather than clearing weeds and plant material off the ground and placing them on the compost, only to use that compost a year later to apply to the very ground the original material came from, chop and drop saves that effort (below). Instead, you let the plant material naturally decompose on the surface, feeding the very soil it came from. It is a wonderfully effective form of mulching, especially for perennial setups, where you may be clearing grass and weeds as well as pruning back growth. It is also incredibly effective for annual plants where slugs are not an issue.

*In the summer, when the grass is growing quickly, it's simple to put a layer of grass clippings around vegetable plants to retain soil moisture and deter weeds.*

# WORM COMPOST

Vermicompost is the name for the compost made by compost worms as they decompose material. This slow-release, nutrient-rich, highly microbial fertilizer is one of the most powerful resources a gardener can use.

A worm bin is the most productive "nutrient factory" a garden can have and is suitable for even the smallest of spaces. Not only can you turn cooked food scraps into a rich natural fertilizer; you can also collect the "worm tea"—the juices from the process—to use as a powerful liquid feed (see p.273).

Worm bins are made up of multiple trays. When the bottom tray has been filled with ingredients, an empty tray is stacked above it and then filled. The tray at the bottom is removed to harvest the casts, and once emptied, it will become the top tray, ensuring a consistent rotation.

*1. Add vegetable scraps and other materials often to the bottom tray of the worm bin. 2. Worms turn the material into highly fertile worm casts, working their way up through the trays. 3. Worm tea can be tapped to use as fertilizer.*

There are many different worm bins on the market, but the Wormcity is the go-to model for the UK. Each model will come with specific instructions, so be sure to check these to know how to start the process with bedding material. You will need compost worms, also known as tiger worms, which either come with your bin or can be purchased separately. Avoid woody materials and feed your worms with:

- Raw and cooked vegetable scraps
- All fruit scraps (avoid citrus)
- Eggshells, coffee grounds, plastic-free teabags, and bread

Aim to collect kitchen scraps from neighbors and friends to keep the bin well fed. The more vermicompost you make, the more productive your garden can become.

### HUW'S TIP

**Position a worm bin out of direct sunlight when outside. In cold climates, move a worm bin into a shed or garage to protect the worms from extreme freezing temperatures. Alternatively, wrap the bin with a thick layer of breathable insulation or place straw bales around it.**

### USING THE CASTINGS

Vermicompost is a fantastic ingredient when potting seedlings. Mix 1 part vermicompost to 5 parts multipurpose potting mix or 4 parts of your homemade compost mix.

It's also an excellent supplement for plants when transplanting. Mix one handful of vermicompost with one handful of soil and place at the base of the planting hole, then plant and water thoroughly before firming the plant into position. Alternatively, top dress the soil around plants with a ½–¾in (1–2cm) layer and lightly rake it into the top 2in (5cm) of soil. For larger plants, such as squash and tomatoes, mulch around their stems with two handfuls every two weeks and then water them.

### USING WORM TEA

Worm tea is rich in nutrients and microbes. Collect and use worm tea right away by diluting it (see p.273) and using it to water seedlings and maturing plants.

### DIY IN-GROUND WORMERY

You can also make a simple in-ground wormery. While the usability benefits are far lower, it will create a nutrient-rich hotspot that you can plant with hungry fruiting crops, such as an outdoor cucumber pyramid around a wormery.

To create an in-ground wormery, start with a drainpipe. Cut the pipe into 24in (60cm) sections and drill a series of holes ½in (1–1.5cm) in diameter every 1–2in (3–5cm) for 18in (45cm) of pipe length, starting from one end and leaving 6in (15cm) undrilled. Bury the pipe vertically, with 20in (50cm) in the ground, and keep the non-drilled part sticking up. Finally, add a couple of generous handfuls of wood chips, then fill with kitchen scraps. Cover the top of the pipe with a cap or stone, and every week or two, top it up with more scraps.

Worms will decompose the material, moving in and out of the pipe, depositing their casts containing nutrients around the wormery. This will result in nutrient-rich soil to plant around. In-ground wormeries are fantastic in the center of raised beds.

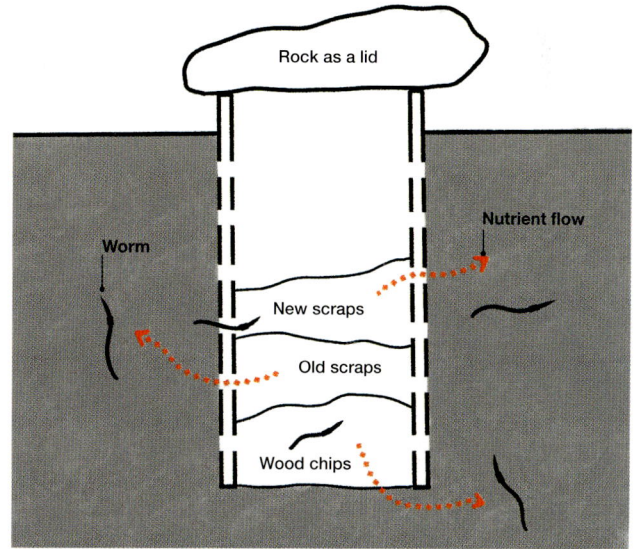

**How an in-ground wormery works**
*Worms move in and out of the pipe, depositing their casts, making the soil more nutrient-rich.*

# WOOD CHIPS

Wood chips are perfect for making pathways, mulching perennial crops, increasing soil carbon by composting over a couple of years, being the carbon source in a chicken composting setup, and serving as a base layer for tall raised beds.

If you can get a reliable source of wood chips from a local arborist, then you have struck gold. For best results, ensure that the wood chips you use are mostly from various hardwood sources and up to 20 percent pine in volume.

## THE CARBON CHALLENGE

Most wood chips have a very high concentration of carbon in relation to nitrogen. This means that if they are mixed into soil, the chips will tie up nitrogen in the soil until they have decomposed. As a result, in the short term, mulching annual crops with wood chips or using chips to build soil organic matter in a kitchen garden is not recommended unless you use ramial chipped wood (see below). If you have the space and time, a very effective way to create a fertile bed is to mulch an area of ground with a 2¾in (7cm) layer of wood chips in year one, incorporate chips into the top 4–5in (10–13cm) of soil in year two, and then grow in it in year three.

## RAMIAL CHIPPED WOOD

Ramial chipped wood (RCW) is made during the dormancy period from the younger tree branches that are under 2¾in (7cm) in diameter. These smaller branches are where the greatest concentration of minerals and nutrients are found in a tree—around 75 percent of the tree's total!

The word *ramial* comes from the Latin *ramus*, meaning "branch." The technique was pioneered by Gilles Lemieux, a former professor of forestry at the Laval University in Canada, who called it "copying and pasting forest soil into agricultural soil, minus the trees."

RCW has a far more favorable carbon-to-nitrogen ratio than wood chips, meaning that it is more suitable for mulching annual vegetables. However, it has many other uses.

*This handful of ramial chipped wood is laden with fungal hyphae in a matter of weeks after chipping.*

### Edible mushrooms

RCW can be used to grow your own edible mushrooms at home. King stropharia (wine caps) are one of the best edible species of fungi to grow by using RCW, and you can make beds under your fruit trees or soft fruit bushes that are inoculated with king stropharia mycelium to enjoy for years to come.

### Heat for hot beds

RCW from slightly thinner branches (2in/5cm and under) makes the perfect bulk material for filling hot beds (see p.61). It produces an excellent, consistent source of heat for up to four months, and at the end of the year, you can use the partly decomposed chips to mulch perennials or to add to the compost bin.

### Compost material

RCW is a must for compost. By running it through a compost system for a year or so, it will be perfect for mulching your annual crops or even in a potting mix. The best way I have seen RCW fully utilized in a garden is by selecting it as the core "carbon" ingredient in a chicken composting setup (see p.78).

### Producing RCW

The downside of RCW is that you need tree prunings and a woodchipper to make it. Garden shredders are a good option for smaller scales and can be rented by the day. If you have a larger garden or space, explore coppicing methods to turn RCW into a regenerative resource. Coppicing is when a tree is cut back to ground level over the winter to harvest all the biomass; it will put on new growth in the spring, to be harvested again a few years later.

*Mulching mature apple trees with ramial chip wood encourages long-term soil health.*

# BIOCHAR

Biochar is a form of charcoal used as a soil additive rather than as fuel. It is effective due to its highly porous structure, which helps retain moisture and nutrients and provides a protected habitat for soil microorganisms.

### BENEFITS OF BIOCHAR

Charcoal and biochar are stable forms of carbon produced through the process of pyrolysis, where organic matter is burned in a low-oxygen environment. It's easy to make it yourself (see right). There are numerous advantages to incorporating biochar within a permaculture kitchen garden.

### Enhanced soil fertility

Biochar is rich in essential nutrients that plants need to grow. Its structure helps in slowly releasing these nutrients into the soil, making them available to plants over a longer period.

### Improved water retention

Its porous nature allows biochar to absorb and retain water much more effectively than ordinary soil. Less watering is needed, making your garden more resistant to drought.

### Enhanced biodiversity

The porosity of biochar also creates the ideal protected environment for soil microorganisms, which are crucial for healthy, resilient soil.

### MAKING BIOCHAR

Biochar is one of the most effective ways of increasing the fertility of your garden soil, and if you can source woody materials, such as brashwood, from your local area, making it should be a priority to help reduce your garden's dependence on compost. Purchasing biochar is expensive. You can make your own by using either the cone method (right) or making it in a can (opposite).

### Making biochar using the cone method

The cone shape helps encourage an efficient burn for pyrolysis and saves you the expense of buying a kiln.

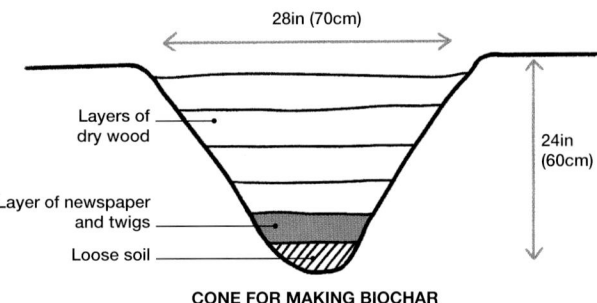

**CONE FOR MAKING BIOCHAR**

**1.** Dig a cone-shaped pit in your garden, about 24in (60cm) wide and 28in (70cm) deep. Loosen the soil at the bottom and then add some layers of scrunched-up paper at the base, followed by some smaller dry twigs. Set them alight.
**2.** Once the fire gets underway, add 4in (10cm) of dry woody material, such as branches, prunings, leaves, and dried plant matter. Avoid treated wood.
**3.** When the top layer of wood begins turning white, add the next 4in (10cm) layer of dry woody material. Repeat until the cone is full.
**4.** Once the top layer has burned, drench it with water to put out the fire. Leave it to cool overnight.
**5.** The following day, remove the biochar from the pit and crush to a coarse gravel-sized consistency. Store in a bucket for use or begin activating it right away.

### BIOCHAR'S BEGINNINGS

The use of biochar in food production stretches back thousands of years to the Amazon Basin, where Indigenous communities cultivated rich, fertile lands known as Terra Preta. These Terra Preta lands remain highly fertile to this day, thanks to the high carbon content promoting healthy soil.

## Making biochar in a can

This simple method of small-scale biochar production is something I learned from John Nitkowski from *Live on What You Grow*. It is a foolproof method of making charcoal whenever you have a bonfire or to place in a lit woodstove where you will get not just charcoal but also heat as a result.

**1.**
Take two steel cans. Pack one with the feedstock (wood chips, twigs, Jerusalem artichoke stems, and so on) and use pliers to crimp around the top of the other so the lip bends inward. Press firmly into the other can.

**2.**
Use a nail to puncture a hole in the base of one can to allow gases to escape. Place on the fire, as close to the embers as possible.

**3.**
After 3 hours, the charcoal will be ready. Use a couple of sticks to carefully remove from the fire and then knock the cans to open them. If the biochar pieces are large, break into smaller parts by placing between two sheets of cardboard and jumping up and down. Activate right away (see below) or store in a bucket to batch activate later.

## USING BIOCHAR

For growing crops, biochar needs to be activated; raw biochar will tie up nitrogen in the soil and reduce plant growth, whereas activated biochar will improve plant growth. To activate, soak it in an undiluted liquid weed feed for at least a month or mix 50:50 with compost for three months.

The best way to use biochar is to incorporate it into your garden's soil. The starting ratio should be 0.25 gallon (1 liter) of activated biochar per 11 sq ft (1 sq m) of growing space, forked into the top 6in (15cm) of soil (this would be 0.5 gallon or 2 liters of activated biochar in compost due to the 50:50 ratio). There are some other uses for it:

**Chicken compost** Add biochar at the start of the chicken compost flow (see p.78). This can be one of the core carbon ingredients, alongside wood chips and sawdust.

**Mulch** Instead of incorporating biochar into the soil, when mulching beds annually, add 1 part activated biochar to 9 parts compost.

**Potting mix** If you only have a small amount of biochar, you can mix it into compost when potting up seedlings before they are to be transplanted. Aim for a 1:9 ratio of activated biochar to your potting mix.

### In the polytunnel

A polytunnel is often where your hungriest crops are growing; think tomatoes, eggplants, and cucumbers. It is also where year-round growing can happen, so you need the highest quality healthy soil to support this. When making your first rounds of biochar, I would strongly suggest that you activate it and add it to your polytunnel beds before your outdoor beds.

# TRENCH AND POCKET COMPOSTING

These two methods are effective for growing food without compost. Rather than waiting for the material to break down in a compost bin, you add it to the soil to decompose in situ, feeding plants at the same time.

## SUITABLE MATERIALS

As with standard compost, ensure that you aim for a balance of greens and browns (see pp.54–55), about half of each by volume. Chop up the material as small as possible to speed up the process. The following are suitable:

- Chopped-up weeds without seed heads: nettle, dock, dandelions, thistle, chickweed, etc.
- Fruit and vegetable scraps
- Crushed eggshells and shells from shellfish
- Fish heads
- Partly decomposed farmyard manure
- Grass clippings (unsprayed)
- Shredded cardboard and newspaper (vegetable-based ink and nonglossy)
- Shredded fall leaves

These materials decompose faster than many used for standard compost, meaning the nutrients will be available more quickly for the plants. Ensure that you follow the composting ratio of 1:1 or 2:1 of greens and browns.

When creating trenches or pockets, you can also add activated biochar (see pp.68–69) to further increase the nutrient and mineral content.

## USING POTATOES IN TRENCHES

If you want to further build soil, I recommend this method. Make a trench and plant maincrop potatoes 4in (10cm) deep in the trench, spaced at 12in (30cm) intervals. Mulch them heavily with a mix of the ingredients listed above. Potatoes will grow through the mulch. When you harvest the potatoes, you will naturally mix this additional organic matter into the soil, creating a highly productive bed for the following growing season. See also other ways to build soil with potatoes on page 81.

## TRENCH COMPOSTING

This method can be used to create new growing areas or to replenish very poor-quality beds. You may need to top up the ingredients over time to prevent the trench from sinking.

**1.**
At least eight weeks before you want to plant, dig a trench 12in (30cm) wide and deep.

**2.**
Fill it generously with well-mixed green and brown material. High-nitrogen and nutrient items, such as fish heads and manure, should be at least 8in (20cm) under the surface.

**3.**
Firm down the materials well. Cover with a 2in (5cm) layer of soil and then cardboard to prevent weeds from growing. After eight weeks, remove the cardboard and transplant directly into the ground over the compost trench.

## POCKET COMPOSTING

Pocket composting follows the same method as trench composting but is used for growing single plants rather than for larger growing spaces—for example, you could create one pocket per tomato or pumpkin plant. Create a hole that is 12in (30cm) wide and 12–18in (30–45cm) deep. Thoroughly fill it with a mix of green and brown materials, press down firmly, and cover with a thin layer of soil. Use a stick to mark the pocket. After eight weeks, transplant the seedling into the pocket. Pocket composting is similar to an in-ground wormery (see p.65), but it is only temporary and used for one plant.

*Use a stick to mark the center of a composting pocket so that you know where to plant at a later date.*

## MICRO-POCKETS

Micro-pockets are where you increase the depth of your usual transplant hole and add one or two generous handfuls of highly nutritious compostable material at the base, covered with a thin layer (1½in/3–4cm) of soil. The seedling is then transplanted above this soil layer, perhaps with a little compost, and over time, the roots will enjoy the additional slow-release nourishment. This method also adds extra organic matter to the soil. It is an ideal way to further supplement good-quality growing areas or to use when transplanting perennials. The proportions of my ideal generous "handful" would comprise 1 part leaf mold, 1 part crushed shells or a fish head, and 2 parts grass clippings or a blend of chopped-up weeds.

# LIQUID AMENDMENTS

These liquid-based methods either improve soil or plant health or provide nutrition directly to plants. Pages 272–273 present all the liquid amendment recipes in one place. Here are guidelines to why and how to use them.

## MICROBIAL AMENDMENTS

These focus on adding biological organisms to the soil or to plants. For the soil, the role is to provide microbes that can kick-start the process of creating a better environment for plants by making nutrients plant-available and occupying space that pathogens could otherwise take up. Microbial amendments need to be used in conjunction with gardening methods that promote good soil organic matter levels to house and feed the biology.

Microbes are everywhere: on the stems and leaves of plants, in the soil, on our skin, in the air. Microbial amendments capture these and propagate them into concentrated liquid quantities for us to use, such as Jadam microbial solution (JMS, see p.273), which propagates microbes from leaf mold to add a diversity of biological life to poor-quality soils.

Some microbial amendments, such as lactic acid bacteria (LAB, see p.273), are also made to protect plants from pathogens. This works by using LAB to populate the leaves and stems of plants with microbes, which makes it harder for pathogens to settle and multiply.

## NUTRITIONAL AMENDMENTS

Nutritional amendments provide plant-available nutrients directly to the roots through watering. Minerals need to be soluble in water for plant roots to access them, which is a process made possible thanks to microbes breaking down complex molecules. Once organic material has been fully decomposed, the nutrients can be mixed into water to form a nutrient tea to feed your plants with.

Nutritional tea can be both aerobic and anaerobic. Anaerobic amendments are far simpler and less expensive for growers to create. One of the most powerful anaerobic feeds you can make for your plants is by decomposing comfrey or nettles in a bucket of water for a few weeks and diluting that liquid to then water your crops with.

## APPLICATION METHODS

Be careful about the water that you used for these liquid amendments. Rainwater is ideal. Mains water contains chlorine, which is severely damaging to microorganisms; see p.272 for how to make mains water safe.

### Drench

The most common application of liquid amendments is via soil drench. In a garden, this is with a watering can, following either a normal watering session or recently after rainfall, so the liquid is quickly absorbed into the soil rather than hydrating the dry surface.

*Watering crops with diluted liquid feed every few weeks helps maintain plant health, especially in poorer soils.*

### Spray/foliar feed

Leaves can absorb nutrients faster than plant roots when applying amendments. The liquid amendment is diluted as normal, but then placed in a spray bottle to be applied to the surface of leaves and stems (make sure you spray the underside of leaves too). Foliar sprays are also how microbial amendments like LAB are applied to plants for biological protection.

### Seedling soak

When watering seedlings with the base watering method, where they soak up water from the bottom (see p.92), the water can be diluted with a liquid amendment. This will also be absorbed into the pots and then available for plant roots to use.

*Applying LAB as a foliar spray to crops (here, bok choy) helps prevent disease outbreaks.*

## SPECIFIC AND MULTIPURPOSE

There are liquid amendments that technically offer both nutritional and microbial benefits. Worm tea (see p.272), compost extract (see p.272), and JMS (see p.273) are some examples; however, the tea and extract sway more toward the nutritional side, with the JMS being more on the microbial side.

*JMS ready for use; this is one of the simplest and most effective amendments a gardener can make.*

# GREEN MANURES AND COVER CROPS

Both green manures and cover crops are grown to improve soil health, structure, and fertility of ground that is to be used for food crops. They are excellent methods for improving low-quality areas of ground.

### COVER CROPS

These are primarily used to cover and protect the soil surface and improve soil structure via their root systems and root exudates. They either protect soil during short gaps within the growing season or for as much of winter as possible. Cover crops are usually terminated by cutting the stems at ground level as a chop and drop (see p.62) in early to midwinter or by mixing them into the soil like a green manure at the start of and during the growing season.

### GREEN MANURES

In a nutshell, these are cover crops that are grown primarily to be cut down and turned into the soil, quickly enriching it with organic matter and nutrients. Green manures are usually planted at the start of the growing season and allowed to grow until just before they set seed. They are then cut down as a chop and drop or mixed into the top 4in (10cm) of soil to produce maximum biomass yield.

### BENEFITS OF COVER CROPS AND GREEN MANURES

They prevent soil erosion by covering bare ground, which can be crucial during off-seasons or between plantings. Their growth can outcompete weeds, suppressing them and keeping beds weed-free during the off-season, reducing the need for weeding. Their roots aerate and bring structure and carbon to the soil, helping prevent compaction and improve water retention. Some attract beneficial insects, from pollinators to pest predators, enhancing the garden's balance and biodiversity.

While they share common applications, green manures and cover crops offer distinct benefits in a permaculture garden, and their timings are slightly different. Cover crops are sown in the late winter or early spring to protect the ground where tender crops like squash are to be planted in the late spring; they are also sown at the end of the season to protect soil over the winter. Green manures can be sown throughout the season. Undercover growing spaces also lend themselves well to cover crops and green manures, particularly over the winter, when the warmer temperature extends the growing season of these crops.

Some cover and green manure crops are not suitable for a permaculture garden, as they are too complex, specific, expensive, or difficult to terminate, so this book only shares the most useful and practical plants to grow. For maximum nutritional benefits from these crops for the soil, just remember to cut them down as they begin flowering.

### KEEP ROOTS IN THE SOIL

Both cover crops and green manures help with adding organic matter for healthy soil. One of the simplest techniques is when it comes to clearing annual crops. Instead of pulling out their roots, cut the plant at soil level and leave the root in the ground. The roots will gradually break down into nutrients and organic matter, helping to maintain a good soil structure. The roots of the majority of annual crops can be treated this way unless they are actual root crops like potatoes or carrots.

*In the late fall, I scythe phacelia to allow it to naturally break down over the winter. Leaving the roots in the ground helps maintain soil structure to reduce erosion from winter rains.*

## Suitable for both cover crops and green manures

1. Phacelia
2. Mustard
3. Crimson clover
4. Vetch winter tares*
5. Buckwheat
6. Field peas*
7. Field beans*
8. Lupin blue
9. Nasturtium
10. Borage

* Winter hardy

## COMFREY

You can't write a book about permaculture without mentioning comfrey! Comfrey is a perennial grown as a green manure and compost ingredient. However, unlike green manures, which grow where they are to decompose, comfrey is grown in a permanent location, and you harvest three or four cuts a year to use where you wish around your garden. The most accessible variety to grow is Bocking 14—its seeds are sterile, so it doesn't spread and take over your garden. It is propagated by root cuttings and crown division. An email to your local permaculture group will quickly connect you to someone who can share some root cuttings if you don't have access to comfrey yourself.

Comfrey grows well in partial shade and likes good drainage, but it will tolerate poorer draining areas. When preparing the ground to transplant your root cutting or division, mix in a little well-rotted manure to get the plants underway, and ensure that the young comfrey is well watered. For the first year, comfrey should be kept free of weeds, mulched generously, and not cut. After this, you will enjoy comfrey harvests for many years with next to no additional work.

Comfrey leaves are an incredible nutrient-rich regenerative resource and have a vast array of uses—most notably as a powerful liquid feed for fruiting crops (see p.272) and a fantastic chop and drop for enriching annual crop beds.

*Comfrey provides an abundance of biomass over the growing season, allowing up to five harvests between the spring and fall.*

**1.** *Divide comfrey by lifting the root and slicing the crown with a spade.*

**2.** *Replant the divided comfrey at the same depth.*

*For comfrey root cuttings, cut lengths of 2in (5cm) and plant them 2in (5cm) deep.*

# CHICKEN COMPOST

Chickens are professional compost machines! Their natural habit of scratching through the soil to search for bugs and seeds just under the surface can be used to make large volumes of high-quality and high-fertility compost.

Chicken composting is working with the foraging instincts chickens have to generate high-quality compost for very little effort. This is an example of the permaculture principle of designing from patterns to details: looking at the natural habits (pattern) the chickens have and then designing a productive fertility system (detail) for the garden around this habit.

While there are many approaches to making compost with chickens, what every system has in common is allowing chickens to access compost material to scratch up as they are looking for bugs, seeds, and leaves. At the same time, they are adding their fertility to the mix from their manure. The scratching of material also helps speed up the decomposition process in the same way that mixing a compost pile does.

There are many different types of chicken composting setups. One of my favorites is by Sean Dembrosky of Edible Acres (see resources, p.280). His setup uses simple stabilized boards to line the path and keep the compost material contained. The material ranges from raw waste that is mixed with nonactivated biochar (see pp.68–69) at the start of the path to finished compost at the end. With the help of a manure fork, the material is flipped along a "nutrient-flow" path, exposing germinating seeds, grubs, and other things that the chickens swoop in and enjoy. This helps keep the chickens healthy by adding a diversity of foods for them to enjoy as well as encouraging their natural behavior. In the process, they also manure the material, adding very rich fertility, resulting in the perfect compost to mulch annual beds with.

## CHICKEN COMPOST DESIGN SYSTEM

This design is small enough for an allotment scale with a handful of chickens, but very productive. Raw ingredients are added at one end, and compost is collected at the other. There is a covered bay to store finished compost away from the rain. The manure fork has a dedicated home to prevent it from being misplaced. The one downside of chicken

compost systems is that they are a shallow layer, and during dry weather, the material can dry out, and decomposition will slow down. The design takes this into account, ensuring that the hose can access the setup so the material can be drenched. Collecting rainwater from the chicken house into a bucket will also help, as will a moveable shade cover, which the chickens will need anyway during hot weather.

At the end of the flow, there is a small fenced-off section— using chicken wire—where comfrey is planted to act as a sponge to soak up any nutrients leached from the system, which you can harvest and use in the garden. In warmer climates, this would also be a good spot to grow outdoor tomatoes, and for larger setups, you could also integrate a willow coppice system.

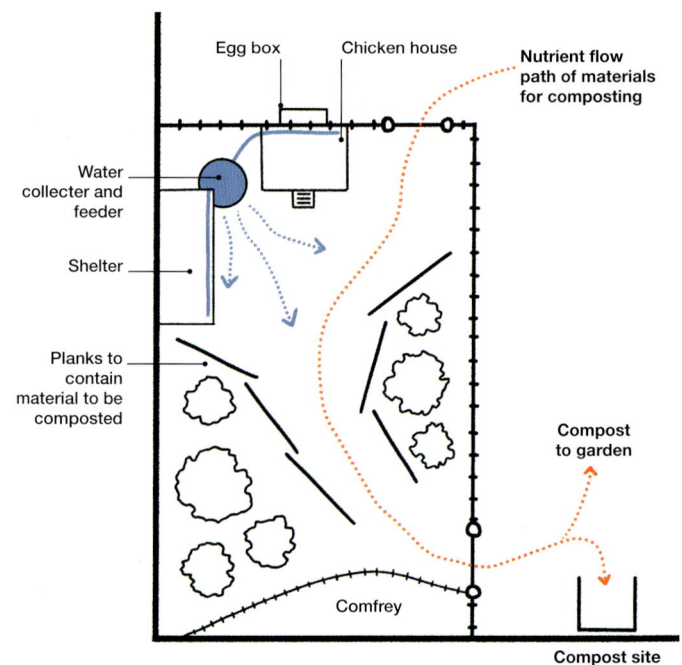

**A chicken compost setup**
*This is a chicken compost system that would work well next to a kitchen garden. The material should flow downhill if on a slope.*

*Harvesting compost for the garden provides hens with another opportunity to hunt for grubs and seeds.*

## HUW'S TIP

Rather than feeding the chickens in a dedicated dispenser, throw their food into the chicken compost system, and they will have a great time scratching around the material to eat, while helping the composting process at the same time.

## WOOD IN THE CHICKEN COMPOSTING PROCESS

Because of the high nitrogen content from the chicken composting process, both from the plant matter and manure, it is a perfect opportunity to add wood chips and sawdust as a carbon material alongside biochar, followed by fall leaves. Paper and cardboard, although high in carbon, contain very few additional nutrients.

# LOW-NUTRIENT GROWING

One of the best ways to reduce compost needs in your garden is knowing which edible crops require very little nutrition for respectable yields.

### PERENNIAL CROPS

In poorer soils, perennials are much better to focus on growing. Provided the crops are kept free of competing weeds, they can all be nourished just by the addition of one layer of mulch annually—with no need for compost. The only time these crops may need compost is at the planting stage if the soil is of particularly poor quality. Use soil tests (see pp.48–49) to find out whether the soil is on any of the extreme ends, and if so, generously amend the transplanting hole with a 50:50 mix of compost and topsoil.

The following crops grow well for me in low-fertility soil:
- Red, black, and white currants
- Gooseberries and jostaberries
- Blackberries
- Raspberries
- Blueberries
- Fruit trees
- Perennial herbs
- Jerusalem artichokes

### BIOMASS AND BIODIVERSITY

Provided you have the space to plan for the long term, low-nutrient soils lend themselves well to growing trees, such as willow, alder, and hazel, for coppicing for RCW (see pp.66–67). Areas of low-nutrient soils are also perfect for sowing wildflower meadow seed mixes that are tailored to your soil and climate. Wildflower meadows, even if small, offer a massive boost to local fauna, helping increase both the diversity and ecosystem.

### ANNUALS

For annual crops, leafy greens and herbs are the least hungry, along with edible flowers. Legumes, such as fava beans and peas, are also a good option for poor soil. In most cases, poor soil offers an excellent opportunity to grow cover crops or green manure. These can be incorporated into the soil to gradually build fertility over two to three growing seasons, giving you more options later down the line.

*Fruit trees are one of the best plant choices for reducing dependence on compost. Edible tree leaves on page 165 are also ideal for this.*

*This medley of leafy greens was harvested from plants growing in soil improved only through mulching with plant matter to add fertility.*

## SOIL BUILDING WITH SPUDS

This idea of growing potatoes in a way that provides a harvest as well as building soil is inspired in part by Nigel Palmer. Potatoes are a unique vegetable, as they can grow and yield well purely in mulch placed on top of the lawn. This method is one I have developed for simplicity, and it can be used with different materials. You will need some cardboard, seed potatoes, and one of the following mulch materials:

- Seaweed
- Comfrey
- Used farmyard bedding
- Wood chips and RCW (mix in grass clippings if possible)
- Fall leaves (shredded when possible)
- Hay and straw
- Grass clippings and chopped-up "weeds," such as nettles

**1.** If planting on grass, use a string trimmer or scythe to cut the grass short, but leave any of the grass cuttings in place.
**2.** Place a couple of layers of cardboard and a thick layer of mulch (at least 4in/10cm) on top and leave for at least four weeks.
**3.** From four weeks on, you can plant your seed potatoes. Make a hole in the mulch and cardboard to plant the potato at the original ground level and cover the hole over with mulch.
**4.** Once the shoots of the potatoes start showing, place an additional 4in (10cm) of mulch on top. This could be the same as or different than the original mulch. If you are using hay, straw, and seaweed, double this depth to ensure that potatoes don't turn green from sunlight.
**5.** Allow potatoes to naturally die back at the end of the growing season, harvest the tubers, and spread the remaining mulch evenly over the ground to continue composting.
**6.** Over the winter, cover with cardboard or natural landscape fabric to prevent weeds from growing.
**7.** The following spring, rake off any clumps of mulch that haven't decomposed and place them on the compost. Then, transplant seedlings or direct sow into the new, fertile ground.

---

### HUW'S TIP

To grow potatoes later in the season, use a blight-resistant potato variety, such as 'Sarpo Mira'.

# Water

# WATER NEEDS AND DROUGHT

Water, light, and healthy soil are the core ingredients for a successful kitchen garden. Ensuring plants get enough water is often an afterthought in the midst of a busy season. Here are some strategies to reduce watering needs.

In a garden that isn't resilient to periods of dry weather or drought, any lack of rain will lead to high watering demands, and plants will not be able to grow at their optimum rate. In the same way that you can build healthy soil (see pp.46–79), there are many methods to reduce water needs of your garden, and, as a result, help drought-proof your crops, too.

## ADDING ORGANIC MATTER

First, I have some good news: Any technique you use to add organic matter to the soil, such as adding compost, incorporating biochar, and chop and drop, will increase its water-storage capacity. This is explained in greater detail under rainwater storage (see p.88), but when you learn that soil organic matter can retain up to ten times its weight in water, focusing on building your soil health suddenly becomes even more impactful.

## MULCHING

While increasing soil organic matter is an important ongoing project to improve in-ground moisture levels, mulching (see pp.62–63) offers immediate results and is the most powerful tool in the short term. Mulches at least 2in (5cm) thick are best for reducing evaporation from the soil. If you're applying mulch in response to drought conditions, thoroughly water the soil in the evening and immediately apply mulch. The cooler night temperatures allow as much water as possible to enter the soil. Most mulches have a high water permeability, helping any rainwater slowly seep down into the roots rather than quickly flow off the surface of dry bare soil. My three go-to mulches specifically for soil moisture are grass clippings, wood chips, and fall leaves.

*Mulching peppers with straw shreds conserves water by covering all bare ground.*

*Perennial herbs such as thyme, lavender, salvia, and Welsh onions (all left) are only ever watered during extreme dry weather. For me in Wales, this is only once every few years.*

## GROWING PERENNIALS

A resilient kitchen garden includes a large percentage of perennials. They have much stronger root systems in comparison to annuals, giving them a greater surface area to access water. They also cope much better due to their genetics. Annuals have a limited time to reproduce, and so whenever conditions become too extreme, they react by bolting (running to seed prematurely) in order to have a chance for their lineage to continue. However, perennials have time on their side and so conserve their energy during extremes rather than using it all up to reproduce. The more perennials you have, the less watering you'll need to do, and if you're trying to conserve water, prioritize perennials.

## ESTABLISHING A WATERING INFRASTRUCTURE

There are many cases where watering is a necessity, regardless of all the points mentioned at left. When you're growing annuals from seed, vulnerable seedlings will need water to maintain their quality and health. This is where having the correct watering infrastructure for both collection and application comes in; setup and use are covered on the following pages.

# RAINWATER AS A RESOURCE

Most rainfall tends to happen in the fall and winter, when we need it least. Capturing this abundant rainwater to use in the spring and summer is one of the most valuable steps toward a resilient, more productive kitchen garden.

## RAINWATER COLLECTION CALCULATOR

One of the most important calculations any gardener can make is figuring out the annual water-capture potential from any roof where the collection of rainwater is possible, which could be a shed, garage, greenhouse, or house. To do this, you need to know the total roof area (length x width) and the average annual or monthly rainfall in your area (in millimeters). Many online resources provide detailed local rainfall measurements. The calculation also includes a deduction of 10 percent from the total to account for the potential loss of rainwater due to water splashing over the sides of roofs and gutters and evaporation. You can reduce water loss from splashes by modifying a roof to include shallow barriers around its edges.

### The calculation
Roof area x average annual rainfall = X liters

### To factor in 10 percent water loss
X liters x 0.9 = Total liter potential

### Example
A garden shed measuring 2 x 3m in an area that receives an average of 1,400mm of rain each year.

6 (m²) x 1,400 (mm) = 8,400 (liters) x 0.9 = 7,560 (total liter potential)

## BUILDING A RAINWATER COLLECTION SYSTEM

Once you have figured out the quantity of water that your roof has the potential to supply, it's time to build a DIY rainwater collection system. There are many systems out there, but I opt to keep it simple and low cost, especially when it comes to the storage container, which is always the most expensive element. Follow these steps to create a setup that suits you and your garden.

### 1. Location
Ideally, place your system near a downspout that carries water from the gutter on your house, garage, or shed to allow you to easily channel rainwater from the roof into your container.

### HUW'S TIP
**Always place water storage in the shadiest possible spot so that it doesn't take up premium growing space. Using a longer pipe to connect the water storage to the downspout gives more flexibility.**

### 2. Storage
Select a storage container for the rainwater. Options include plastic barrels, intermediate bulk container (IBC) tanks, metal tanks, and even wooden barrels. Use the rainwater collection calculator (see left) to determine the water-holding capacity you will need to make the best use of rainwater from a given roof space; remember to at least double up your tanks so that if one leaks, you don't lose everything (see p.23).

### 3. Setup
Place the water storage container in its chosen location and ensure that the ground or base is level so that the tank will be stable. Consider how you will access the water. For example, I raise IBC tanks on stacked wooden pallets to allow space for a watering can under the tap. Connect the downspout from the roof to your container by using a diverter. This allows water to continue down the drainage pipe when the tank is full rather than causing the tank to overflow.

### 4. Filter
It is important to create a simple filter to prevent debris, such as leaves, moss, and twigs, from entering your tank. A wire mesh filter placed at the end of the pipe feeding into the container works well. Use wire to hold the filter in place and allow for easy removal to clear any blockages.

*Here, I am measuring the total water collection potential of my shed roof to use as another element in my off-grid water setup.*

Create a lid for tanks with open tops to keep animals from falling in and getting trapped and help prevent evaporation. A sheet of wood secured with a few bricks is my go-to cover.

### 5. Maintenance

Once your collection setup is complete, all you need to do is ensure that the system remains leak- and block-free. I always check my water infrastructure in late February to make sure everything is in working order, ready for spring.

## TEMPORARY RAINWATER COLLECTOR

A large tarpaulin attached between four poles creates a temporary roof space to capture heavy rain and divert it into a container if you need extra water. This can even be done over part of your garden as a temporary method to capture rain over a day or two. During particularly dry periods, have the tarp ready to install so that when it does rain, you can capture precious water.

## USING IBC TANKS FOR WATER STORAGE

For years, my go-to low-cost water storage containers have been 264-gallon (1,000-liter) IBC tanks. These large plastic containers are used for storing and transporting bulk liquids, which makes them ideal for holding water. They can be bought second-hand, but it is vital you know that any tank you buy hasn't been used to store something nasty. Fortunately, most sellers specify what tanks have been used for previously. To prevent algae from building up inside the translucent tank, purchase an IBC cover or use a long-handled brush to give it a quick rinse in winter. I know that a full tank will fill my 2.5-gallon (10-liter) watering can 100 times, so during dry weather, I can keep track of how much water I am using and how much is left.

## SOIL AS WATER STORAGE

Soil is also a natural rainwater collector, as its organic matter acts as a sponge that soaks up and holds rainwater, which plants can use during dry weather. Adding organic matter by mulching and following no-dig methods (see p.52) increases the soil's water-holding capacity. According to the US Department of Agriculture Natural Resources Conservation Service, conservative estimates suggest that a 1 percent increase in soil organic matter can result in an additional 20,000 gallons (75,000 liters) of available soil water per acre. On a garden scale, this means an extra 5 gallons (18 liters) of water per 11 square feet (1 square meter)! Results can vary depending on soil type and initial soil organic matter percentages, but upping soil organic matter considerably increases soil's ability to hold onto water, which means that my most important water tanks are the raised beds themselves.

*Many people think IBC tanks and other water storage units are ugly, but their appearance can easily be improved with climbing plants, such as sweet peas, shown here, or by covering them with pallet wood.*

# WATERING TOOLS

There are a few watering tools to have in every garden to ensure all needs are covered. It is about quality over quantity, so you want a few tools that will last you for as many seasons as possible. This is what's in my watering arsenal.

## HOSES
### Garden hose
I have one trusted garden hose that can reach from my main water tank to the farthest corner on one reel; larger gardens may need a connecting hose. I have a wall mount that allows my hose to quickly reel in, keeping it clean and off the ground.

### Spray nozzle
One high-quality spray nozzle with multiple settings will cover almost every watering task. Ensure that your nozzle includes a delicate function for gently watering seedlings as well as a sprayer setting for more mature plants.

### Long wand
A long wand spray nozzle is an underrated garden tool. It allows you to direct water right to the base of the plant while saving your back! It's perfect for rows of seedlings, individual plants, and medium to large pots and containers.

### HUW'S TIP
When purchasing hoses and nozzles, look for ones that have frost and UV protection.

### MICRODRIP HOSE
A microdrip hose system is perfect for pots, as it allows you to install a water outlet at any chosen point along the hose that irrigates at the base of the plant. This means you only need to turn on the tap to water all your containers at once.

### BATTERY PUMP

If your garden, like mine, does not have access to mains water, you may want to consider a rainwater tank battery pump. This allows you to have a 2 bar water pressure—more than enough for powerful watering. It's also useful if you wish to move water uphill, either for watering or to fill another storage tank. The alternative is a solar water pump, which is far more expensive but requires no battery and is better suited for larger gardens.

*A wall-mounted hose box with a battery pump makes an effective watering setup for smaller gardens without mains water.*

*This soaker hose is being laid in a polytunnel bed in late winter in preparation for summer-fruiting crops, such as cucumbers.*

## WATERING CAN AND DUNK BUCKET

A durable 2.5-gallon (10-liter) watering can allows you to be quick and nimble when doing targeted spot watering rather than needing to reel out the hose. Coupled with a dunk bucket—a trash can filled with water from an IBC tank that has a water stop float so it is always full—you can quickly fill a watering can and water exactly what is needed.

## TRAY

A large deep-sided tray that can be filled with water is the final watering tool and is reserved for watering modules and pots of seeds and seedlings from the base (see p.92).

## SOAKER HOSE

This type of hose has permeable walls, allowing a gentle, consistent drip irrigation over the area it covers. Roughly every 3ft of length will irrigate 11 square feet of ground around it. Soaker hoses are best placed on the surface of the bed and then mulched or buried around 2in (5cm) below the surface to prevent evaporation during hot weather and to ensure the water goes directly to the roots. They are particularly useful under cover (see p.92).

*This dunk bucket naturally fills due to a water stop float, meaning it is always ready when I need it.*

# HOW TO WATER

The advice here is all you need to know to ensure success with watering. In later chapters, there will be crop-specific watering tips, such as the "plank method" for direct sown vegetables.

### SEEDS AND YOUNG SEEDLINGS

Newly sown modules and young seedlings require gentle watering to avoid damaging their leaves and stems. For seedlings in modules and pots, the best option is to fill a large, leak-proof tray with 1–2in (3–5cm) of water, place the trays in the water, and set a timer for 10 minutes. The water will naturally be absorbed by the potting mix and available for the roots of seedlings. If watering from overhead, either for modules or seedlings in the ground, make sure the water is going down into the roots. A damp surface may give a false impression of effective watering, so use your finger to ensure the soil below the surface is not dry.

### CONTAINERS

Large pots and containers are much thirstier than raised beds, so mulch is an absolute must for saving both time and water. If your garden is on a patio or balcony with multiple containers, then I recommend that you look into microdrip systems (see p.90). Otherwise, water containers of both annuals and perennials when the top 2in (5cm) of soil is dry.

### POLYTUNNEL BEDS

Polytunnel beds and hoop beds don't have the luxury of rainfall to help cover the water demands of your crops. Watering plants that are under cover should be done thoroughly, at least once a week during the growing season. Watering time can be slashed if you use a soaker hose (see p.91) for a couple of hours every two days during the growing season. Over winter, reduce watering to a biweekly activity to prevent mold growth but maintain soil health.

### RAISED BEDS/GARDEN BEDS

As for containers, water annual crops when the top 2in (5cm) of soil is dry. Perennials will almost always be mulched, and so watering is only needed for young, developing perennial plants when there has been a noticeable lack of rain.

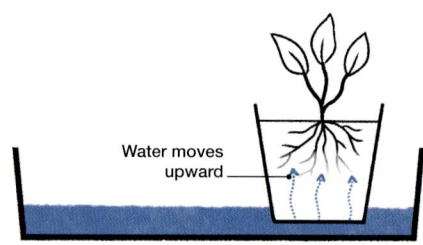

**Watering seedlings**
*The compost in pots acts as a "wick" to draw up moisture to the roots.*

Water moves upward

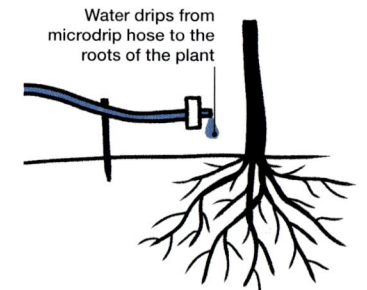

Water drips from microdrip hose to the roots of the plant

**Watering a container**
*Microdrip systems target water as close to the root system as possible to minimize any water loss.*

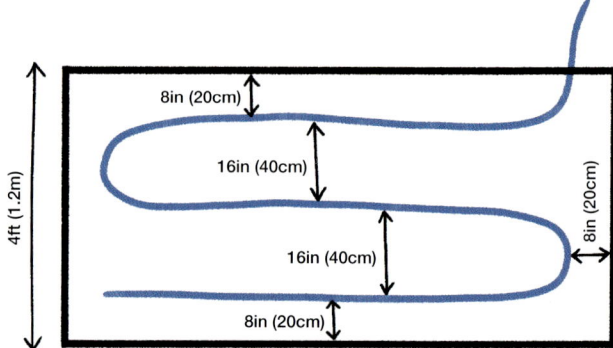

8in (20cm)
16in (40cm)
16in (40cm)
8in (20cm)
4ft (1.2m)
8in (20cm)

**Watering a polytunnel bed**
*This is my soaker hose layout to ensure maximum range of watering with no dry spots for a 4ft-wide (1.2m) raised bed.*

*If seedlings just need a little top up, overhead watering (above) works well.*

*Semi-mature seedlings (above) respond best to watering close to their base.*

## TIMING

Whenever possible, water on overcast days, either early in the morning (particularly if your garden suffers from slugs) or in the early evening. This is to avoid watering in intense sunlight or around midday, when evaporation levels are highest and your time spent watering is least efficient.

## HUW'S WATERING TIPS

**1.** Water as close to the base of the plant as possible so the water targets the roots. If the water runs off the leaves, less will be available for the roots.

**2.** To ensure your water goes deeper into the soil, water once thoroughly and repeat in 10–15 minutes. The first watering will help condition the permeability of the surface to accept more water.

**3.** Water the outer edges of beds a little more thoroughly than the middle, as the edges will dry out more quickly.

# The hierarchy
# of growing space

# GARDEN OVERVIEW

As a permaculture gardener, your job is to use the strengths and challenges of your garden to create the most resilient, productive system you can. Understanding each type of growing space will greatly help you create a productive garden.

The hierarchy of growing space is my approach to organizing what I grow. It's a scale of quality. Per square meter or foot, some growing spaces are multiple times more productive than others, but each offers specific benefits that allow you to design a garden in the most efficient manner. Soil health is also a key consideration, and this is explained under pots and containers (see p.115) and in the undercover section (see p.100). Toward the end of the chapter, I also recommend where other elements could best fit, such as a shed, compost area, and water tanks.

This hierarchy is tailored to a temperate climate where there is a distinct difference between summer and winter and the growing season is limited by the last and first frost dates.

## THE HIERARCHY

This chapter follows the hierarchy of growing space from most to least productive. It goes as follows:

1. Undercover: large structures
2. Undercover: small structures
3. Vertical spaces
4. Raised beds
5. Non-sided beds
6. Soft boundaries
7. Pots and containers
8. Shade

There are multiple opportunities to increase the potential of your growing spaces: A raised bed could be converted into a hoop bed, a sunny wall could be painted a brighter color to reflect more light, and you could install trellises in beds to increase vertical growing.

*This aerial view of my original kitchen garden shows the key elements from undercover, bed, and vertical growing spaces to soft boundaries and water storage in a shady corner.*

## HIERARCHY OF SUN EXPOSURE

Most crops in a temperate garden thrive with as much sun as possible, and the sunniest spots are the most productive. There are four core types of sun exposure that also form a hierarchy: full sun, partial shade, dappled shade, and full shade (fewer than four hours of sun a day). Even in full shade, you can grow certain crops (see p.116). Which crop to plant where is covered in the chapters on perennials (see pp.124–173) and annuals (see pp.176–225).

# LANDSHAPE

One essential element of designing a productive garden is understanding the shape of your land. Is it on a steep slope, is it mostly flat, or is it a mix of both?

Flat and sloped ground each offers its own benefits and drawbacks, which I have summarized below. Understanding its characteristics helps give you direction on how to best approach your land.

| Type of ground | Key benefits | Key drawbacks |
|---|---|---|
| Flat | • Better accessibility for people and materials<br>• More suited for building structures, such as polytunnels<br>• A more even spread of water throughout the area | • Prone to becoming waterlogged<br>• Limited microclimates to work with<br>• Reduced sun exposure |
| Sloped | • Low chance of waterlogging<br>• Different parts of the slope offer different microclimates<br>• Improved sun exposure if south- or east-facing | • More work may be required for establishment<br>• Harder to maintain the site<br>• Likely to have uneven water distribution |

## POSITIONING BEDS IN A SLOPING GARDEN

If you have a gentle slope that levels off at the bottom of your garden, this level part will hold the most moisture. If it gets swampy after heavy rainfall and during the wettest months, raised beds will combat this. Alternatively, you could create beds on the slope and grow plants on the level ground that are more suited to wetter conditions, such as comfrey, blueberries, and willow.

For gardens on a hillside, make sure that beds are built horizontally rather than angled downhill (see right). If soil or compost is placed at an angle, excessive heavy rains can cause erosion, washing away your most fertile ground.

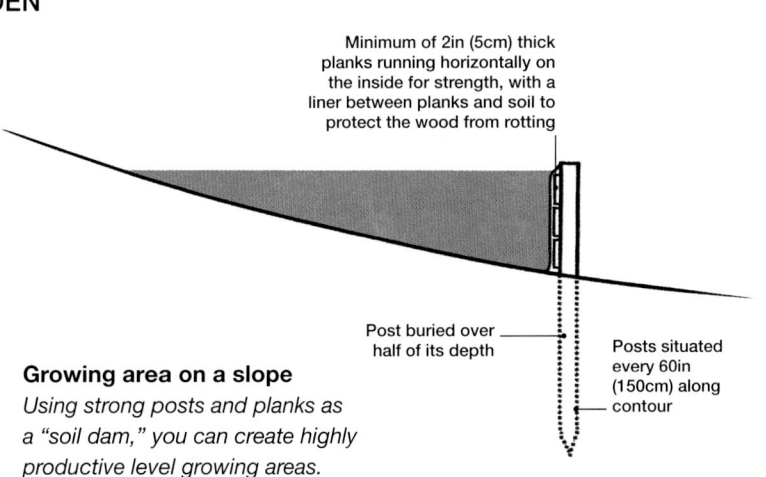

Minimum of 2in (5cm) thick planks running horizontally on the inside for strength, with a liner between planks and soil to protect the wood from rotting

Post buried over half of its depth

Posts situated every 60in (150cm) along contour

**Growing area on a slope**
*Using strong posts and planks as a "soil dam," you can create highly productive level growing areas.*

## CONTOUR LINES

A contour is a specific line of equal elevation; contour lines on a map are often described as the fingerprint of the land.

How does this affect gardening on a slope? First, planting along the contour yields a natural aesthetic; instead of growing in straight lines, you work with the natural shape of the land, embracing the curves.

Planting on the contour can also help slow the flow of water as it moves downhill, allowing the water to be retained in the soil rather than running off the land. Soft boundaries and linear food forests are often planted on the contour, and you can create beds or borders along the contour for similar benefits, including ease of harvesting by moving along the row rather than walking uphill or downhill.

### Identifying a contour line by using an A-frame

An A-frame is a simple, ancient DIY tool that allows anyone to find contour lines on their land without other technical equipment. To make an A-frame, you need two pieces of wood around 6ft (1.8m) in length, a shorter straight piece around 3ft (1m), and a length of string with a weight (such as a rock) tied at the base. Assemble as shown in the diagram.

Calibrate your A-frame by placing a spirit level on the horizontal plank, leveling it by moving one leg higher or lower. Use a pen to mark the point on the plank where the string hangs steady when completely level.

To use the A-frame, place it down at the starting point of the area you wish to measure, move the leg (closest to the direction in which you are heading) until the string is steady in line with the pen mark, and then use that outer leg as a pivot to swing 180 degrees. Repeat this process, moving along the contour line. Every time you pivot, mark the location the leg was at with a stick, and when you come to the end, the sticks mark out your contour line.

I am using an A-frame here to identify contours along which to plant a soft boundary (see pp.112–113).

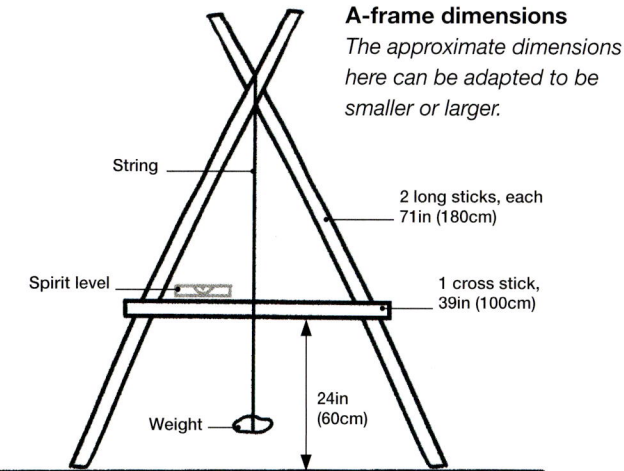

**A-frame dimensions**
*The approximate dimensions here can be adapted to be smaller or larger.*

String

Spirit level

Weight

2 long sticks, each 71in (180cm)

1 cross stick, 39in (100cm)

24in (60cm)

# UNDERCOVER: LARGE STRUCTURES

Polytunnels and greenhouses are often the centerpiece of a kitchen garden. They offer a seedling-raising factory, a place for sun-loving crops like tomatoes, shelter in unsettled weather, and even winter accommodations for poultry!

The one rule for situating an undercover growing structure is that it needs to be in a location that enjoys full sun and isn't a frost pocket. The orientation, as long as it is in a sunny location, matters less. Undercover growing space requires a large initial outlay and brings a lot of potential to a garden, so it is important to carefully plan what you want from this space every growing season. You need to prioritize the soil fertility of your beds over any containers undercover, following the hierarchy of growing space.

I would always recommend polytunnels for new gardens, as they are so cost-effective. When purchasing a polytunnel, aim to get the largest you can fit in your space and that works with your budget. Note that when buying polytunnels, there is a massive savings per square yard when you extend the length of the tunnel. For example, a 200 sq ft (18 sq m) polytunnel only costs 30 percent more than a 100 sq ft (9 sq m) polytunnel if sticking with the same width.

A greenhouse can easily cost ten times as much as a polytunnel per square yard of undercover space. For example, as a rough comparison, about $2,480 would buy you 60 sq ft (5.5 sq m) of growing space in a greenhouse, but this same amount would buy you 600 sq ft (55 sq m) of growing space in a polytunnel. However, if you want a greenhouse or already have one, the approach to growing inside a polytunnel or a greenhouse is much the same.

## SOIL FERTILITY UNDERCOVER

I demand more from my undercover growing spaces yield-wise—and often I am growing the hungriest crops, such as tomatoes and cucumbers. To ensure that the soil remains as productive as possible, I add a thicker layer of compost (2in/4–5cm) annually, amend with activated biochar (see pp.68–69), and add more organic matter when transplanting seedlings, either pocket composting ahead of time (see pp.70–71) or a few handfuls when planting out.

Mulch is an essential aspect of successful undercover growing. Polytunnels and greenhouses have higher temperatures that result in greater evaporation. Applying mulch (see pp.62–63), coupled with soaker hoses, keeps the soil moist and biologically active.

## MAKING THE MOST OF SPACE

Another major benefit is that you have space to propagate a large number of seedlings. You can start earlier in the season, so you have semi-mature seedlings ready for transplanting as soon as outside conditions become favorable. You can also increase the seedling numbers by using shelves to stack modules or by creating a temporary vermin-proof hanging mesh platform suspended above a raised bed to maximize productivity.

A nice idea for polytunnels and greenhouses over the winter is to create a seating corner for you to use as a garden office or a reading nook. Stacking functions is a core element of permaculture (see p.27), and the seasonality of undercover growing spaces allows you to get creative and use them in multiple ways.

## HUW'S TIP

North–south or east–west? The orientation of a polytunnel is up to you. An east–west orientation maximizes winter temperatures, as the large south-facing side will have more consistent sunlight due to the sun being lower in the sky. A north–south aspect provides equal sunlight to both sides over the summer but is less effective for winter growing. The majority of mine are east–west.

## TWO EXTRA MONTHS

It's estimated that a layer of protection, such as a polytunnel, can provide you with at least an additional four weeks of growing both at the start and at the end of the growing season. Additionally, this single layer creates a more ambient winter temperature, allowing you to overwinter crops that wouldn't survive the elements outside in raised beds, such as salads, pea shoots, carrots, and beets.

## VENTILATION

One of the biggest undercover growing issues is a lack of ventilation, which leads to either stagnant air that can cause disease issues or, during the peak of summer, overheating. During the cool start of the growing season, the four weeks on either side of the average first frost, I will always keep the doors closed overnight, have one door open on cool days, and on warm days keep both ends open. From mid-June, I usually keep the doors open overnight to save time having to close them. When temperatures begin to drop in September, I begin to close the doors in the evenings, and around the last average frost date, the doors are closed permanently overnight but opened as much as possible during the days of winter and early spring to maintain airflow.

*For gardens in temperate climates, a polytunnel becomes the most valuable growing area.*

# UNDERCOVER: SMALL STRUCTURES

There are many types of small-scale undercover growing spaces that provide multiple benefits, from extra propagation space for seed sowing to extending the season and overwintering potential.

### THE HINGED HOOP BED

A hinged hoop bed converts a standard raised bed into a mini-polytunnel by attaching a hoop frame with polytunnel plastic over the bed (for how to assemble a hoop bed, see pp.276–277). You can enjoy all the same growing benefits of a large polytunnel, but you are limited to plant height; rather than growing cordon tomatoes, you would grow bush tomatoes, for example.

A hinged hoop bed is usually a permanent feature, extending the growing season and creating a warmer ambient temperature over the winter months. However, if all, or at least some, of your raised beds are of the same dimensions, you can move the cover to different beds by unscrewing the hinges. This means that you can be flexible about which bed has the cover and even use it for providing temporary warmth.

The skeleton design of a hoop bed means that you can interchange the cover you place over it. Usually, I go for polytunnel plastic, with the focus on increasing the growing season, but you can install other types of covers, such as a shade net if your garden has little shelter from the sun and you want to grow salads throughout summer, or an insect mesh to protect brassicas from cabbage white butterflies or carrots from root fly.

**Ventilation of a hoop bed**

The approach to ventilation of a hoop bed is very similar to a polytunnel. Rather than keeping doors open, you prop the cover up around 2in (5cm) off the base of the raised bed on cooler days and 12in (30cm) on warmer days.

*A hoop bed can be easily propped up for ventilation by using a single post.*

*A cold frame is being used here to create a mini-greenhouse over a raised bed to protect salad crops through the fall and into the winter.*

## COLD FRAME

A cold frame is a lightweight, versatile square or rectangular growing box of glass or polycarbonate. It's weatherproof, offers insulation, and lets in light. The top opens for ventilation and access (see hoop beds, opposite, for ventilation).

The traditional use for rectangular cold frames is for hardening off tender seedlings. This is a process of helping adjust cold-sensitive seedlings, such as squash and tomatoes, to increased sunlight and the cooler daytime temperatures outside to reduce the shock of transplanting them into the ground outside. While hardening off the most tender seedlings (squash and tomatoes) by gradually increasing their exposure to the outdoors over a one to two-week period is useful, it is something I rarely (if ever) do for hardier seedlings, such as beets and brassicas, and I still have excellent results (and have saved a lot of time). Granted, the seedlings may experience a bit of shock, but in my experience, they quickly bounce back.

I use a cold frame in other ways in my garden. First, it forms an additional protected space for starting off seedlings in modules or as a space for seedling overflow from the polytunnel. Second, a cold frame can act much in the same way as a hinged hoop bed, but for a smaller growing area. Because a cold frame is lightweight, you can move it around the garden to help bring on directly sown seeds faster, so it is perfect for starting off an early sowing of carrots or salads, for example, and can be removed once conditions are warmer. A cold frame is also the structure I use on top of a hot bed to create that protected growing zone and retain heat (see pp.274–275).

## MINI-GREENHOUSE (SEEDLING SHELVES)

A mini-greenhouse is an excellent answer to starting a lot of seedlings in a small footprint. It is a vertical structure with several shelves and a covering that offers a small, protected environment. You can further insulate mini-greenhouses by saving bubble wrap from packaging and placing it around pots and modules on cold nights. If you are using your mini-greenhouse outdoors, it is essential that the base be weighed down and that it is in a sunny, sheltered position. The upright nature of the structure means it can be susceptible to tipping in the wind. To ventilate, open the the front on warmer days.

# VERTICAL SPACES

I have placed vertical growing above raised beds in the hierarchy because vertical growing is increasingly valuable in smaller spaces—such as a city, where the buildings are forced to go high due to a lack of available footprint.

The term *vertical* encompasses anything in a garden from a wall, fence, side of a compost bin, and trellises to other small-scale growing methods, such as hanging baskets or gutter gardens. The greatest challenge with gutter gardens and hanging baskets is that they are incredibly thirsty, as they have a small volume of soil, and water evaporates more quickly in containers in mid-air compared to those on the ground. A permaculture kitchen garden prioritizes in-ground vertical growing first and foremost, followed by larger containers, and finally the gutters and hanging baskets.

## SOUTH-FACING BOUNDARY

South-facing boundaries provide gardeners with a suntrap that will support an exciting range of crops that relish warm conditions. Cordon, fan, and espalier-trained fruit trees and soft fruits are the usual go-to for perennial options, while outdoor varieties of tomatoes are a common choice, with much higher success rates compared to growing in raised beds in the middle of a garden. For best results, create a raised bed at the foot of the boundary for a large volume of soil to plant into.

### Fake walls

You can create additional south-facing boundaries within a garden by making smaller wooden walls painted a light color. These micro-suntraps offer additional prime space for dwarf fruits and trained soft fruits as well as sun-loving vegetables, while providing welcome shade in exposed sites.

*Harvesting my first 'Jumbo Pink Banana' squash of the season, which grows in front of my south-facing boundary.*

## CASCADE RAISED BEDS

These beautiful yet practical raised beds have several tiers on different levels that allow you to maximize the vertical and encourage the planting of crops that overflow. There is also more surface area in a raised bed presented to the sun, resulting in increased warming of the soil, which will benefit the plants overnight. My favorite way of using cascade-style beds is to have a beautiful impact plant on the top tier (such as dwarf sunflowers), cascading crops on the outer edges (such as tumbling tomatoes), and high-yielding crops in the remaining space (such as root vegetables).

## A-FRAME BUCKET SETUP

Some growing spaces may have areas of concrete ground where raised beds are unsuitable. An A-frame bucket growing setup is a simple way to create a productive space by having two or three tiers of potato buckets oriented to maximize south-facing exposure. These are large enough to grow most crops, and you can ensure preferred growing conditions.

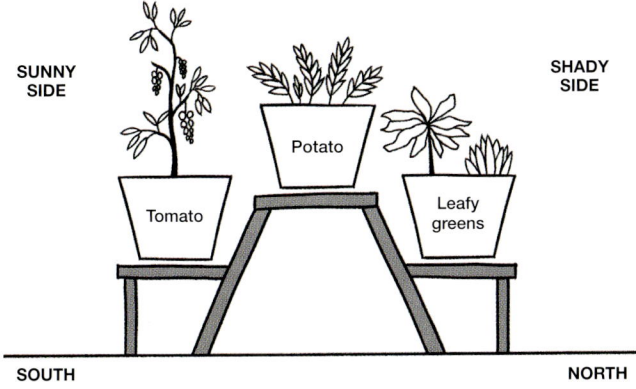

### Crops in potato buckets on an A-frame
*The potato in the middle helps by creating a warm and sheltered microclimate for the tomato to enjoy. Leafy greens grow in the partial shade.*

## TRELLIS-TYPE GROWING

The other most common vertical options come in the form of trellises for growing climbing crops. A-frames, wigwams, obelisks, propped-up pallets, and pyramids are other options, which can be sunk into the ground (see pp.180–181). Whenever you add a vertical aspect to your garden, you are creating a microclimate: a suntrap on the south side and a shady spot on the north. Use this to help prioritize what you plant around the vertical structure. Trellises also increase the visual interest of a garden, so I like to bear this in mind when I plan where I place my structures at the start of each growing season.

*Vertical supports, clockwise from top left: a fence of netting and bamboo canes; a wigwam made with bamboo canes; and a frame using hazel poles and string.*

# RAISED BEDS

Raised beds are the ultimate growing space for intensive cropping of annual vegetables in small to medium gardens. They do not need sides (see pp.110–111 for non-sided beds), but sides offer many benefits that help produce high yields.

## PROS AND CONS OF BEDS WITH SIDES

Beds with sides offer a large number of benefits:

- A permanent size that allows for easy planning, and you don't need to worry about weeds or grass creeping into the edges.
- A seat for the gardener, as well as bringing the plants closer to you to reduce how far you need to bend.
- Solid sides allow you to attach a greater option of accessories, such as trellises and hoop beds.
- Above ground level to avoid saturation of water during extreme rainfall, but still allow roots to spread freely.
- Edges allow you to increase growing area in a similar manner to cascading beds.
- Mulching is much easier and more accurate, especially with compost, as the sides keep the material in.
- A physical edge to a bed allows you to compartmentalize your garden, meaning you can just focus on the bed in front of you rather than everything blending together, which can lead to distraction or overwhelm.

There are two core arguments against raised beds with sides: slugs and cost. First, let me address the slug concern—that they hide between the side of the bed and the soil. To me, this is a perfect opportunity to set up dedicated plank traps (see p.262) to capture slugs. Also, with my experience in a wet, humid climate, slugs much prefer hiding under mulches, in long grass, and under rocks and logs rather than the soil pressed against the edge of a bed.

Cost is a valid argument, but there are many different materials you can make raised beds out of, and many can be sourced for low costs, or even for free (see overleaf).

*Metal raised bed frames (above) are lighter and easier to transport if moving compared to wooden raised bed frames (right), but they come at a greater cost.*

*Mixing up raised bed materials can create nice visual contrasts in the garden, such as the metal and wood pictured here.*

## MATERIALS FOR RAISED BEDS

### Wood

Wood is the most common option for the sides of raised beds. Boards work best, while logs offer a nice aesthetic. I source my timber from an online merchant that makes thicker versions of scaffold boards that last, untreated, up to ten years. I also have two local contacts who offer a fantastic price on larch wood because I am buying direct. Pallet collars are a fantastic option for smaller gardens. Railroad ties contain harmful chemicals, so avoid using them for beds for edibles, though you could use them for ornamentals.

### Stone

Stone can encompass such materials as bricks and breeze blocks, which can be sourced from some building projects, especially renovations or demolitions. They offer a unique aesthetic, as you don't often see garden beds made from stone. If you're using bricks, cement them together, but a single layer of breeze blocks can be used without cementing.

### Metal

Metal raised beds are the most expensive to buy as kits, but they will last much longer than wood. If you have the means to cut corrugated metal, then this is a far more affordable option, and these sheets can be screwed into wooden corner posts, which will need replacing after many years but are still much more cost-effective than wooden-sided beds.

### IBC tank bed

With a few simple power tools, you can turn IBC tanks (see p.88) into raised beds. You have the option to cut them to whatever height you desire, and the tops can be used as temporary covers to help protect seedlings in your raised beds. Keep the base of the tank for rigidity, but drill holes in it for drainage. An IBC tank bed is basically a big container, but because of its depth and size, it's treated more like a raised bed.

## THE "IDEAL" RAISED BED

My ideal size that I have settled on for intensive annual crop production is about 4 x 10ft (1.2 x 3m). The bed is narrow enough for me to comfortably reach the middle from either side and is just short enough so that I am not tempted to hop over the bed to the other side. These dimensions lend themselves to using vertical support structures and trellises, alongside hoop beds and net covers. On a lawn or soil, I would make the bed around 1ft (30cm) deep, and on a hard surface, I would make it 2ft (60cm) deep.

## FILLING BEDS

### Option 1: Topsoil and potting mix

Fill with a 50:50 mix of peat-free multipurpose potting mix and screened local topsoil. You can either mix this thoroughly before filling or place topsoil in the bottom half and potting mix in the top half. Both work excellently, but I find that the mixing version suits a greater range of crops in the first year, after which you will be adding organic matter or compost in layers. If your budget is tight, you can get away with a 2in (5cm) layer of potting mix in your first year if you mix it into the top 2in (5cm) of soil.

### Option 2 : Material and compost

Fill two-thirds of the raised bed with material that will break down well. Examples include used farm animal bedding, leaves and seaweed, ramial chipped wood, or even filling the bed like you would a compost bin by adding cardboard, vegetable scraps, and so on (see p.54). Then, fill the top third with compost. Over time, the material underneath will decompose, and while the level will sink down a little as it settles, you will have an incredibly fertile garden bed.

## Option 3: Low compost option in year one

In a similar approach to soil building with spuds (see p.70), you can fill a raised bed with organic material and plant potatoes directly. Alternatively, create one hole per square yard in the organic material, add a couple of shovels of compost, and plant summer or winter squash. At the end of the season, most of the material will have decomposed, and you can add more mulch over winter. In the second year, you can treat it like a normal garden bed.

*As you create more compost, you can use it to fill shallower raised beds, topping them up gradually over time.*

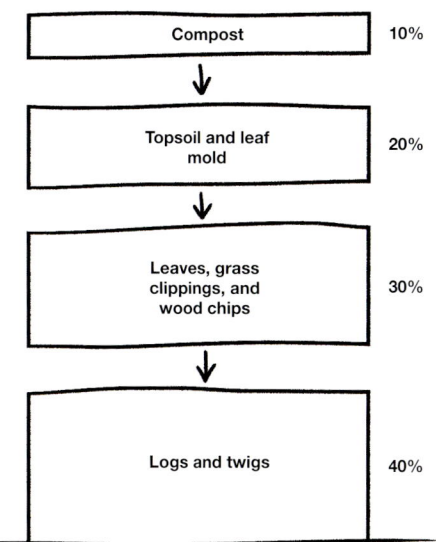

| Compost | 10% |
| Topsoil and leaf mold | 20% |
| Leaves, grass clippings, and wood chips | 30% |
| Logs and twigs | 40% |

### Hügelkultur layers
*Here are the layers of different materials (in proportion) for filling a raised bed.*

### The Hügelkultur approach

Hügelkultur was originally developed by Austrian permaculturalist Sepp Holzer as a way of making fertile mounds on which you grow food (see above). People have adapted this approach as a way of filling raised beds. While this does work, and it is excellent for creating a rich and high-carbon growing medium, expect the level of the bed to drop significantly in comparison to when it was first filled. Aim to overfill the bed to help mitigate this, and at the end of the first growing season, mix in a generous load of organic material to help replace the initial lost mass of the bed.

### HUW'S TIP

Whenever you fill beds, aim to incorporate 0.25–0.75 gallon (1–3 liters) of biochar into the top 6in (15cm) of the bed, per square yard (see pp.68–69).

# NON-SIDED BEDS

Raised beds without physical sides usually consist of a shaped mound of soil and organic matter sloping gently to the ground at the edges. These edges help reduce erosion, particularly during heavy rainfall or harvesting.

The slightly raised nature of these beds helps protect crops from waterlogging, which is essential for wetter climates or gardens on level ground. Below, I describe several ways to create non-sided beds; think about the paths and edging (right) before you decide which type to make.

## IN-GROUND BEDS

For gardens with a gentle slope to carry excess water away, in-ground beds are excellent for growing bulk staple crops, such as potatoes or winter squash, and for edible perennials. To create a ready-to-go in-ground bed on a lawn, wait for a period when there has been no rain for three or four days, as the soil will be much easier to work. Remove the turf (this can be used upside down to create mounds to plant up or to make the base layer if you are filling raised beds with sides) and then fork over the top 12in (30cm) of soil, breaking up large clumps and removing any oversized stones. Then, incorporate a 2–4in (5–10cm) layer of compost or well-rotted manure into the top 8in (20cm) of soil. Add biochar, if available (see pp.68–69). Give the bed a final rake, and it is ready for growing.

### No-dig beds

Creating a no-dig bed on a lawn is simple. Place down three or four layers of cardboard stripped of all tape, give it a good watering, and then place a thick mulch (4–6in/10cm–15cm) of compost or well-rotted manure on top of the cardboard. Tidy up the edges with a rake, and the bed is ready for sowing or planting up. If you are creating multiple beds, you can make a wooden frame as a tidy way to keep the material together when filling your bed. Alternatively, invest in metal bed edging (see suppliers, p.281).

### Potato box

You can use the potato method (see p.81) to create new in-ground beds. The following year, you can mound the material to lay down cardboard for pathways, shape up the beds, and then add the wood chips.

### Turf and flip beds

A simple way of creating individual in-ground beds in the fall for the following spring is to de-turf and flip the turf upside down in situ, cover with a 2–2¾in (5–7cm) mulch, and then cover this mulch with a tarpaulin to prevent weed growth. Uncover the tarp in the spring and plant into the bed. Allowing the turf to decompose in place will provide additional soil fertility.

## EDGING AND PATHWAYS

As they have no physical sides, these beds need managing to avoid encroaching grass. Use a bed-edging spade once a year to keep on top of this. An easier way to reduce encroaching grass over the long term is to create paths around the perimeter of (and between) your beds.

### Wood-chip pathways

Wood-chip paths can be created on soil or lawn. They make a tidier, more efficient growing space and contribute directly to the soil health of the beds. Being high in carbon, wood-chip paths hold on to moisture well and promote a thriving microbial community that can extend into the beds either side.

If creating more than one in-ground or no-dig bed, it is a good idea to mulch the entire area with cardboard, use two wooden frames as containers to tidily fill beds 1 and 2 with compost, and then add a 2–2¾in (5–7cm) layer of wood chips between these two beds before removing one of the frames to form bed 3, followed by the path between beds 2 and 3, and so on. The outer perimeter of the beds should be wood-chip paths. It is easier to maintain the grassy edge of the outer wood-chip paths than if all of your beds had grass paths— mowing grass paths is a pain and time-consuming. For example, if you had ten raised beds, it would take you less than half the time to edge the perimeter compared to every side of each raised bed.

*Clockwise from top left: non-sided beds in a polytunnel; harvesting from outdoor market-garden-style beds; and in-ground beds with wood-chip paths.*

# SOFT BOUNDARIES

A soft boundary or hedge is an edible crop or useful plant grown in the ground in a linear fashion to define garden areas and boundaries while contributing to the garden's productivity.

An edible soft boundary could be made up of fall raspberries or Jerusalem artichokes, or useful plants could be comfrey for smaller gardens, or a row of willow coppice for larger spaces. Soft boundaries can also be used as a visual screen, for wind protection, and for adding visual interest.

Soft boundary plants are always perennial and need to be low maintenance. The goal is to plant once and enjoy yearly harvests, with an annual prune and mulch being the only ongoing maintenance. Planting soft boundaries in grassy areas means that when the grass is cut, you can rake the clippings to the base of the soft boundaries as additional mulch and fertility for the plants.

## CHOOSING PLANTS

The most suitable plants I have come across for soft boundaries are soft fruits; dwarf fruit trees; some perennial herbs, such as rosemary and lemon balm; perennial vegetables, such as Jerusalem artichoke, rhubarb, and kale; comfrey; and trees that can be coppiced or pollarded, such as willow, hazel, and small-leaved lime (which has edible leaves).

When thinking about locations for soft boundaries, consider what plant would make most sense. Comfrey would be ideal close to your composting area, while willow can occupy the wettest corner. Black currants grow well in partial shade, but rosemary prefers full sun.

## Fall raspberries

My go-to soft fruit for soft boundaries is fall raspberries (see p.157). They crop on the current year's growth, meaning that pruning is as simple as cutting back all growth in the early winter. Fall raspberries do have a tendency to spread, which is excellent for thick boundaries, but if you have unwanted wandering shoots, they can just be cut back during the normal grass cut.

## Comfrey

Comfrey makes an excellent low-growing soft boundary. As it's in a neat line, you can easily harvest the comfrey with a scythe or sickle from one end to the other and then use a hay rake or similar to make a pile and pitchfork the comfrey into a wheelbarrow to move to other locations.

## Roses as a soft boundary

For a more formal or ornamental aesthetic, consider roses, specifically *Rosa rugosa*. They are vigorous growers, are easy to prune, provide edible flowers and hips, and look incredible, especially when planted up in color schemes or themes.

## PLANTING SOFT BOUNDARIES

The simplest way to prepare ground for planting soft boundaries, which works for anything but dwarf fruit trees, which are planted in individual holes (see pp.162–164), is to create narrow in-ground beds. Slice off and remove the top layer of turf, at a width of about 12in (30cm). Make the boundary as long as you wish and use a large fork to break up the topsoil. Then, either mix 2–2¾in (5–7cm) of compost or well-rotted manure into the top 8in (20cm), or add a generous handful to each plant when planting.

Rosa rugosa *produces large hips compared to other roses, making it the most suitable for processing in a kitchen.*

## LINEAR FOOD FORESTS

Soft boundaries can be upgraded into highly productive and functional linear food forests (which are discussed more in the polyculture chapter, see pp.240–241). However, where this may not be suitable (for example, if trees may cast too much shade), you can use two or three plants within a soft boundary to maximize the edge productivity. One example would be to plant strawberries on the south-facing side, with rosemary behind and then comfrey behind that (right). There are no real rules for planting schemes, as long as you understand the growing characteristics and needs of each plant.

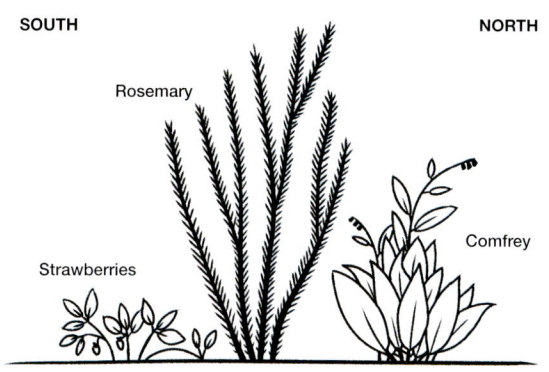

SOUTH     NORTH

Rosemary

Strawberries

Comfrey

# POTS AND CONTAINERS

Pots and containers can be very productive but need far more attention than beds, particularly for watering. It's vital to build enough fertility to overcome the fact that it's very hard to create a thriving soil in a small area, such as a pot.

Containers and pots allow you to grow food in spaces where it is not possible to grow in raised beds or in the ground. For small gardens, even balcony gardens, the value of containers to the kitchen gardener is far greater than it would be for those who are growing in bigger spaces.

*When planting up polyculture containers, keep the plants in their pots to find your favorite arrangement before planting them out.*

## CHOOSING A CONTAINER

For efficiency and productivity, the goal is simple: Aim to grow in the largest pots and containers within the space you have. Rather than having a collection of pots that each contain its own perennial herb, get a larger container and plant all of the herbs within the one container. Not only is this much easier to water (and will retain that water better); you will begin to create a more biologically diverse and active soil.

Large potato tubs and fabric planters are good for growing multiple plants in one space. Square or rectangle-shaped fabric planters allow you to join several side by side and are a fantastic option in rented accommodations or for growing plants on hard surfaces, such as a patio, driveway, or balcony.

For healthy soil, there needs to be a critical mass for a soil ecosystem to work in a balanced manner. It's hard to define the critical mass of soil volume you may need in a container, but you are far more likely to get closer to a diverse soil ecosystem in a large container that has a polyculture of plants in comparison to one plant squeezed into its own pot that spends most of its life rootbound.

To fill a pot or container, add a 4in (10cm) layer at the base with leaf mold or composted wood chips. This will act as a carbon bank for housing soil life and a sponge for water and provide long-term fertility. Fill the remaining space in the pot with a 50:50 compost and loam/soil mix. You can also add biochar, up to 10 percent of total volume.

*After fending off an early slug onslaught in the spring, I set up a microdrip system and grass-clipping mulch for all my pepper plants in pots undercover.*

## MULCHING AND WATERING CONTAINERS

Add at least 2in (5cm) of compost annually as a topdressing mulch for your containers to replenish nutrients and promote a good environment for the microorganisms. You can also mulch containers with other materials, such as grass clippings and wool, to help retain water, which I recommend for any perennial in a container. For any container growing, installing a microdrip watering system (see p.90) is essential for a stress-free experience. Choose a system that allows you to place watering points where needed, and then, for a collection of pots, tubs, and containers, you only need to turn on the tap to water everything and then turn it off afterward.

## CHOOSING WHAT TO GROW

Herbs, flowers, vegetables, soft fruits, and even dwarf fruit trees can all be successfully grown in containers.

| Container depth | Suitable crops |
| --- | --- |
| ~12in (30cm) | Almost all annual vegetables and herbs, plus strawberries |
| ~20in (50cm) | Perennial herbs, potatoes and tomatoes, perennial tubers |
| ~28in (70cm) | Shrubby soft fruits and dwarf fruit trees |

In a larger garden, the role of container growing requires case-by-case decisions regarding their relevance or purpose. My primary reason for growing in containers is to increase the aesthetics of certain awkward corners of my garden, using things like whisky barrels as a permanent feature that is planted up with a stunning flower display. I also use containers for growing a proportion of my potato crop, allowing me to start them in a polytunnel early and then move them outside when the weather warms up.

### Containers for "invasive" crops

Some crops can have a tendency to spread and then be hard to control. Mint, Jerusalem artichokes, and strawberries are common examples. Growing mint in a large container on a non-soil surface, such as paving stones, allows you to keep it contained. Jerusalem artichokes can grow from small pieces of tuber left in the ground after being missed at harvest, so growing in larger potato buckets is a simple solution. Strawberries send out a plethora of runners that can take over, but keeping them restricted to a container allows you to easily see and remove any runners making an escape, using them for propagation if desired (see p.129).

# SHADE

Shady areas of the garden are just as important to design for productivity as sunny areas are. While sunny areas lend themselves to growing the tastiest of crops, shady areas offer a more supportive role to the rest of the garden.

## CROPS TO GROW IN THE SHADE

I have been surprised by how well I have managed to grow numerous crops in areas where conventional gardening would say it is virtually impossible to grow anything. A simple rule of thumb is that if you have clear sky above (i.e., not an overhanging tree or building), many crops can be successfully grown.

My most important piece of advice for growing in the shade is to try growing a range of different crops and see what does and doesn't work well in your situation. I have had success with many perennial herbs, red currants and gooseberries, rhubarb, wild garlic, Jerusalem artichokes, leafy greens, comfrey, and even beets in what would usually be considered near-permanent shade. Granted, these crops won't be as productive as they would be in a sunnier position, but their yield is more than respectable enough to make the effort worthwhile.

## INFRASTRUCTURE

With sunlight being so important for gardens, especially in cooler temperate climates, you want as few nongrowing gardening elements taking up valuable growing space as possible. Water storage, composting, and tool storage are all best placed in the shadiest parts for the majority of domestic gardens. If you have a very sunny plot, put these practical items on your north- or west-facing boundary.

I would also recommend creating a nice seating area in the shade, even if it's just a simple bench, to offer respite from the intense midday summer sun. Creating a workbench in the shade can also help keep you cool during the growing season when you're sowing, potting up, and processing harvests.

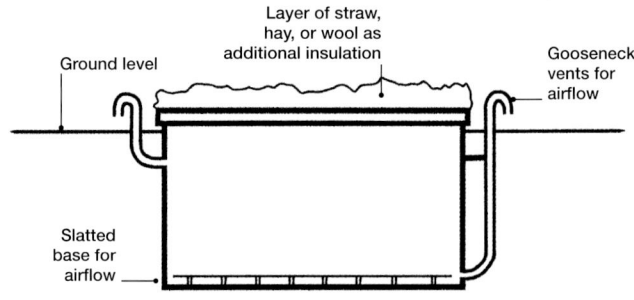

**OLD CHEST FREEZER SETUP FOR ROOT STORAGE**

### Chest freezer root cellar

Another way to make use of a shady spot is to create extra storage space for your harvests. Old chest freezers are perfect for this, providing a cool, waterproof storage solution that is relatively simple to install by burying it in the soil. Note that the freezer will need to have the refrigerant/compressor removed by a professional beforehand. It is important that you add ventilation, as good airflow will help keep the food fresher for longer. Once built, you can use the freezer to store root vegetables and tubers throughout the winter months in jute sacks (see p.198).

### Odds and ends area

Every garden needs an area for storing things that are useful (and valuable) but only needed from time to time. This could be insect netting, certain pots, horticultural fleece, and wood. You can use pallets placed on landscape fabric to store items that can be in the open or add a protected shelter that keeps off the brunt of the weather. See pages 118–119 for tool storage.

*My shady corner acts as a key area for water storage, composting, tool storage, and creating liquid amendments.*

# GARDEN TOOLS AND STORAGE

On this page, I share with you my ultimate tool list, split into core categories based on their uses in the garden. For a smooth growing experience, you also need to have a simple space-saving tool storage system.

## TOOLS

Quality is always more important than quantity when it comes to garden tools. Many tools serve multiple tasks —for example, secateurs can be used for pruning, harvesting, cutting string, propagating cuttings, and deadheading.

| Cutting | Soil and compost |
|---|---|
| Pruners* | Garden rake* |
| Pocket knife | Tarmac rake |
| Bushcraft knife | Broadfork |
| Box cutter | Manure fork |
| Snips | Garden fork* |
| Loppers* | Digging spade* |
| Hedge shears | Shovel |
| Pruning saw | Wheelbarrow |

| Weeding | Sowing and planting |
|---|---|
| Oscillating hoe* | Trowel* |
| Push-pull hoe | Dibble* |
| Hand hoe | Stick and string* |
| Hand fork | Pencil* |
| | Waterproof pen* |

*Essential tools

## CREATIVE TOOL STORAGE

A tool shed can be an expensive outlay and take up valuable growing space. Here are three alternative or additional tool storage methods I use to keep things organized and accessible.

### Mailbox

Installing a mailbox on top of a post is useful for hand tool storage for larger gardens. It can be placed in a central point for ease of access where something like a tool shed wouldn't make sense in the middle of a garden space.

### Vertical tool storage

If space is very limited, you can install an angled overhang to a fence or wall and use nails and wire to create simple hooks to hang your garden tools from. Ideally, locate this vertical tool shelter on the opposite side of where the prevailing wind comes from to keep your tools in the best condition possible.

### Polytunnel

I have found that the area under a potting bench in the polytunnel is a great location for all the smaller hand tools, and long-handled tools can be leaned up against one of the sides of the bench so everything is in one place.

*I use a tool tidy as an easy way to access my long-handled tools during the busy parts of the growing season. These tools will then be stored undercover over the winter.*

## HORI HORI KNIFE

This is a fantastic Japanese gardening tool that serves many uses. It can be used for weeding, planting bulbs, transplanting seedlings, separating perennials, harvesting, chop and drop (see p.62), and all kinds of other garden jobs. I know many a gardener who now can't be without one sheathed on their belt.

# BRINGING IT ALL TOGETHER

By combining the hierarchy of growing space and using zones to ensure maximum efficiency (see pp.42–43), this design gives you an idea of how every element has a dedicated place but works harmoniously with the other elements next to it.

A permaculture garden consists of multiple parts that all work together toward the goals you have set. The garden shown on the opposite page is a concept permaculture design for how a suburban garden might look like for a household aiming to produce as much of their own homegrown food as possible. There are four distinguishable zones, with zone 1 consisting of the kitchen garden, recreation area, and chicken coop. These will be the most frequented areas and are close to the house as a result. The hot bed and polytunnel are another core part of year-round production, with an option of installing hoops over raised beds for the winter months. Soft boundaries of fruits, perennial vegetables, and herbs contribute to the diversity and yield of the area for minimal work.

The in-ground beds in zone 2 form the main garden for growing bulk staple crops, which will only need attention a few days a week, and the chicken composting setup will be the primary source of fertility for these beds and the kitchen garden. Additional compost bins adjacent to the chicken area are for storing finished compost and for composting anything that is unsuitable for the chickens, such as kitchen scraps. With grass paths and some grass lawn areas, there will be ample mulch material for all containers and perennials, including the pots and trained fruit trees along the south-facing side of the house and garage. Water, being one of the most important resources, is stored in multiple locations, including a pond that is fed by run-off from the house roof.

In the front garden (zone 3), a couple of linear food forests with dwarf fruit trees and perennial vegetables will bring a steady flow of supplemental nutrition through the year.

There is no zone 4; not all gardens need to have all five zones, and in most cases, this is not practical or possible on smaller scales. A small corner of zone 5 is left for wildlife.

*A productive garden consists of multiple elements working together to optimize space. Here are raised beds, a hot bed, a polytunnel, and a boundary with a water source attached.*

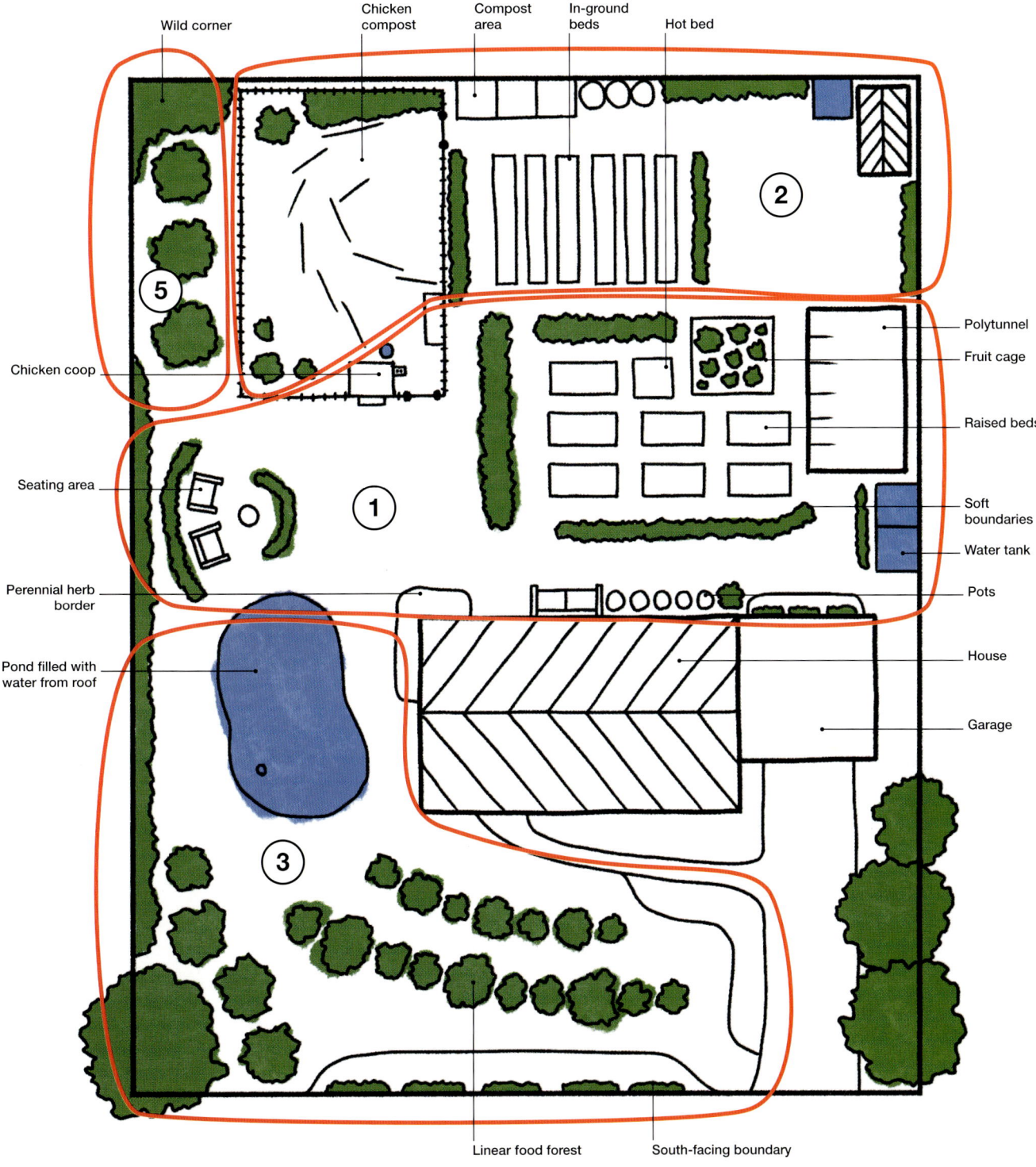

SOUTH

Wild corner

Chicken compost

Compost area

In-ground beds

Hot bed

5

2

Chicken coop

Polytunnel

Fruit cage

Raised beds

Seating area

1

Soft boundaries

Water tank

Perennial herb border

Pots

Pond filled with water from roof

House

Garage

3

Linear food forest

South-facing boundary

**Concept permaculture design**

*An example of a permaculture design including defined zones, as shown by the sections outlined in red and the corresponding number.*

# Perennials

# WHY GROW PERENNIALS?

Perennials offer a huge diversity of crops to grow in a permaculture kitchen garden, from the short-lived Asturian tree cabbage to grape vines that can live for more than 100 years.

Although perennials take longer to mature than annuals, they offer consistent harvests for many years. Perennials play an ever-increasing role in my garden, and the benefits outlined here help highlight why this is the case.

## LESS COMPOST

Because perennials don't need compost, you can focus all of your compost production on the nutrient-hungry annual plants. Compost can, of course, be used for mulching perennials, and most will perform better with a mulch of compost than a mulch of another organic material, but it isn't a necessity, and you will still experience respectable harvests without it. By converting more of your garden to perennials, you will reduce the pressure on the amount of compost you need to produce or purchase.

## RESILIENCE

Perennial crops tend to be more resilient than annuals because they typically form deeper and more extensive root networks, helping them access water during dry weather. There is also going to be far less soil disturbance, contributing to long-term soil health, particularly as many perennials form symbiotic relationships with fungi, further increasing the "surface area" of their root network.

## BALANCING YOUR WORKLOAD

The nature of perennials means that once planted, they need very little attention apart from mulching and pruning. Pruning is mostly done during the dormant season, when there is little to do with annual crops, whereas in the spring and early summer when the annuals are demanding attention, perennials can just be allowed to grow.

## VARIETY OF FLAVOR

The pursuit of flavor should be at the forefront of all kitchen gardens, and the sheer number of flavors in perennials, many of which are impossible to buy, is enough of a reason to include them within your space. There are almost limitless flavors for you to explore, with more than 2,500 varieties of apple alone grown in the United States, each having its own distinct taste.

## BETTER FOR WILDLIFE

Perennial plants contribute hugely to the biodiversity and health of your garden. From the spring blossom of fruit trees to the flowers of herbs, pollinators will truly appreciate a garden rich in perennials. And other insects, invertebrates, and microscopic life also thrive in perennially dominated areas.

## PROPAGATION

Many perennials are easily propagated by cuttings, tubers, or division, all of which clone the DNA of the parent plant so the new plants are the same as the parent (see p.128). This is in contrast with saving seeds from annuals, which can become time-consuming and complex if you are aiming for true-to-type seeds (see pp.222–223). The simple propagation methods for perennials allow you to save huge costs if expanding your plantings as well as ensuring that you have fresh stock to replace older plants. You also have a renewable resource that can be bartered or even sold.

*Clockwise from top left: globe artichoke; pears; grapes; Welsh onions; raspberries; blackberries; apples.*

# MAINTAINING PERENNIALS

The goal when growing perennials is to find the sweet spot where you have the maximum output for the least input. If you follow the basics of mulching, pruning, and protecting as necessary, you will be rewarded with productive harvests.

## MULCHING

Perennials and mulch are a match made in heaven. Mulch enhances the performance of perennials in every way you want (see pp.62–63). You can mulch perennials throughout the year, multiple times, but the bare minimum should be a generous mulch in the late winter/early spring to ensure that weed pressure is kept low. Remember, you want to make sure that the mulch remains clear of the stems to promote good airflow and avoid rotting the stems, but you only need a about an inch between mulch and stem, and therefore you will have very little weed competition. A layer of cardboard as a mulch can go right up against the stem, and such material as manure or wood chips on top of the cardboard will prevent it from being blown away.

### The summer spruce

Around midsummer, you may notice that some grass and weeds have made their way through the mulch that was placed before the start of the growing season. I deal with this by using a pair of hedge shears to cut down the weeds around the base of the stem and leave them there (see p.62). I could add more mulch, but this is not necessary, and the chop-and-drop plant material will act as a mulch regardless.

## PRUNING BASICS

Many perennials, such as herbs, brassicas, and tubers, are hands-off as soon as you plant them, requiring attention only for harvesting or mulching. But many of the soft fruits and tree fruits are made more productive through the process of pruning. This is a method in which certain parts of the plant are removed (or retained) to promote the highest yield possible in the available space. Pruning styles, such as creating goblet-shaped apple trees or training a plum in a fan shape to grow against a wall, increase productivity within the space as well as being aesthetically beneficial.

It is easy to get overwhelmed when it comes to pruning, but I have good news: The Pareto principle (80/20) rule (see p.46) works perfectly when applied to pruning. The

3 Ds pruning rule applies for all fruit trees or bushes: If a branch is damaged, dead, or diseased, then it needs to be removed. This can be combined with the COWs pruning rule, which focuses on branches that are crossing, odd, and weak. Crossing branches can rub and provide a place for disease to enter, so one of the branches needs to be removed. Odd branches are ones growing at a strange angle or away from the shape you wish for; removing these helps the visual balance of the plant, if that is important to you. If in doubt, weak growth should be cut back to promote stronger growth. Weak growth poses a danger of branches breaking under the weight of fruit, too.

The pruning diagrams that accompany each type of fruit on the following pages show you what you need to know to get high yields. Always work with sharp, clean pruning tools (like a knife and pair of pruners), take a step back every so often to look at the shape of the plant, and if you're in doubt, do not cut it out.

## PEST PROTECTION FOR PERENNIALS

Many fruits may need protection from birds. The best option is to have a permanent netted fruit cage with doorway access. This provides a nice working space, offering good height, and saves you from having to pull up netting when harvesting. It is the most expensive option, but it will save you the most time.

For smaller gardens where a large walk-in fruit cage isn't possible, then the next option would be to create a netted structure that contains a few soft fruit bushes; you can access

*Taming a climbing rose growing high above my garden boundary.*

the fruit by lifting up one of the sides. These structures are inexpensive to make and, if treated carefully, will last many growing seasons, or they can be taken apart and reassembled each year.

The final option, which is the least aesthetically pleasing, is to drape netting over the plants and pin it down with wood or stones. You can use pipes or bamboo to help create a temporary netted structure. Birds may access some of the fruit close to the netting boundary, but most of your fruit will be protected. As this is the least secure option, I would recommend checking at least once a day to make sure a bird has not gotten itself stuck inside.

For more advice on pests and diseases that may affect annual and perennial crops, see pp.262–267.

**Under cover pest protection**

For fruit such as grapes growing within a greenhouse or polytunnel, you can create an internal netted structure as described above.

An alternative I use is to create a doorway frame from wire mesh and scrap wood. This acts as an inner bird-proof door that I can slide across when I want to enter the polytunnel. In this way, I can keep the doors open in warm summer temperatures to allow the crops to be well ventilated.

# PROPAGATION SIMPLIFIED

With many perennials being so simple to propagate, you can be completely self-sufficient in a wide range of plants. Tubers, herbs, and soft fruit are particularly straightforward to multiply.

Before looking at individual crops, I will share the most common propagation methods. Throughout the chapter, I will indicate how each plant is best propagated.

## DIVISION

Division involves digging up a mature plant and then slicing it into smaller sections (usually with a sharp spade), with each section including some root mass and a growing node. When a section is planted, it will grow into its own mature plant. The best time to divide plants is in the early winter and early spring, at either end of the dormancy period.

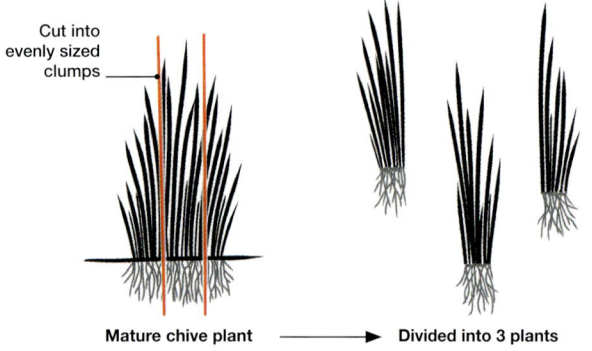

Cut into evenly sized clumps

Mature chive plant ⟶ Divided into 3 plants

## CUTTINGS

A cutting is a length of stem removed from a parent plant. When placed in soil or compost, the cutting will grow roots and then new top growth to create an independent plant.

Softwood cuttings are taken during the growing season, usually in the spring to midsummer, when the stems are soft and the plant has leaves. The ideal length for plants such as herbs is about 4in (10cm); they may start to root within a few weeks and can be planted out the following season. Mint is so easy to propagate that the cutting will root in water (you can also do this with basil). Other softwood cuttings can be placed in soil and will need a clear bag placed over the pot to help keep in the humidity while the cutting starts to form roots and grow. Semi-ripe cuttings are similar to softwood cuttings but

are taken from woodier stems towards the end of the growing season, from the late summer to mid-fall. Hardwood cuttings are taken during the dormancy season, and because they have no leaves, they do not need to be kept in humid conditions. An example is black currant. Hardwood cuttings can be 8–12in (20–30cm) long and start rooting in early spring, but they are not planted out until the following winter.

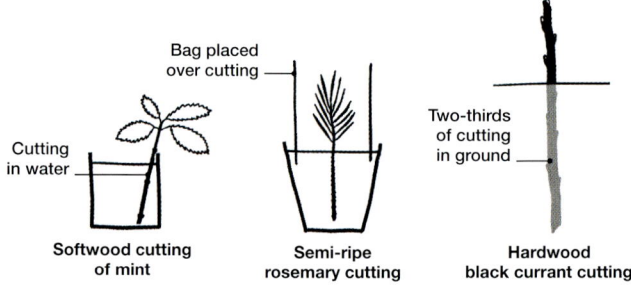

Bag placed over cutting

Cutting in water

Softwood cutting of mint

Semi-ripe rosemary cutting

Two-thirds of cutting in ground

Hardwood black currant cutting

## TUBERS

Tubers are the easiest crop to propagate. When harvesting the crop, select healthy individual tubers to plant elsewhere to create new plants. Some tubers, such as oca, mashua, and yacon, are more sensitive to poor winter weather in a temperate climate. Mild and wet weather can rot the tubers, while hard freezes can cause them to turn to mush. Therefore, harvest tubers in the early winter and store them in a cool, dry, and dark space before planting out again in the spring. Jerusalem artichokes are the hardiest tubers and do not need this extra care.

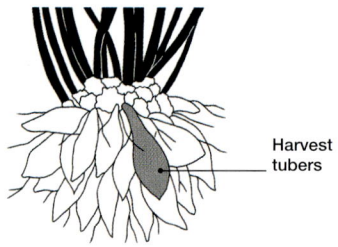

Harvest tubers

## GRAFTING

Grafting (joining) is the most common technique for propagating fruit trees. It is the most complex propagation method, as it requires precision in order to graft what is essentially a cutting onto a living plant (known as a rootstock). An apple grown from seed will grow into a large tree that is not true to type. Grafting allows you to grow true-to-type apples while also being able to control the vigor of a tree. The vigor is controlled by using a rootstock, which provides a root system that influences how the grafted plant material (scion) then grows (see also p.161). The rootstock and scion are bound until they grow together.

Grafting is a technique also used for some annual crops. The pomato, where a tomato is grafted onto a potato, allows you to grow both spuds and fruit from the same plant. In the commercial growing world, many tomatoes are grafted onto tomato rootstocks, such as Maxifort, Beaufort, and Estamino, which offer specific disease resistance while promoting more vigorous growth than if the chosen tomato variety were to grow by using its own root system.

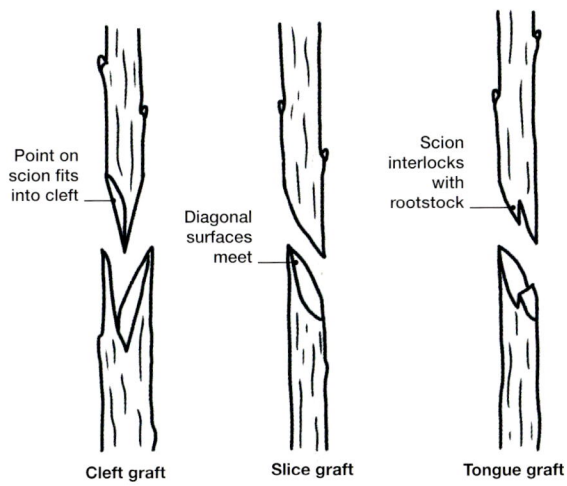

Point on scion fits into cleft

Diagonal surfaces meet

Scion interlocks with rootstock

**Cleft graft**       **Slice graft**       **Tongue graft**

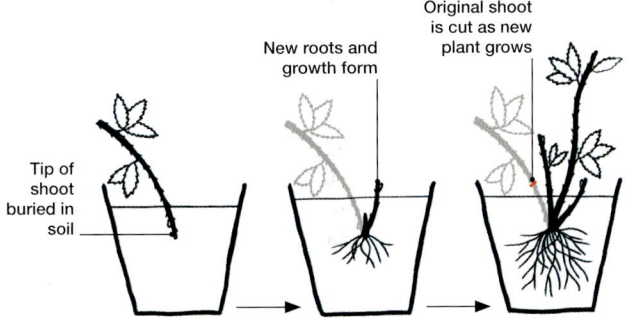

Tip of shoot buried in soil

New roots and growth form

Original shoot is cut as new plant grows

## PROPAGATING STRAWBERRIES BY RUNNERS

Many varieties of strawberry spread by a form of layering known as runners. Runners are sent out by the plant for the purpose of propagation; fruit will not grow on those runners until a new plant has developed and rooted. This is different than a blackberry, for example, where the layers will also yield fruit. You can pot up a plant from a runner, cutting it away from the parent when it is growing new leaves (see below).

## LAYERING

Layering takes advantage of a natural process in some plants: When a growing tip comes into contact with the ground, it sends out roots and creates a new plant in that spot. The parent temporarily provides all the nutrients the layered plant needs until its root system has developed and it can survive independently and be transplanted elsewhere. This works for any trailing berries. In fact, layering, along with suckers (plants that pop up from shallow roots sent away from the mother plant), is how brambles quickly take over if left unchecked.

# TUBERS

A tuber is a thicker part of an underground stem that acts as an energy reserve for new growth. Some tubers are delicious to eat, allowing us to capitalize on that energy reserve for our own nourishment.

For maximum yield, this group of crops requires a full growing season and enjoys plenty of organic matter in the soil. Harvest from the late fall onward. The typical eating period for perennial tubers in a temperate climate is during the dormant season, unless they are preserved. The foliage isn't frost-hardy, so start planting tubers around two weeks before your last average frost date. All the tubers mentioned here will survive a light frost in that period.

To give them a longer growing season, you can start all these tubers off undercover in 4in (10cm) pots from early April and then transplant them to their final growing position once the risk of frost has passed. Full sun is preferred, but they will grow well in partial shade. Propagation is done by saving some tubers when harvesting and planting these to grow on and create new plants.

### JERUSALEM ARTICHOKE

Also known as sunchokes, Jerusalem artichokes (*Helianthus tuberosus*) are in the same family as sunflowers and are known for their height. They put on a fantastic display in the early fall of small sunflower-like blooms, which make for a lovely backdrop or seasonal screen. For windy sites, you can cut back growth to 4–5ft (1.2–1.5m) in midsummer. The plants will respond by bushing out, but you will be less likely to enjoy a flower display. There is also a naturally compact dwarf Jerusalem artichoke (2ft/60cm), which produces incredible maroon-colored tubers. These are incredibly productive, and when cooked, they have a sweet, nutty, creamy flavor.

**Plant spacing** 12in (30cm)

**Planting depth** 6in (15cm)

**Height** 10ft (3m) in a sunny position

### MASHUA

Also known as the perennial nasturtium and in the same family, mashua (*Tropaeolum tuberosum*) is one of the most beautiful vegetables you can grow. Its climbing habit makes it a valuable crop aesthetically, and it's suitable for small gardens. Mashua plants grow incredibly quickly and provide you with edible leaves over the summer, flowers in the fall, and tubers over the winter. The tubers are best enjoyed roasted or boiled and have a sweet, cabbage-like flavor. A fun way you could grow it is in two potato buckets, with an archway trellis in between to create a stunning living archway. Mashua also trails beautifully if there is no structure to climb.

**Plant spacing** 12in (30cm)

**Planting depth** 2in (5cm)

**Height** 13ft (4m) if grown on a trellis

## YACON

Yacon (*Smallanthus sonchifolius*), also known as earth apple, has been a long-time staple crop in South American diets. The tuber can be eaten cooked or raw. If raw, leave in a sunny warm spot for a week or two (like a polytunnel potting bench), and the initial starchy state will turn into a juicy and crunchy sweet fruit, which can be enjoyed whole. Yacons are hungry tubers, and a generous 4in (10cm) mulch of a blend of well-rotted manure and composted wood chips every year in their growing bed will be appreciated. Weather depending, you may get to enjoy their beautiful yellow flowers in the fall. If you want to save tubers for planting, choose the smaller red tubers. For eating, use the larger bulbous tubers deeper in the ground.

**Plant spacing** 20in (50cm)

**Planting depth** 4in (10cm)

**Height** Up to 6ft (1.8m)

## OCA

A common name for oca (*Oxalis tuberosa*) is New Zealand yam, although, like many tuberous crops, oca originates from the Andes region in South America. One of my favorite perennial vegetables, oca has leaves that offer a beautiful visual texture, perfect for growing as an edible ornamental, while the plants produce a great yield of small, tasty, nutty tubers. Oca is suitable for growing in large pots and potato tubs. The tubers come in multiple colors, depending on the variety; the most common are white, red, and yellow. Toward the end of the growing season, it also produces a lovely display of small, delicate yellow flowers.

**Plant spacing** 8in (20cm)

**Planting depth** 2in (5cm)

**Height** 12in (30cm)

## CHINESE ARTICHOKE

Small, white tubers of Chinese artichoke (*Stachys affinis*) can be eaten raw, with a refreshing nutty crunch, or pickled and cooked. Its herbaceous growth looks similar to mint.

**Plant spacing** 12in (30cm)

**Planting depth** 3in (7cm)

**Height** 20in (50cm)

## CINNAMON VINE

A vigorous climber, cinnamon vine (*Dioscorea polystachya*) has beautiful heart-shaped leaves, stunningly scented tiny white flowers, and tubers that are edible when cooked, tasting similar to water chestnuts. It likes particularly deep soils.

**Plant spacing** 20in (50cm)

**Planting depth** 4in (10cm)

**Height** 13ft (4m)

## GROUNDNUT

An amazing nitrogen-fixing climber with beautiful flowers, the groundnut (*Apios americana*) originates from North America. For best results, harvest tubers from the second year after planting.

**Plant spacing** 12in (30cm)

**Planting depth** 2in (5cm)

**Height** 10ft (3m)

## SKIRRET

A popular vegetable in Europe before the potato, skirret (*Sium sisarum*) tastes like a slightly peppery carrot. It is best propagated by division of plants that are two years old.

**Plant spacing** 16in (40cm)

**Planting depth** 2in (5cm)

**Height** 36in (90cm)

# PERENNIAL BRASSICAS

These highly productive leafy plants grow well in full sun or partial shade. Being evergreen, they bring welcome life to the winter garden and can be harvested throughout the year, including the hungry gap.

These brassicas all enjoy a soil rich in organic matter, but tolerate poorer soils. Even though these are leafy, slug issues are very rare, making them all the more favorable for a resilient and productive garden. They can be grown from seed (and stem cuttings, see below). and new plants may need some slug protection. Once these brassicas are mature, keep the ground beneath them well mulched. Cabbage white caterpillars (see p.264) may show interest, so keep an eye out.

## HUW'S TIP

These brassicas are hardy down to around 21°F (-6°C), so on colder nights, it is worth protecting them with fleece. Growing them in large containers to move into a polytunnel is a suitable option too. Taking cuttings in the fall and overwintering them undercover will act as an insurance policy against potential loss.

## STEM CUTTINGS

All of the perennial brassicas listed here can be easily propagated by stem cuttings. In the mid-fall and early to mid-spring, take cuttings from the smaller sideshoots (tear them off the main stem so they have some old growth attached) and root in pots of compost, keeping them out of the harsh midday sun for the first four weeks to prevent drying out. They do not need to have a clear bag placed over them for humidity, but remove all but the top three or four leaves.

## ASTURIAN TREE CABBAGE

The Asturian tree cabbage (*Brassica oleracea* 'Asturian') is the shortest-lived perennial brassica at around three years, and it's easily grown by seed and cuttings. It is fast to grow and provides leaves that can be eaten raw when smaller or cooked when larger. In the early spring, it sends up a forest of deliciously sweet, tender flower shoots, similar to purple sprouting broccoli, but I think tastier! Harvest all the flower shoots, and it will continue for another growing season. It is one of my favorites, and I cannot have a growing season without a few Asturian tree cabbages.

**Plant spacing** 20in (50cm)

**Height** 3ft (1m)

## NINE STAR BROCCOLI

A very hungry plant, nine star broccoli (*Brassica oleracea* 'Nine Star') needs generous mulching with compost or well-rotted manure. It is said to be much hardier than the other perennial brassicas. Although the leaves are edible, it is grown for its cauliflower-like florets, which appear around the early spring. These must be harvested to keep the plant growing, and from the second year will provide up to 10 florets a year for a few years. I recommend staking the plants to protect from winter storms.

**Plant spacing** 32in (80cm)

**Height** 3ft (1m)

## TAUNTON DEANE KALE

This large, sprawling plant (*Brassica oleracea* var. *acephala*) is also known as cottager's kale. A single plant can keep you well supplied with leaves through the year. Harvest the younger, tender leaves and cook—they taste lovely. Perennial brassicas, such as Taunton Deane, are a must-grow for anyone on a journey toward self-sufficiency.

**Plant spacing** 3ft (1m)

**Height** 6½ft (2m)

## DAUBENTON KALE

There are two versions of Daubenton kale (*Brassica oleracea* var. *ramosa*) available to gardeners: a variegated and a standard leaf. The variegated version creates a real impact plant, allowing it to fit easily into an ornamental garden. This is a small shrub that works well for borders and more exposed sites. Delicious leaves.

**Plant spacing** 3ft (1m)

**Height** 3ft (1m)

## PURPLE TREE COLLARD

This is a purple-green colored leafy plant (*Brassica oleracea* var. *acephala*) with deep purple veins. During colder weather, the leaves become more purple. Tree collards usually require staking due to their upright growth habit. There is also a green tree collard known as Jersey kale or walking stick kale, as its long stem used to be dried and made into walking sticks, which can be found in some museums to this day!

**Plant spacing** 3ft (1m)

**Height** 6–8ft (1.8–2.5m)

# LEAFY AND OTHER PERENNIAL VEGETABLES

There are many great leafy perennial vegetables that provide edible and aesthetic yields. Here are my top ones to try out. They are very easy to grow, are not nutrient-hungry, and grow in full sun and partial and dappled shade.

## SEA BEET

Like a perennial version of a chard, sea beet (*Beta vulgaris* subsp. *maritima*) provides you with useful chard-like leaves for much of the year. In well-draining soil, this is a very hardy, productive crop that will return year after year. Remove flowering stems to focus on leaf production, and cut it back in the late summer to encourage more growth. Careful division is possible (see p.128).

**Plant spacing** 16in (40cm)

**Height** 24in (60cm)

## GOOD KING HENRY

This species of goosefoot (*Blitum bonus-henricus*, also known as *Chenopodium*) produces leaves similar to spinach. If you find the flavor too bitter, soak the young leaves in salted water for around an hour and then rinse and cook. It creates lovely structural tower spikes, which can also be picked and cooked. It dies back in the winter. Very easy to grow from both seed and division (see p.128).

**Plant spacing** 20in (50cm)

**Height** 28in (70cm)

## CAUCASIAN SPINACH

This leafy green climber (*Hablitzia tamnoides*) needs partial shade to thrive and, ideally, damp soil, so mulching is essential. It can grow vigorously if support is given and provides edible shoots at the start of spring, followed by delicious spinach-like leaves. Older plants can be easily divided with a spade (see p.128).

**Plant spacing** 12–16in (30–40cm)

**Height** 10ft (3m)

## MUSK MALLOW

Musk mallow (*Malva moschata*) is very hardy and dies back over the winter. While the leaves are edible and look fantastic, the real stars are the edible pink flowers. It can be easily grown from seeds or by taking basal cuttings about 4–6in (10–15cm) long in the late spring to early summer: For these, cut the stem of new shoots just underneath the soil and treat each as a normal softwood cutting.

**Plant spacing** 20in (50cm)

**Height** 36in (90cm)

## PATIENCE DOCK

This is a very hardy leafy perennial (*Rumex patientia*). Its young leaves are harvested and cooked, tasting similar to sorrel. They are perfect for adding to stews or curries, or even as a side-dish green. Patience dock sends up giant flowering stems that make an incredible visual impact, but the flower stems take away from leaf production. If you don't want the flower stem, it can be removed and old leaves cut back in midsummer to encourage a second flush of leaves before it dies down over thge winter, reappearing early the following spring. It is best propagated by division (see p.128).

**Plant spacing** 20in (50cm)

**Height** 8ft (2.5m)

## GLOBE ARTICHOKE

The globe artichoke (*Cynara cardunculus* Scolymus Group) is a striking plant grown for structure and its edible flower buds, which are treated as a delicacy. Each plant can produce up to 12 buds over the summer and will remain productive for at least five years. It thrives in a sunny position and responds well to receiving a generous amount of organic matter to improve fertility when planting out. Due to its growth habit, which blocks out the light underneath, the ground remains weed-free if you give the plants a generous mulch of compost, wood chips, or manure in the late winter just as the new shoots begin to emerge. It is best to mulch the crown (see p.139) over the winter with straw or leaves, as spells of freezing temperatures can damage or kill artichoke plants.

Artichokes make a great plant for filling an underused area with a tasty, low-maintenance crop. Varieties such as 'Violet de Provence' offer additional beauty with their purple buds. When growing multiple plants, or for the last few buds of the season, allow artichokes to flower. Their large thistle-like purple flowers are a magnet for honeybees, bumblebees, and butterflies. Keep them productive by dividing older plants; mature plants also send up suckers that can be dug out and moved away to avoid them competing for the same space.

**Plant spacing** 36in (90cm)

**Height** 5ft (1.5m)

## NETTLES

Although this isn't a book on foraging, it's worth knowing just how incredible nettles are if treated as a "wild" perennial vegetable. If you have lots of nettles growing, then treat them as a valuable harvest! Their younger leaves and tender growing tips, when cooked by either steaming or boiling to remove the sting, make a great alternative to spinach and are available during the entire hungry gap.

## OTHER PERENNIALS TO TRY

I have only scratched the surface of the hundreds that are worth growing. Here are more recommended perennial vegetables:

- Babington leek (*Allium ampeloprasum* var. *babingtonii*)
- Bulbous nettle (*Laportea bulbifera*)
- Dents de Kyoto (*Elatostema umbellatum*)
- Everlasting onion (*Allium cepa perutile*)
- Garlic cress (*Peltaria alliacea*)
- Japanese wild parsley (*Cryptotaenia japonica*)
- Korean celery (*Dystaenia takesimana*)
- Sorrel 'Abundance' (*Rumex acetosa*)
- Turkish rocket (*Bunias orientalis*)
- Udo (*Aralia cordata*)

Many of the perennials mentioned in this chapter cannot be found at your local garden center. Here in the UK, my go-to for high-quality perennial plants is ordering online from Incredible Vegetables. For any crops I struggle to track down, eBay and Etsy have impressed me with just how many rare seeds and plants are available to purchase. My top tip is to search under Latin names, as often these plants are sold as "ornamentals" and not under their common name. For more nursery recommendations, see suppliers (p.281).

*Korean celery flowers in dappled shade (above) and bulbous nettle growing beside nasturtiums and purple tree collard (left).*

# RHUBARB AND ASPARAGUS

These two prized perennials emerge in the spring, offering reliable harvests for the hungry gap (see pp.220–221). Rhubarb appears first and can be forced (see below) for an even earlier harvest. Asparagus follows a few weeks later.

## RHUBARB

Rhubarb (*Rheum rhabarbarum*) is an incredibly popular staple of the hungry gap, and depending on the variety, you can enjoy a regular supply of tender sweet stems from the early spring until midsummer. Like asparagus, it grows from crowns. Rhubarb performs well in full sun and partial or dappled shade, making it suitable for growing under fruit trees, as you would comfrey (see p.230). The key to rhubarb abundance is simple: plenty of mulch and even liquid feeds. Cover the area around rhubarb crowns generously (4in/10cm deep) with manure, seaweed, a mix of grass clippings and leaves, or compost in the late fall and again in the early spring, if possible.

There are many great varieties to choose from, but for the earliest crops, I opt for 'Timperley Early'. 'Victoria' is a popular "maincrop" variety that is widely available and has also been a consistent performer for me. Harvest stems by snapping them off at the base and place leaves on the compost. Occasionally, rhubarb will send out a flower shoot, taking energy away from stem and leaf production. Cut out these flower shoots with a sharp knife and add to the compost. Finish harvesting rhubarb around midsummer to ensure that the plant has time to send as much energy as possible down to the roots before the leaves naturally die back over the winter, reappearing the next spring.

**Plant spacing** 30in (75cm)

**Planting depth** Top of crown, just below soil surface

**Height** 24in (60cm)

*Lifting a potato container to reveal forced rhubarb stems early in the spring.*

### Forcing rhubarb

Forcing is a technique to encourage the early growth of plants by preventing light from reaching them, causing them to grow long stems, which also taste sweeter. Forcing rhubarb can be as simple as placing a couple of potato containers or a large bucket upside down over the crown from the late winter. For bigger crowns, you can even use a trash can. Check growth every few days, and then remove the chosen light inhibitor and harvest the stems.

### Dividing rhubarb

To maintain productivity, divide crowns every five or six years. Gently lift the rhubarb plant in the late winter, before growth starts, and use a sharp spade to slice the crown into two to four chunks. Plant the largest chunk in the same location, with spare divisions planted elsewhere or sold. If you have two rhubarb patches, divide them two or three years apart. This means you won't have a lull in productivity the year after dividing.

### HUW'S TIP

Victorians used to place large rhubarb leaves on garden beds and leave them overnight. When they turned them over the following day, they collected the slugs that had gathered underneath. If you have chickens or ducks, you can throw the leaves with slugs into their enclosure.

## ASPARAGUS

Asparagus (*Asparagus officinalis*) is one of the most delicious harvests a gardener can enjoy, and it is made extra special by being available during the hungry gap. The most common way of planting asparagus is by crowns (see diagram below). Growing asparagus requires patience because it takes four growing seasons to go from the initial crown planting to a mature and productive plant. You can sow asparagus seeds, but you will need to wait an additional year before the plant reaches maturity.

Asparagus is harvested by either snapping or cutting each spear just above the ground. At the end of the growing season, after the stems have turned yellow, cut them back to the base. Chop and drop this material. The plants can be mulched annually over winter with a 2–3in (5–7cm) layer of composted wood chips, well-rotted manure, seaweed, or compost. There are many varieties available, but reliable performers include 'Connover's Colossal', 'Backlim', and 'Purple Passion'.

**Plant spacing** 16in (40cm)

**Planting depth** Just below the surface; see cross section, below

**Height** 48in (120cm)

### Dividing asparagus

Older crowns, around six or seven years old, can be divided into two or three crowns in the late winter. Take care when dividing, as the roots can break easily: A sharp knife is better in this instance than a spade.

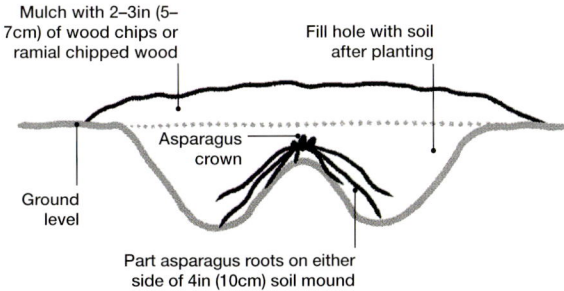

*Above is a cross section of an asparagus crown planted just below soil level, with its roots spread over a mound of soil.*

## HUW'S TIP

The best way to enjoy an asparagus spear is to eat it raw immediately after harvesting! The taste is sublime. I will never forget the first time I tried raw homegrown asparagus, and it is a taste I eagerly await each spring.

*Asparagus spears appearing from their crown and ready for harvest.*

## WHAT IS A CROWN?

Both rhubarb and asparagus grow from crowns, which are a collection of lateral rhizomes (the underground parts of the stem that spread and send up growth), with nodes from where new growth appears. This creates a coppice style of growth—a group of stems rather than one single stem. Another example of a plant that grows from crowns is comfrey (see p.77).

# PERENNIAL HERBS

Perennial herbs encompass a vast range of plants whose leaves, seeds, and/or flowers are used for food, flavor, medicine, and perfume. Many offer multiple harvests and uses and are magnets for beneficial insects when they flower.

Traditionally, kitchen gardens have an adjacent herb garden, or at the very least a dedicated herb bed for ease of harvest when it comes to needing fresh herbs. A permaculture kitchen garden can have a dedicated herb area (see p.232) but will often have herbs throughout the garden in places where it makes sense: mint in a shady corner, chives under soft fruit, lemon balm under an apple, bergamot in the salad bed for a splash of color. The polyculture section of this book explores the integration of perennials and annuals in more detail (see pp.244–247). Most of these herbs thrive in full sun to partial shade and fertile well-draining soils, but I have added plant-specific information where this rule of thumb does not apply.

## CHIVES

Chives (*Allium schoenoprasum*) offer a delicious allium flavor, and I use both the leaves and flowers regularly in my kitchen—in fact, it's probably the herb I use most often. Chives die back in the winter, emerging early in the spring. After flowering, they can be cut down to encourage a second flourish. Their purple flowers are particularly popular with pollinator insects, and the plant is very winter-hardy. Propagate by seeds and division (see p.128).

**Plant spacing** 12in (30cm)

**Height** 12in (30cm)

## CHINESE GARLIC CHIVES

Deservedly gaining in popularity, Chinese garlic chives (*Allium tuberosum*) are a hardy herb that comes back early in the spring and offers succulent grass-like leaves. They offer (you guessed it) a tasty, garlicky chive flavor and can be used like normal chives. Their stunning delicate white flowers are also edible and loved by pollinators. Propagate by seeds and division (see p.128).

**Plant spacing** 8in (20cm)

**Height** 16in (40cm)

## WELSH ONION

The Welsh onion (*Allium fistulosum*) is a perennial bunching onion originally from China and Siberia. Both the leaves and the flowers are edible, with a white onion flavor. To harvest, remove a few stems per clump. Use a sharp knife to cut low down or carefully twist away, ensuring that the surrounding stems don't get damaged. After a while, new stems will sprout—hence the alternative name of cut-and-come-again spring onion. Propagate by seeds and division (see p.128).

**Plant spacing** 12in (30cm)

**Height** 16in (40cm)

## WILD GARLIC

Wild garlic (*Allium ursinum*) can be grown as an herb. In the wild, it enjoys partial shade and moist soil, and the same applies in a garden. Emerging in the late winter, and flowering until the late spring, it is excellent ground cover under a tree and will naturally spread over a period of years. Leaves, buds, flowers, and seed heads can all be eaten. Propagate by division (see p.128).

**Plant spacing** 4in (10cm)

**Height** 12in (30cm)

## SOCIETY GARLIC

Society garlic (*Tulbaghia violacea*, below) has a garlic-like taste and scent, but it doesn't make the breath smell. Use the leaves as you would chives, and its flowers are edible too. It's a must for anyone with an allium allergy, as it's not in the allium family. It can be propagated by division (see p.128).

## MINT

There are said to be over 30 different varieties of mint (*Mentha*), from Moroccan mint, which is a must for fresh tea, to basil mint, which is a great alternative to basil when cooking, as the heat removes much of the mint taste but retains the basil flavor. Mint will spread if given the opportunity, so if you have a small garden, you may want to grow it in a pot to contain it. Harvest leaves as you need them. The flowers are particularly valuable to insects. Propagate by softwood cuttings and division (see p.128).

**Plant spacing** 16in (40cm)

**Height** 16in (40cm)

## CATNIP

Famously loved by cats, this herb (*Nepeta*) provides flowers from the mid-spring to late summer and has beautiful silvery leaves. It is an excellent supplemental herb for aesthetics and attracts beneficial insects. The flowers make a great herbal tea, while young leaves can be added to salad. Propagate by seeds and division (see p.128).

**Plant spacing** 16in (40cm)

**Height** 16in (40cm)

## KOREAN MINT

A must-have herb in the garden, Korean mint (*Agastache rugosa*) has aniseed-flavor leaves and incredible purple flower spikes. It brings generous color throughout the summer and into the fall, meaning it is also a perfect border plant. Propagate by seed and division (see p.128).

**Plant spacing** 20in (50cm)

**Height** 36in (90cm)

## BERGAMOT

Bergamot (*Monarda*) is in the same family as mint. Its distinctive flower heads, which come in a multitude of shades and colors, depending on variety, flower for an extended period, making it a real eye-catcher. Use the leaves and flowers for tea, oils, and vinegars in the kitchen and as a cut flower. Propagate by division (see p.128).

**Plant spacing** 16in (40cm)

**Height** 36in (90cm)

## LEMON BALM

A beautiful bushy evergreen herb with a fresh lemon aroma, lemon balm (*Melissa officinalis*) is great for ground cover within a food forest, and the variegated version looks incredible too. It comes back to life every spring and is one of the easiest herbs to grow, but, like mint, it should be contained in a pot in smaller gardens. Propagate by division (see p.128).

**Plant spacing** 20in (50cm)

**Height** 32in (80cm)

## ROSEMARY

You cannot have a kitchen garden without rosemary (*Salvia rosmarinus*). Not only do the needle-like evergreen leaves look striking and have many culinary uses; the edible early spring flowers are an important nectar source for native bumblebees. Rosemary thrives against a sunny boundary in well-draining soil. Propagate by softwood and semi-ripe cuttings (see p.128).

**Plant spacing** 20in (50cm)

**Height** 3ft (1m)

## LEMON VERBENA

The citrus flavor of lemon verbena (*Aloysia citrodora*) is far stronger than that of lemon balm, and it's one of the best herbs to grow for tea or making an herb oil. It will need protection during colder months by mulching with straw or growing in pots and taking them into a polytunnel over winter. Cut stems back every winter to encourage strong regrowth. Propagate by softwood cuttings (see p.128).

**Plant spacing** 16in (40cm)

**Height** 3ft (1m)

## LAVENDER

Although it's not used much in the kitchen apart from the flowers flavoring foods, such as cookies and ice cream, lavender (*Lavandula*) is a fragrant and beautiful herb to grow. It requires particularly good drainage to thrive, so pots are the best option for wetter climates. Propagate by softwood cuttings (see p.128).

**Plant spacing** 16in (40cm)

**Height** 16in (40cm)

## THYME

Thyme (*Thymus vulgaris*) is one of my favorite herbs to grow, and there are many great varieties to try. My favorite is lemon thyme, bringing together two exceptional flavors, which I add to a roast dinner or when roasting veggies. Thyme makes for excellent ground cover under taller perennials, like rosemary or currants. Propagate by softwood cuttings and layering (see pp.128–129).

**Plant spacing** 12in (30cm)

**Height** 8in (20cm)

## MARJORAM AND OREGANO

These two herbs (*Origanum majorana* and *O. vulgare*) grow in much the same way, but marjoram has a sweeter and milder taste than oregano. The flowers are popular with bees, while the leaves are great for pizza toppings or to add flavor when roasting. Propagate by softwood cuttings and division (see p.128).

**Plant spacing** 12in (30cm)

**Height** 12in (30cm)

## VIETNAMESE CORIANDER

One of the most tender perennial herbs, Vietnamese coriander (*Persicaria odorata*) is also one of the most visually striking. The plants form a mass of green leaves, each with a purple horseshoe pattern toward the base. My favorite way to grow this delicious aromatic herb is on the edge of a container or raised bed, allowing the foliage to flow over the side. Lift roots in the late fall and keep potted undercover, replanting after the last frost the following year, or overwinter cuttings. Prefers damp soil but enjoys full sun. Propagate by semi-ripe cuttings (see p.128).

**Plant spacing** 20in (50cm)

**Height** 20in (50cm)

## TARRAGON

Known as the "King of Herbs" in France, tarragon (*Artemisia dracunculus*) is an easy herb to grow. It's popular in fish and chicken dishes and is used for many different sauces, including Béarnaise. For the best flavor, opt for French tarragon rather than the hardier Russian tarragon. Propagate by semi-ripe cuttings and division (see p.128).

**Plant spacing** 32in (80cm)

**Height** 16in (40cm)

## SAGE

Sage (*Salvia officinalis*) is a lovely, traditional herb to grow, often underrated, but it has many uses in the kitchen. One of my favorite foodie memories was when I first ate crispy-fried sage leaves—an absolute must for everyone to try! There are many varieties that offer differences, such as variegated or purple leaves. Propagate by softwood cuttings (see p.128).

**Plant spacing** 20in (50cm)

**Height** 20in (50cm)

## BLACK CURRANT SAGE

Related to common sage, black currant sage (*Salvia microphylla*) is easily in my top five perennial herbs. The leaves have the most incredible black currant aroma—perfect for cold drinks in summer. The profuse, edible, dark pink flowers are also loved by bees, and it's a joy in the garden. Propagate by semi-ripe cuttings (see p.128).

**Plant spacing** 16in (40cm)

**Height** 32in (80cm)

## FENNEL

Fennel (*Foeniculum vulgare*) is one of the most impactful and useful perennial herbs. It is closely related to the fennel vegetable but comes back every year. The main parts to harvest are its feathery leaves, flowers, and seeds. The towering flower stalks are loved by beneficial insects and may need support in exposed locations. Keep an eye out for bronze fennel, which has purple leaves when young that turn to a dark gray-green later in the season. Propagate from seed (see pp.178–183).

**Plant spacing** 20in (50cm)

**Height** 6½ft (2m)

# PERENNIAL FLOWERS

Although many perennial flowers are not edible, they serve other key functions for a thriving kitchen garden, such as supporting a diverse insect ecosystem and creating splashes of beauty.

The value of aesthetics should not be underestimated; you want to have a garden that inspires you to visit at any spare moment, and flowers really help with that attraction. A mistake some people make with permaculture is thinking that *everything* must have more than one purpose, but I believe nothing is more important than having a space that evokes a deep sense of joy that energizes the gardener. An inspired gardener is a force to be reckoned with. As a starting point for you, here is a collection of some of my favorite perennial flowers to grow, which happen to be loved by pollinators too.

## 1. Coneflower
Daisy-like coneflower is a group of flowers that includes several types of *Echinacea* (shown here) and *Rudbeckia*, both from the aster family. They are easy to grow, are loved by pollinators, and produce long-flowering stems, perfect as cut or dried flowers.

**Plant spacing** 12in (30cm)

**Height** 2–5ft (60–150cm), depending on variety

## 2. Lupin
One of my favorite early summer flowers, lupins (*Lupinus*) come in a range of different colors and produce fantastic flower spikes that stand out in a border. The sun-ray leaves add more visual interest.

**Plant spacing** 18in (45cm)

**Height** 2–3ft (60–90cm), depending on variety

## 3. Dahlia
Dahlias (*Dahlia*) are tuberous flowering plants that come in an incredible variety of colors, patterns, and shapes. They are one of the most popular back garden and allotment flowers for a reason —the hardest thing about them is picking which ones to grow!

**Plant spacing** 16–20in (40–50cm)

**Height** 1–5ft (30–150cm), depending on variety

## 4. Yarrow
Yarrows (*Achillea*) are traditional border plants offering long-lasting flat-topped flowers that are enjoyed by pollinators. There are many colors available, and they are very easy to grow. Divide every four or five years to keep them productive.

**Plant spacing** 12–18in (30–45cm)

**Height** 1–3ft (30–90cm), depending on variety

## 5. Verbena
The variety *Verbena bonariensis* is a butterfly magnet and looks particularly stunning when grown in larger clumps of plants or along a whole border. A great option for cut flowers, it can be easily propagated by semi-ripe cuttings that are overwintered in a polytunnel.

**Plant spacing** 18–24in (45–60cm)

**Height** 6ft (1.8m)

## MEADOWS

Natural meadows are one of the most important habitats for insects and birds. If you have a large garden, let an area of lawn grow wild and enjoy all the flowers that naturally grow up. Alternatively, you can sow perennial native wildflower mixes. To make a meadow look fit for purpose (sometimes neighbors have issues with "unkempt" lawns), just mow a curved path through it.

6

7

8

10

9

### 6. Salvia

On the ornamental side of the sage family, *Salvia* offers wonderful color displays that last well into the fall and are a haven for pollinators. There are many types available, including annuals, biennials, and perennials, and they range from deep blues to vivid reds.

**Plant spacing** 12–18in (30–45cm)

**Height** 4–5ft (1.2–1.5m)

### 7. Sea holly

A beautifully structured plant, sea holly (*Eryngium*) is, in my eyes, an ornamental version of a thistle, with lovely silvery-green leaves and striking blue flowers. These flowers are popular for drying and using in winter floral displays.

**Plant spacing** 12–18in (30–45cm)

**Height** 16–39in (40–100cm), depending on variety

### 8. Aquilegia

*Aquilegia* was one of the first perennial ornamental flowers I ever included within a kitchen garden, and the bell-shaped flowers (or nodding bonnets) are both lovely to look at and enjoyed by bees. It self-seeds readily but doesn't invade.

**Plant spacing** 16–20in (40–50cm)

**Height** 18–36in (45–90cm), depending on variety

### 9. Oxeye daisy

This perennial wildflower (*Leucanthemum vulgare*) blooms through the summer months and is a popular choice in cottage gardens, attracting hoverflies, bees, and butterflies. It is easy to propagate by division (see p.128) and looks incredible when planted in clumps.

**Plant spacing** 12in (30cm)

**Height** 24in (60cm)

### 10. Poppy

Oriental poppies (*Papaver orientale*) are a lovely addition to any kitchen garden and offer an abundance of accessible pollen for pollinating insects. The most bees I've ever counted on a flower (14) was, in fact, on a large ornamental poppy in my mom's front garden. They can be propagated by division (see p.128).

**Plant spacing** 20in (50cm)

**Height** 20–39in (50–100cm), depending on variety

*A beautiful tulip display in my bulb beds in early spring.*

## BULBS

This massive category of flowers includes everything from allium flowers to tulips. There are bulbs for every season, and those that flower during the late winter through to mid-spring are great to focus on first while much of the kitchen garden is still asleep or, at the very least, rather green! Some of my favorite bulbs that flower after the spring window include alliums, agapanthus, and irises.

## DEADHEADING

Deadheading is a technique used to extend flowering and keep plants looking tidy. Whenever a flower goes past its best, and if you don't need the plant to set seeds, simply cut the flower head, or whole flower spike for something like lupins. However, for maximum wildlife benefit, it is best to leave as many suitable seed heads standing as possible for birds to feed on over the fall and winter. Coneflowers, sea holly, and poppies are all sought out by birds.

# ROSES

Out of all the flowering plants, roses are my favorite. My choice is justified because roses are also edible. Every rose petal is edible, and the hips are useful for making a range of food and drinks, from delicious jam to summer wine.

The sheer number of rose varieties can be overwhelming to start with, but there are some core characteristics that help when deciding which variety to grow. These include:

- **Longevity**—does it flower during a short stint, have a second flush, or continue throughout the season?
- **Habit**—does the rose grow as a shrub, or is it a climber?
- **Resistance**—how well does it fare against common rose pests and diseases?
- **Fragrance**—the better smelling the rose, the tastier it is when it comes to eating or infusing.
- **Pollinators**—how attractive is it to pollinating insects?

## CULINARY ROSE GARDEN

Because of my love for roses, I have a whole rose garden of carefully selected varieties for culinary uses. This includes a collection of shrub and climbing roses with a wide range of fragrances, each delivering a unique flavor, as well as roses chosen for large hips, which are more efficient when it comes to prepping in the kitchen. I keep work to a minimum by mulching around the base of the roses twice a year with grass clippings or well-rotted manure and just use a string trimmer to keep the grass down if the rose is grown in the ground. Roses can be easily propagated by softwood and semi-ripe cuttings (see p.128).

## PRUNING ROSES

Pruning roses is important to promote vigorous healthy growth and to maintain a certain shape for aesthetic reasons, to improve yields, or both. It is usually done in the dormant season, and roses are a great beginner starting point if you have never pruned before.

Use a sharp, clean pair of pruners and just remember the golden rule of pruning to maintain plant health: Always cut just above a bud at a slight angle away from the bud so rainwater doesn't pool on the top of the shoot or drip into the bud below, which may cause it to rot.

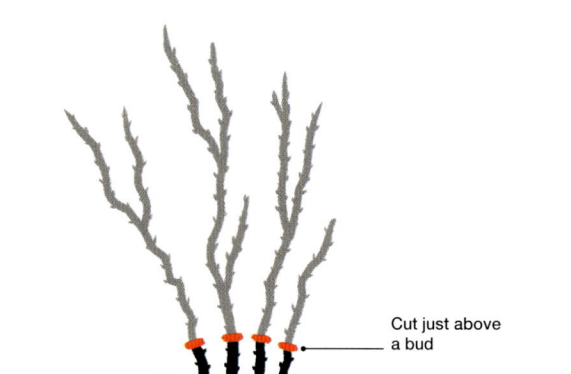

Cut just above a bud

**Shrub rose first year**
*Cut all stems to around 2–4in (5–10cm) above ground level.*

**Established shrub rose**
*Reduce the overall bush size to around half of its original size.*

*Cutting multiple different varieties of rose to make an edible bouquet for the kitchen.*

## BUYING BARE-ROOT ROSES

The most cost-effective way to purchase roses, as well as any other perennial shrubs and trees, is bare-root. Bare-root plants are only available during the dormant season and because of this do not need to be transported in pots filled with compost. This makes them cheaper to buy. Bare-root plants can be bunched together, and their roots are wrapped to prevent them from drying out.

When a bare-root plant arrives, you can plant it out immediately as you would a fruit tree (see pp.162–165), but with no stake, and bury the bottom stems 2in (5cm) below soil level. If it's not possible to plant it out, you can heel it in temporarily. This involves digging a hole in the ground and placing the roots in the hole, gently covering them with the soil that has just been excavated. Choose a free-draining area so as not to rot the roots, especially during the winter, when rainfall is greater and evaporation is slower. Lift the rose just before you are ready to plant it.

## ROSA RUGOSA

A readily available variety of rose that is excellent for a permaculture kitchen garden is *Rosa rugosa*. It produces beautiful delicate yet fragrant pink flowers for a long period that go on to form excellent-sized hips. It is a wild rose type and makes a great addition to any border, hedgerow, or food forest planting scheme. Another beautiful wild rose is the dog rose (*Rosa canina*), a native climbing hedgerow rose in the UK.

# CURRANTS AND GOOSEBERRIES

Currants and gooseberries are a staple of any kitchen garden. They are very simple to grow, don't require lots of soil fertility, yield consistently, and root easily from hardwood cuttings.

Ideally, currants and gooseberries prefer to grow in a sunny position, but they tolerate partial shade well. Because of this, they are a great option to grow beneath fruit trees on the south side of the trunk. Currants include black, red, white, and pink currants, while gooseberries come in three colors: green, yellow, and red. A jostaberry is a cross between a gooseberry and a black currant. Almost every variety of these fruits crops around midsummer, and all may need protection from birds leading up to fruiting (see p.264). All are easy to freeze, providing a valuable source of fruit over the winter months. Propagate them from hardwood cuttings (see p.128).

### BLACK CURRANT

The most popular of all of the currants and the easiest to prune, the black currant (*Ribes nigrum*) is a heavy cropper and can live for at least 20 years. The fruits have a strong grape-like flavor with good tartness.

**Plant spacing** 5ft (1.5m)

**Height** 5ft (1.5m)

### JOSTABERRY

Forming an incredibly vigorous and productive bush, the jostaberry (*Ribes × nidigrolaria*) yields gooseberry-sized black fruits with a sweeter, deeper flavor than gooseberries.

**Plant spacing** 6½ft (2m)

**Height** 5ft (1.5m)

## PRUNING BLACK CURRANTS AND JOSTABERRIES

Pruning is done to encourage vigorous plants and to make harvesting easier. These two plants produce new growth almost like suckers, with stems appearing from beneath the ground. They can both be pruned in much the same way every winter.

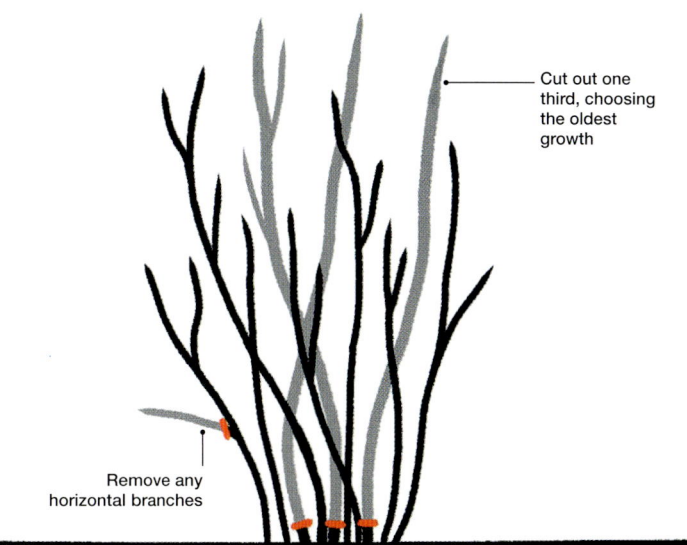

Cut out one third, choosing the oldest growth

*The focus is on removing around one-third of the stems at the base, taking out the oldest. Remove any that touch and any damaged or low-growing branches.*

Remove any horizontal branches

## RED CURRANT

A favourite of mine, but also a favorite of blackbirds, red currants (*Ribes rubrum*), with their vibrant transparent berries, are deliciously sweet and boast impressive yields.

**Plant spacing** 5ft (1.5m)

**Height** 5ft (1.5m)

## WHITE CURRANT

Less common than red and black currants, white currants (*Ribes rubrum* cultivars) are also less vigorous, but they taste delicious, and due to their color, they usually go unnoticed by birds.

**Plant spacing** 4ft (1.2m)

**Height** 4ft (1.2m)

## PINK CURRANT

The rarest currant of them all—in fact, most gardeners haven't heard of pink currants (*Ribes rubrum* cultivars). They grow with similar vigor to the white currant but will need bird protection.

**Plant spacing** 4ft (1.2m)

**Height** 4ft (1.2m)

## GOOSEBERRY

A heavy-yielding soft fruit well known for its tartness, the gooseberry (*Ribes uva-crispa*) also has red and yellow varieties that are noticeably sweeter. Be careful of the spikes when harvesting!

**Plant spacing** 5ft (1.5m)

**Height** 5ft (1.5m)

## PRUNING RED, WHITE, AND PINK CURRANTS AND GOOSEBERRIES

Unlike black currants, these soft fruits are pruned to have a single "trunk" and then a crown shape of branches coming from this trunk. Prune in the dormant season. They can also be pruned into cordons to save space (see below).

*When establishing a crown shape, cut the main branches by one quarter and side branches to 3 or 4 buds.*

### Training as a cordon

A great way to grow red currants and gooseberries is as a cordon, which is a single trunk growing up a support stake. This is created by choosing one main stem as a leader and cutting back sideshoots before the spring to one bud. In the summer, once seven or eight leaves are on the new growth, cut back to four or five leaves and prune developing sideshoots to one leaf. The following winter and winters thereafter, take off around half of the new growth of the leader back to a bud and prune all sideshoots back to one or two buds, not forgetting to also follow the same summer pruning approach annually. An alternative way of training them is in a fan shape.

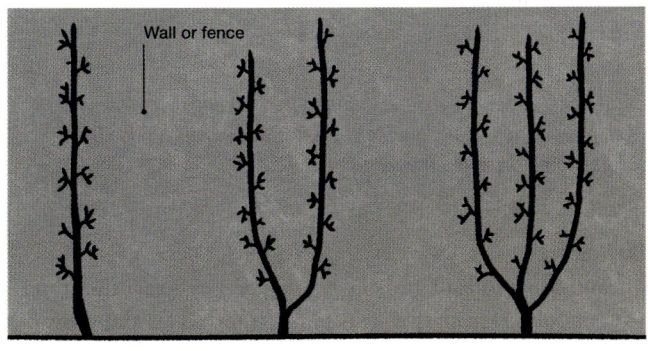

**Single-stemmed cordon:** plant spacing 16in (40cm)

**Double-stemmed cordon:** plant spacing 24in (60cm)

**Triple-stemmed cordon:** plant spacing 36in (90cm)

*You can train currants and gooseberries as either single-, double-, or triple-stemmed cordons.*

## CAPE GOOSEBERRIES

The cape gooseberry (*Physalis peruviana*) is a plant in the nightshade family (not related to the gooseberry) that grows as a perennial in its native habitat in Chile and Peru. It needs to be carefully overwintered in cooler climates. The easiest way to grow it is by starting it off by seed every spring and growing it inside a polytunnel. Cape gooseberries grow up to 6ft (1.8m) tall and more than 3ft (1m) wide, and the fruits are ready to harvest when their "cape" turns to a pale yellow papery texture. Homegrown cape gooseberries taste miles better than the ones you sometimes find on top of your dessert in a restaurant!

# TRAILING BERRIES AND RASPBERRIES

If your garden has a sunny boundary, such as a fence or wall, then you have to grow some trailing berries or try a row of raspberries.

## TRAILING BERRIES

These berries come in many different varieties related to and including blackberries (*Rubus fruticosus*), such as tayberries, silvanberries, boysenberries, and loganberries. Trailing berries like deep, rich soil but don't need much fertility once established. They are vigorous and produce long, trailing stems known as canes. They are best grown against a trellis, fence, or wall for easy harvest and training. Fruit appears on the two-year-old canes. Trailing berries are easy to propagate by layering (see p.129).

**Plant spacing** 6½ft (2m)

**Height and spread** 8ft (2.5m) tall by 10–13ft (3–4m) wide

## Training and pruning trailing berries

Training and pruning are done at the same time. First, cut out all the two-year-old canes that have just fruited at ground level; these are easily identifiable by the stems appearing less fresh. Once you have more space, tie up the new canes with garden twine at several points against a wall or fence, starting at 24in (60cm) up from the ground, spacing canes 6–12in (15–30cm) apart. When you have used all the available space, cut out any excess canes or use these as layer tips (see p.129) to start off new plants. If you don't tie the canes, they will flop on the ground.

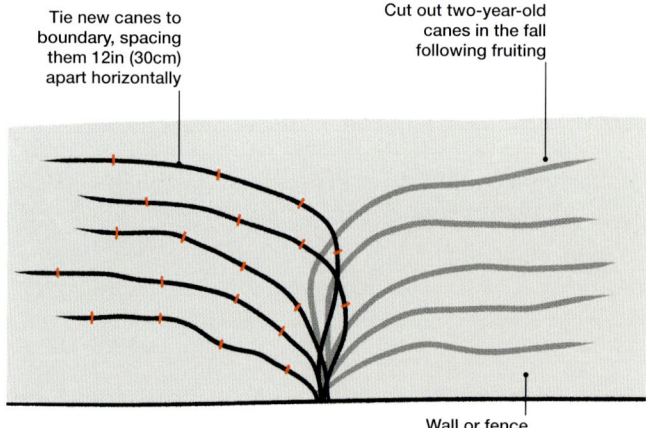

Tie new canes to boundary, spacing them 12in (30cm) apart horizontally

Cut out two-year-old canes in the fall following fruiting

Wall or fence

*Each year, cut out the older canes after fruiting. The following year, new canes will grow up in their place. Fruit will be borne on alternate sides from year to year.*

## Suckers

The only downside of growing trailing berries is that they can send up suckers from their roots, which spread far and wide. Suckers are new shoots that appear a few steps away from the plant, and these are in part how wild versions of trailing berries like brambles can spread quickly. While growing them in a large container is possible, I've found that cutting out suckers below ground level as I spot them will keep things in check.

*'Joan J' fall-fruiting raspberry*

*'Golden Everest' summer-fruiting raspberry*

## RASPBERRY

Raspberries (*Rubus idaeus*) are one of the tastiest fruits you can grow, and they are always a joy to harvest and eat when in the garden. There are two basic types of raspberries: summer-fruiting and fall-fruiting. The two types are pruned very differently (see right). Although red raspberries are the most common, golden varieties are equally tasty and attract fewer birds. That being said, I have found birds are far less interested in red fall raspberries compared to strawberries, red currants, and summer raspberries. Propagate raspberries by layering or by dividing mature clumps from two years after planting (see pp.128–129).

**Plant spacing** 16in (40cm)

**Height and spread** Summer-fruiting raspberries: 6ft (1.8m); fall-fruiting raspberries: 4–5ft (1.2–1.5m)

## Pruning raspberries

Summer raspberries are similar to trailing berries, fruiting on second-year growth. This means that when you are pruning in the winter, you cut down all the old growth, leaving only the new stems that emerged the spring before. Fall raspberries are perhaps the easiest fruit to prune, as they fruit on the new canes that emerge each spring: Just cut back all growth to ground level in the winter.

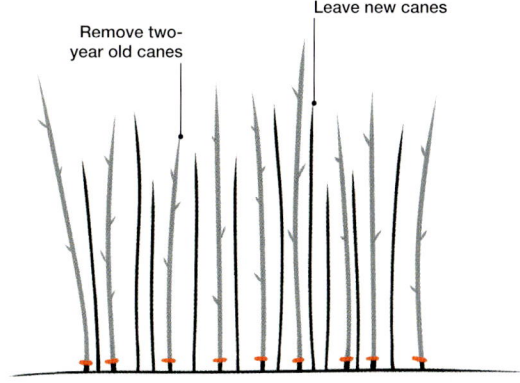

Remove two-year old canes

Leave new canes

### Pruning summer raspberries
*Cut back the two-year old, fruited canes at the base to leave the new canes that will fruit the following year.*

### Support

Summer raspberries can be easily supported by running a few wires on either side of the raspberry patch just to keep them from being blown over. In more sheltered sites, raspberries can be grown without support. Fall raspberries are shorter than summer raspberries, and I don't bother supporting them in more exposed locations.

## JAPANESE WINEBERRY

Japanese wineberries (*Rubus phoenicolasius*, right) are gaining popularity for good reason. Not only is their flavor described as unbelievably sweet, a reason in itself to grow them; they have attractive red stems that are a lovely sight during the winter. If you want to add taste and interest to your garden, then get yourself a plant!

# OTHER BERRIES

A berry is a simple, plump, and juicy fruit, and there are many delicious options that can be easily grown. I've featured my favorites below.

## STRAWBERRY

Strawberries (*Fragaria × ananassa*) are an excellent ground-cover fruit, perfect for growing under currants or at the base of fruit trees. They grow best in fertile soil and full sun. Mulching under fruit isn't necessary, but straw is a common option and can be used if you want perfect-looking berries. To guarantee a harvest, strawberries must be netted, as otherwise the birds will beat you to it. You can grow strawberries in a polytunnel for earlier crops, but ensure that you keep on top of watering.

There are many different varieties available (see below), and the key harvest season is from early to midsummer. Strawberry plants start to lose vigor and productivity by their third year, so separate rooted runners (see p.129) from the mother plants in the early fall, discard the mother plants, and replant the runners. For the first two years, when you don't need to do a big replant, pot up runners into individual pots to plant elsewhere, swap, or sell.

**Plant spacing** 12in (30cm)

**Height and spread** 8 x 12in (20 x 30cm)

### June-bearing and everbearing strawberries

There are two key categories of strawberry. June-bearing strawberries tend to have one big flush of fruits earlier in the season, which is perfect for when you need a quantity of strawberries for preserving or cooking. Everbearing strawberries, on the other hand, provide a continuous crop of berries throughout summer, and although you won't get as many in one go, they are great for ensuring that you always have some to snack on. If you have the space, it is worth having one June-bearing and one everbearing strawberry bed.

### Alpine strawberries

Alpine strawberries yield tiny fruits over the summer—a lovely option if you want to enjoy mini-bursts of intense flavor. They work well within an herb bed and grow well in partial shade. Some varieties do not send out runners but grow as a clump that can be divided every two or three years (see p.128).

## BLUEBERRY

Growing your own blueberries (*Vaccinium corymbosum*) has to be one of the highlights of a kitchen garden. They require a more acidic soil to thrive than most other crops. I tend not to buy specific compost for different plants, but blueberries are perhaps the one exception. I buy potting mix for acid-loving plants, as it means I can guarantee successful harvests for years to come. Blueberries can be grown in the ground if you prepare the site adequately. This means digging a large hole, at least 20in (50cm) wide and deep, and filling it with potting mix for acid-loving plants before planting your blueberries. Alternatively, you can invest in sulfur chips to amend the soil and then mulch the plants generously every two or three years with potting mix for acid-loving plants. If you have heavy clay soil and a neutral pH (see p.48) you are often better off growing blueberries in large containers rather than trying to change the pH of the soil. Varieties come in all sizes, from smaller 20in (50cm) high ones up to 60in (1.5m) in height.

**Plant spacing** 36in (90cm)

**Height** 20–60in (50–150cm)

### Pruning blueberries

Start pruning blueberries once plants are two years old. The best time to prune them is in the late winter, as it is easy to distinguish the fruit buds (fat) from the leaf buds (smaller and flatter). As a simple rule, any branches that have lots of fruit buds and are attached to a strong, healthy stem should be left on. For general pruning guidelines, see page 126.

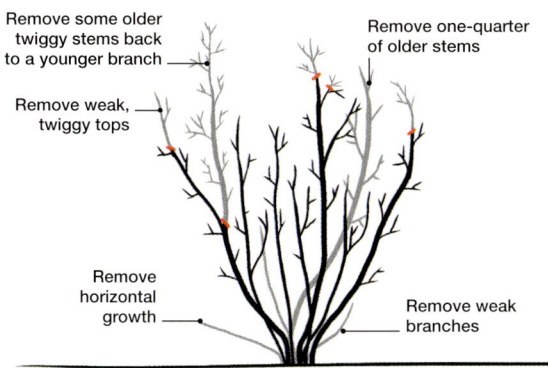

Remove some older twiggy stems back to a younger branch

Remove one-quarter of older stems

Remove weak, twiggy tops

Remove horizontal growth

Remove weak branches

*Aim to have a bush that has one third older stems, one third stems that are 2–3 years old, and one third newer stems.*

### HONEYBERRY

Also known as the edible honeysuckle, honeyberries (*Lonicera caerulea*) have a moreish zingy taste that is both sweet and tart and don't require the stricter soil conditions of blueberries, making them easier to grow for most people. Pruning is easy and is only needed for plants older than three years. In midsummer,

after fruiting, remove any weak growth and overcrowded branches and then cut back the tips of shoots by a few buds to encourage more fruiting in future years.

**Plant spacing** 36in (90cm)

**Height** 20–60in (50–150cm)

### GOJI BERRY

Goji berries (*Lycium barbarum*) are hardy soft fruits that begin to fruit two or three years after planting. They can be grown successfully in the UK if they are trained against a sunny fence or wall, tying in the stems to their support so the plant can spread out and enjoy as much sun as possible. You can also grow a goji berry bush within a box-like frame (see p.187) to retain some structure and support, but with a more natural look. Fruit appears on the previous year's stems, so when pruning, ensure that you keep these. Every winter, follow the 3 Ds of pruning (see p.126) and tidy up the plant by removing the oldest stems, any congestion, and any weak growth and tying up canes as needed. The leaves can be cooked and eaten.

**Plant spacing** 6½ft (2m)

**Height** 10ft (3m)

### POLLINATION OF HONEYBERRIES AND BLUEBERRIES

Some fruits require pollination from other plants (and varieties) to ensure a healthy yield. If the flowers are not adequately pollinated, they won't form fruit. Honeyberries and most blueberries (with the exception of self-fertile varieties) require other plants in close proximity for successful pollination. As a result, honeyberries should be planted in trios, and blueberries should be planted in pairs of two different varieties.

# TREE FRUIT

Fruit trees offer multiple benefits for a permaculture kitchen garden in addition to their crops. It's even possible to grow them in small or balcony gardens.

First, fruit trees add a vertical dimension, providing perching opportunities for birds, visual interest over the winter, and blossoms in the spring. They also form microclimates within a garden. Occasionally, a garden may be so exposed to the sun that planting some trees to form natural shade is necessary to grow certain shade-loving crops as well as to provide a respite for humans and wildlife during the intense midday sun. Trees also act as a natural windbreak, protecting weaker annual crops within the garden as well as offering delicious harvests.

Some varieties of fruit trees follow a pattern of biennial bearing; they alternate a noticeably productive year with a less productive year.

## LOCATION

When it comes to laying out your garden, it is worth remembering that out of all the perennials listed in this book, trees are the most permanent and the most prominent. Never rush when it comes to placing a tree, as once planted (see pp.162–164), you don't want to be moving it! The polyculture chapter will give you more ideas on where to plant fruit trees and how to best use the microclimate they offer, starting with fruit tree guild planting (see pp.230–231).

Fruit trees thrive in sunny, sheltered locations with good drainage. Sun is essential for ripening. Shelter is essential for both preventing the blossoms from getting blown away and protecting the tree from damage. Good drainage is a must because fruit trees that have "wet feet" will succumb to disease or die. If in doubt, conduct a percolation test.

*Once established, apple trees will produce for generations to come. I'm harvesting apples here from a tree my dad planted when I was a baby.*

## Percolation test

To know whether your ground is suitable for fruit trees, one morning, following a couple of days without rain, dig a hole 12in (30cm) deep and wide and fill it with water (see right). The following morning, refill the hole with water and place a tape measure or ruler to track the rate of drainage, using a stick laying across the hole as the starting guide. Measure the depth every hour. Ideally, you want a drainage rate of 2in (5cm) per hour. Less than 1in (2.5cm) is too slow, and faster than 4in (10cm) is too fast. If the rate is too slow, explore deep raised beds for growing fruit trees. If it's too fast, dig the planting hole twice as big as usual and incorporate generous amounts of compost, ideally decomposed wood chips. For larger gardens, it's a good idea to conduct a few tests to see whether there are any areas more suitable for fruit trees than others.

## Undercover growing

In temperate climates, polytunnels open up the range of fruit that can be grown, especially in the UK, which has cooler and darker summers compared to North America. Fruits such as peaches, nectarines, and pomegranates are surprisingly hardy, but they struggle to produce fruit outside without enough warmth. A polytunnel solves this.

## PROPAGATION AND ROOTSTOCKS

Most trees are propagated by grafting a scion (a one-year-old stem of the variety you want) onto a suitable rootstock. A rootstock is the roots of a different species, and it controls the vigor of the tree. Dwarf rootstocks mean that even balcony gardens can have fruit trees growing in pots. In fact, dwarf trees are highly productive for the little space they take up, as their energy is put into fruiting rather than growth.

Different fruits have different rootstocks, and you need to match the correct rootstock with the correct fruit. A quince rootstock is suitable to graft an apple onto, for example, while a cherry is not. Depending on the rootstock, grafting can also improve a tree's resilience to common diseases or poorer soil conditions. More details are available under each tree fruit.

Trees are sold already grafted onto rootstocks with various qualities; it's possible to graft fruit trees yourself, too. Although grafting is a more complex propagation method than cutting, it is simpler than many people think. If you have a more extensive growing area and are looking for a low-cost method to create multiple fruit trees, you can purchase inexpensive rootstocks online and graft scion wood from the prunings of your current fruit trees onto these. For three simple grafting joins that can be used for grafting apples, pears, and plums onto rootstocks, see page 129.

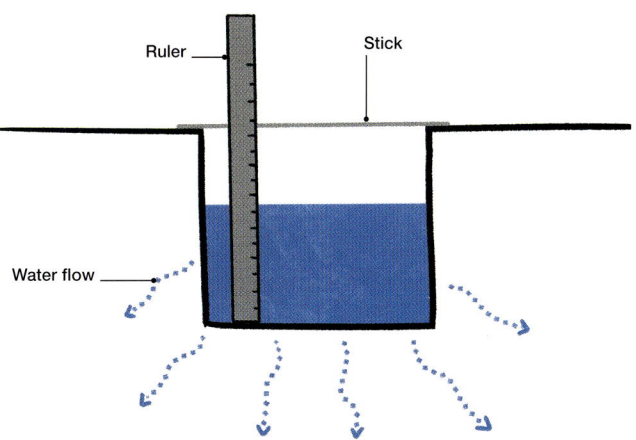

Ruler — Stick

Water flow —

**Testing drainage**
*Check the rate of drainage by measuring every hour to see how quickly the water percolates into the soil around.*

## POLLINATION

Pollination is an important subject when it comes to growing fruit trees successfully. In the simplest terms, trees are either self-fertile (just need their own pollen) or require a pollination partner (a different variety growing nearby that flowers at the same time). For those that need a pollination partner, if they don't have one nearby, there will be no fruit. For growing individual fruit types, such as one cherry tree and one apricot, you must grow a self-fertile variety in order to guarantee fruit.

Some apple varieties are also self-fertile, but many require another apple tree (of a different variety) to pollinate successfully. The biggest challenge when it comes to apples is that there are different pollination groups. Each group is made up of varieties that flower around the same time, so they are compatible for cross-pollination. There is crossover between each of the five pollination groups, and so apples in group 3 are pollinated by groups 2 and 4, and so on.

The good news is that if you are in a suburban area or have an allotment, then you will more than likely have other apples in close proximity that will take care of the pollination for you. Otherwise, growing a flowering crab apple nearby will also solve the issue, as they flower for an extended period and will pollinate your apple trees. Wild crab apples in the hedgerow will do the same job, too.

# PLANTING A FRUIT TREE

A fruit tree in the garden is a real centerpiece that requires minimal effort to look after and no further expenses once planted. That's why it's important to get it off to the best start by planting it with care.

My preferred method of planting a fruit tree is the zero-fertility method, in which the tree is planted without extra nutrients. This encourages the tree to spread out its roots to search for nutrients rather than enjoying all the goodness from the compost in the hole for the first couple of seasons. The better the root system, the more resilient the tree.

## BARE-ROOT TREES

These are purchased and planted in the dormancy season (late fall to early spring) and are far more affordable to buy (and easier to source) than fruit trees in pots of compost.

### You will need

| |
|---|
| Spade |
| Bare-root fruit tree |
| Stake (and post rammer or sledgehammer) |
| Can of water |
| Tree tie |
| Tree guard (optional but recommended) |
| Ramial chipped wood (optional) |

**1.**
Select the site for the tree; it should be a sunny, sheltered spot with well-draining soil.

## PLANTING A POTTED FRUIT TREE

Follow the exact same steps as shown here, planting the tree at the same depth as it is in the pot. If the tree has become rootbound, with roots circling around the edge of the pot, gently tease out some of the roots before placing the rootball in the hole. Potted fruit trees can be successfully transplanted all year, but October to April are the best months for planting.

**2.**
Cut out a square of turf twice the width of the root system and place it over the bare roots while you work. Dig a hole 2in (5cm) deeper than the root system measured from the root collar (seen by a change in bark color where the roots start).

**4.**
Fill back some of the loose soil and then place the tree upright, checking the roots by placing a handle or stick across the hole to ensure that the root collar is in line with the ground level.

**3.**
If your tree needs a stake (this depends on its rootstock, see p.161; the tree seller will also be able to advise you), bang the stake in at the corner closest to the prevailing wind. This means that during windy weather, the tree blows away from the stake rather than into it, which could damage the branches.

**5.**
Continue filling the hole up with the excavated soil, gently shaking the tree up and down so that the soil falls between the roots to get rid of any air pockets.

**6.**
Once the loose soil is all back around the roots, gently pat it down and then flip the turf upside down to place it around the base of the tree. You may need to cut up the turf to fit nicely around the base.

**7.**
Gently step around the stem of the tree on the flipped turf to fully anchor the plant and then give it a generous watering.

**8.**
Add the tree tie to secure the tree to the stake; the spacer on the tree tie helps to protect the trunk. Add a tree guard around the trunk if you wish.

**9.**
Mulch with compost, grass clippings, hay, or wood chips to retain moisture and keep the stem weed-free.

## RAMIAL CHIPPED WOOD

Like all perennials, trees like fungally dominated soil and form associations with mycorrhizal fungi where nutrients are exchanged. Mulching the ground around a fruit tree with ramial chipped wood (see pp.66–67) is a low-cost way to encourage more fungi in the soil, thus creating a more favorable growing environment for the tree.

# TREES AND SHRUBS FOR EDIBLE LEAVES

Who said you can't eat trees? The following trees and shrubs are my recommendations for anyone looking to grow an abundance of edible leaves for very little effort.

## WHITE MULBERRY

The young leaves of white mulberry (*Morus alba*) can be eaten after cooking and treated as a "greens" vegetable crop in a similar way as nettle leaves. For small gardens, you can coppice mulberry back each year to encourage vigorous growth that will provide you with an abundance of leaves.

## SMALLED-LEAVED LIME

A must-have for any food forest or soft boundary, the small-leaved lime (*Tilia cordata*) has young leaves that have a nice texture with a slight lemony taste. They can be harvested and used raw in the same way you would lettuce. As for the mulberry, coppicing small-leaved lime is the best method for an abundance of leaf production. Since it's a perennial, this is a great way to increase your salad self-sufficiency without needing the compost or maintenance that annual salads need. The young flowers are also edible raw and can be dried to make linden tea.

## SALTBUSH

The saltbush (*Atriplex halimus*), with edible raw leaves that have a salty tang to them, is a popular ornamental plant that also offers an ingredient to add to your salads. To thrive, saltbush likes a well-drained spot and will work very well in a polytunnel. Because it is

evergreen, you can harvest it year-round, and it responds well to hard pruning if it ever gets too large.

## GRAPE

Grapevines (*Vitis*, see also p. 171) offer edible raw leaves. There is considerable difference between varieties in terms of taste and texture. Trials by Martin Crawford (see resources, p.280) found that the young leaves of the popular grape variety 'Chardonnay' had wonderful edible qualities, with "lemony" and "juicy" being noted. His advice is to look for *Vitis vinifera* varieties recommended for their vine leaves. *Vitis vinifera* 'Rondo' is a suitable variety for growing in cooler and wetter climates.

## HUW'S TIP

In early spring, the young leaves of beech (*Fagus sylvatica*) and hawthorn (*Crataegus monogyna*) can be foraged and eaten raw as another tasty addition to spring salads.

# APPLE AND PEAR

When you visit walled kitchen gardens on large country estates, you will always find a collection of apple and pear trees. However, you don't need a huge space to grow them: They can be cleverly added into any scale of garden.

There are more than 2,500 apple (*Malus domestica*) and 500 pear varieties (*Pyrus*) growing in the UK alone, each one offering unique flavors, textures, and characteristics. Many varieties are rooted in a specific geographical region, and this used to be the case with vegetable varieties, although many of these have been lost forever.

Visiting local gardens, heritage orchards, and allotments is a great starting point to see which varieties thrive in the conditions in your area. When buying fruit trees, opt for local or leading fruit tree nurseries that can offer advice on pollination, rootstock options, pruning, and care for each variety (see suppliers, p.281).

*A stunning display of apples on this Welsh heritage variety 'Pig Aderyn', which translates to Bird's Beak.*

## ROOTSTOCKS

Dwarf fruit trees have a shorter life-span than larger specimens, but they do come into full production much faster. The largest rootstock can take up to seven years to reach full production, while very dwarfing rootstocks only need a couple.

### Apple rootstocks

Below is a diagram of the most common apple rootstocks with the final tree size to help you decide what size trees suit your garden. For the best results in the smallest of spaces, I recommend avoiding the most dwarfing varieties and instead growing M26 as cordons. M26 make a good bush tree for small gardens, and MM106 for medium gardens.

### Pear rootstocks

Pears use different rootstocks than apples. The most common are Quince C, growing 8–10ft (2.5–3m) tall, Quince A, 10–13ft (3–4m) tall, and the confusingly named Pyrodwarf, reaching around 13–16ft (4–5m) tall.

### Propagating your own rootstock

Rootstock compatibility for some pears can be confusing, but propagating your own rootstock for apple production is easy. Order your chosen rootstock, such as M26, plant it in the ground, and let it grow for a year. The following winter, cut it to around 2in (5cm) in height and mound up over the short stem with 12–16in (30–40cm) of sawdust.

The harsh cut will force the stem to coppice, with each stem rooting into the sawdust. The following winter, carefully remove the sawdust, cut the rooted stems where they connect to the original stem, and you will now have rootstocks ready to graft on to (see p.161).

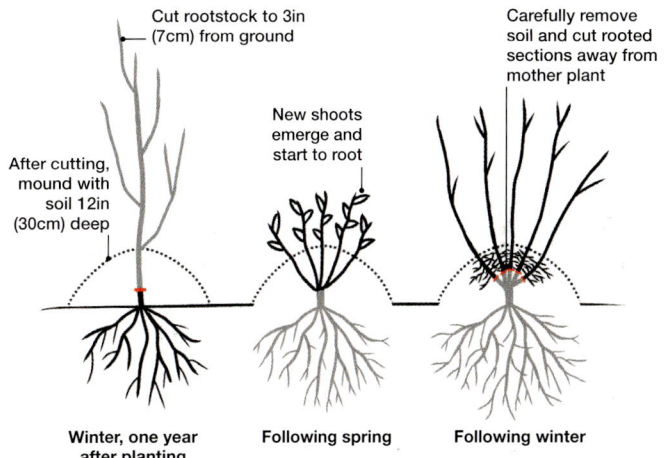

CHOOSING ROOTSTOCKS

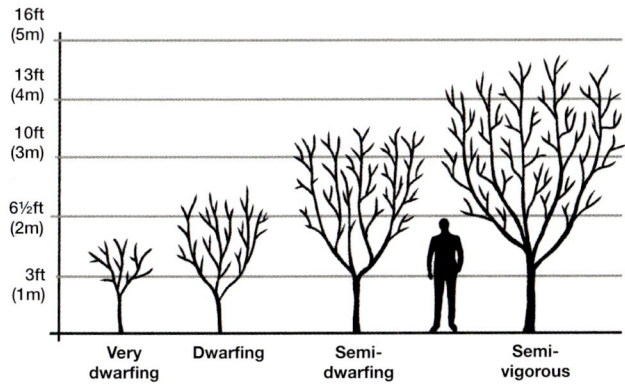

| Height | 5–6½ft (1.5–2m) | 6½–10ft (2–3m) | 10–11½ft (3–3.5m) | 13–15ft (4–4.5m) |
|---|---|---|---|---|
| Rootstock type (apple) | M27 | M9 | M26 | MM106 & M116 |
| Rootstock type (pear) | N/A | Quince C | Quince A | Pyrodwarf |
| Tree spacing | 6½ft (2m) | 10ft (3m) | 13ft (4m) | 16ft (5m) |

*The graph shows the different sizes of rootstocks to scale with a corresponding table of apple and pear types.*

*Fresh pears make a delicious garden snack.*

## PRUNING APPLES AND PEARS

Pruning is useful for many reasons. First,you promote good airflow and light levels around the tree, reducing disease issues and aiding ripening. It also makes it easier for you to access the fruit when harvesting rather than battling countless branches.

### Pruning after planting

Prune during the dormancy season. When you've planted an apple or pear, you will need to prune it. The tree will either be what's termed a maiden, which is one single stem, or a bush. For a maiden, your aim is to establish the first stage of formative pruning, which is when you encourage the plant to begin to bush out rather than continue upward. To do this, cut the maiden back by one third to a half, just above a bud, and then rub off this bud and the next two down (the longer you leave the maiden, the taller the trunk). This will encourage the new branches to grow outward rather than vertically, creating a better shaped tree.

For trees that are already trained into a bush shape, follow the steps below for the first three years to establish a strong framework shape. For subsequent years, follow the same approach as in year three.

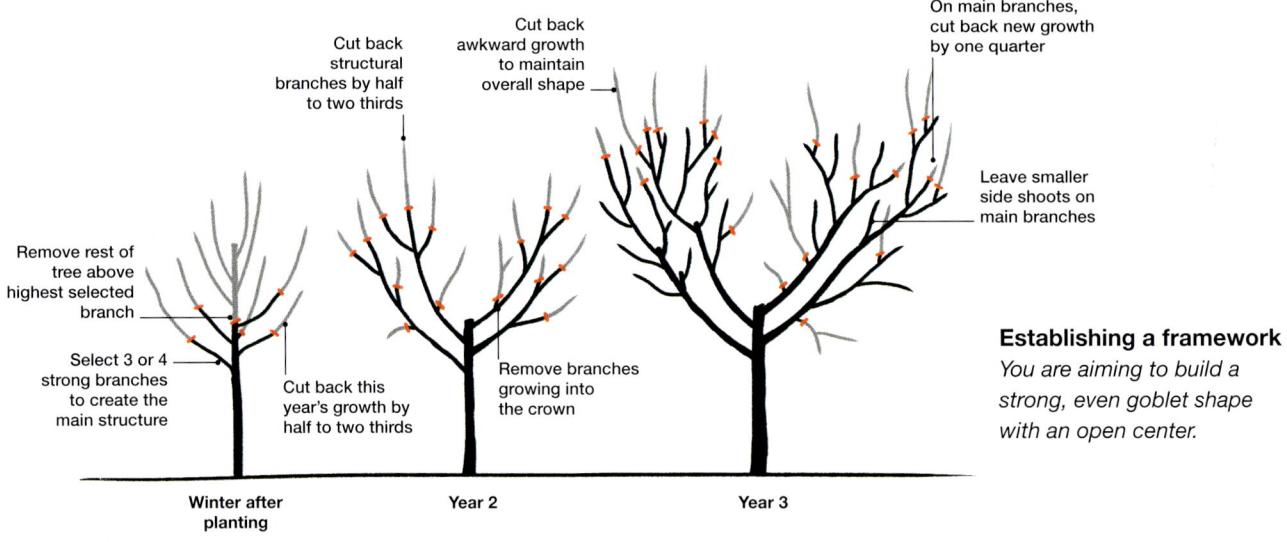

Remove rest of tree above highest selected branch

Select 3 or 4 strong branches to create the main structure

Cut back this year's growth by half to two thirds

**Winter after planting**

Cut back structural branches by half to two thirds

Cut back awkward growth to maintain overall shape

Remove branches growing into the crown

**Year 2**

On main branches, cut back new growth by one quarter

Leave smaller side shoots on main branches

**Establishing a framework**
*You are aiming to build a strong, even goblet shape with an open center.*

**Year 3**

### Pruning spur bearers, partial tip bearers, and tip bearers

The majority of apples and pears are spur bearing. This means that there are fruit spurs (short and stubby buds) along the branches, from where the blossoms and then fruits appear. Some varieties are tip bearing, which is where the fruits form only on the tip of shoots that grew the previous year. These different ways of bearing fruit mean that you need to approach pruning slightly differently for tip bearers after the first three years of formative pruning. The easiest approach is to leave any of last year's shoots less than 8–9in (20–23cm) long to bear fruit the next growing season; any shoots longer than 9in (23cm) can be pruned back to five buds. Partial tip bearers can be pruned as for spur bearers. There are many different apple pruning styles; I have shared what I think works best if you have a few trees in your garden and want the space to plant a guild below.

### Fruit thinning

When apple and pear trees appear laden, it is worth thinning fruit clusters to promote larger, more useful fruit rather than having lots of small fruit. The aim is to produce the highest quality possible. Thin fruits around midsummer, following the "June drop," which is when apples naturally shed some excess fruit. Thinning also reduces the chance of the tree having an off-season (biennial bearing) the following year and branches snapping under the weight, which can lead to misshaping or disease. I like to keep things simple: Thin clusters of apples down to the two strongest and healthiest fruits by pinching out smaller and misshapen fruitlets with your fingers. For wilder planting schemes, like a food forest, you do not need to thin.

## SUPPORTING OVERLOADED BRANCHES

Even after thinning, some branches may need more support due to the weight of fruits. For a rustic but effective prop for laden branches, use forked hazel sticks, with the base on the ground and the fork at the top with the branch resting on it.

## Cordon pruning

Cordon apples and pears are a fantastic option for small permaculture gardens looking to include as many perennials as possible (though this method isn't suitable for tip bearers). While these trees can be shaped in multiple ways, such as stepovers and fans, the cordon is simple to manage, and you can grow multiple varieties in a very small space, spacing them 24in (60cm) apart and growing them at an oblique angle. Cordons are also an excellent option against a sunny boundary. There are many ways of supporting cordons, from a single stake in the ground to using horizontal wires along a wall spaced every 12–16in (30–40cm) upward (see p.170). You can tie the tree to these wires as it grows.

Unlike bush trees, cordons follow a summer pruning regime—around midsummer for pears and late summer for apples. For the first two or three winters of a cordon's life, prune back the previous summer's growth on the main stem by one third to encourage more fruiting and branching buds beneath.

## U-cordons

If you want to take training to the next level, explore U- and then double U-cordons. These are a form of vertical cordon that, due to having more than one branch, will naturally be less vigorous in vegetative growth but more productive when it comes to fruiting.

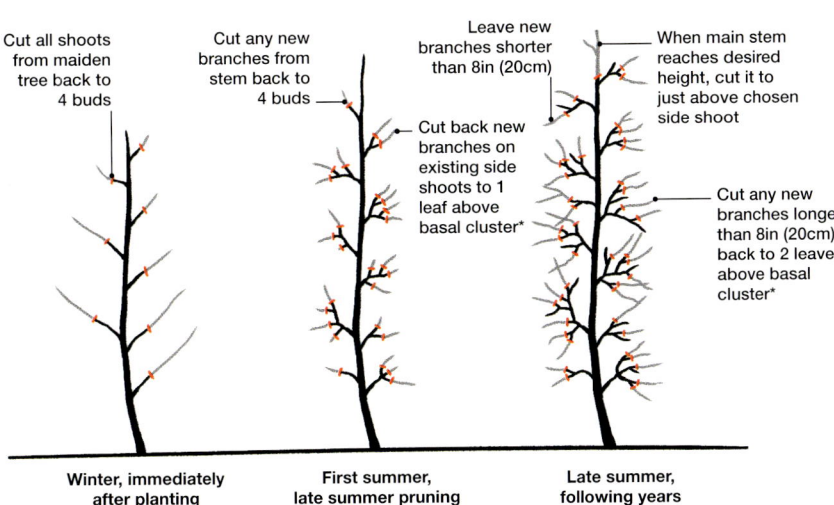

Cut all shoots from maiden tree back to 4 buds

Cut any new branches from stem back to 4 buds

Leave new branches shorter than 8in (20cm)

When main stem reaches desired height, cut it to just above chosen side shoot

Cut back new branches on existing side shoots to 1 leaf above basal cluster*

Cut any new branches longer than 8in (20cm) back to 2 leaves above basal cluster*

**Winter, immediately after planting**

**First summer, late summer pruning**

**Late summer, following years**

### Establishing a cordon shape
*Follow this guidance to form the shape of the cordon with a main stem and short fruiting branches. The detail below shows where to prune new growth in summer.*

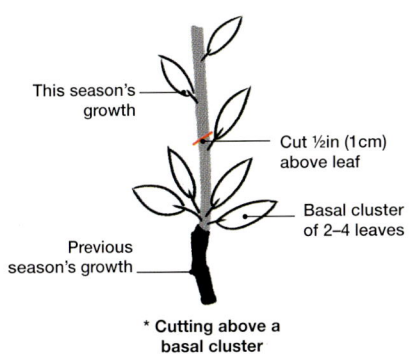

This season's growth

Cut ½in (1cm) above leaf

Basal cluster of 2–4 leaves

Previous season's growth

\* Cutting above a basal cluster

## CRAB APPLE

The crab apple (*Malus sylvestris*, right) is a hedgerow plant that has been domesticated into hundreds of different varieties. These varieties are usually chosen for their ornamental values of long-flowering blossoms over the spring as well as apple displays that stay on the tree well into the winter and come in a range of colors from bright yellow to deep pink. What isn't talked about enough is that all crab apples are edible. Some are rather sharp, but others, like the variety 'Butterball', have a delicious balance of sweet and tart and can be used in many ways in the kitchen.

Pruning crab apples can be very simple: Remove any dead, diseased, or damaged wood and thin out any branches that are crossing or causing congestion. When deciding which of the two crossing branches to remove, take a step back and consider which offers the most structure to the tree.

# PLUM

Plums, and the related damsons, are a wonderful fruit to grow, and most varieties are self-fertile.

For pruning plums (*Prunus domestica*) you can follow the same bush-pruning regime as for apples and pears (see pp.168–169). The only difference is that it's best to prune plums (up to three years old) around mid-spring and older plums around early summer. This is to reduce the chances of infection from silver leaf disease, which is much more likely to enter pruning cuts in the winter. When growing plums, you may notice suckers at the base of the stem. This is a natural part of the rootstock growth: Gently pull them up as and when they appear.

*Damsons, paired with apples, make a wonderful country chutney.*

## TRAINING PLUMS AS CORDONS

Plums, like apples and pears, work well when trained as cordons against a wall or fence or up a permanent stake. They can be trained vertically or grown as an oblique (45-degree angle) cordon. Vertical cordons are great for taller boundaries and to squeeze into small spaces, as they take up less width, but they grow with more vigor and will require heavier pruning. If you want an eye-catching archway, vertical cordons are the ideal option, as they can grow up to 10ft (3m) tall. Oblique cordons follow the same pruning regime, but in general the vegetative growth will be less, and the tree will divert more energy into fruit production.

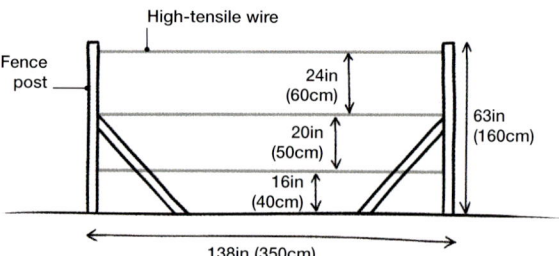

**Support for cordons**
*This structure will support all types of tree fruit cordons trained against the wires.*

**A cordon fence**
If you lack suitable boundaries to plant a vertical cordon against, then you can make a post-and-wire cordon support structure. Ideally, run these east-to-west to create a south-facing boundary so the trees gain the maximum sunlight for the greatest health and productivity. You will need strong, durable posts at either end and high-tensile wire.

**DAMSON**
Damsons (*Prunus insititia*) are a subspecies of plums, with smaller fruits. Their yields are impressive, and they are perfect for preserving—especially frozen for winter desserts and for making one of the best-tasting chutneys out there!

# GRAPE

Although not a tree, a grapevine has the ability to grow huge—the leading branch of the vine in my dad's polytunnel has been trained along the top of the tunnel and has gone 23ft (7m) from one end to the other, and the whole way back!

Grapes (*Vitis*) are almost all self-fertile and excellent for polytunnels, where pruning makes it easy to control their size. I would recommend planting a grapevine in the northernmost corner of a polytunnel and training it along the back so as to not cast shade onto all your sun-loving crops. Alternatively, grow a grapevine along a section of your polytunnel ceiling and train it back to create a shady space for helping regulate the internal temperature during the hottest summer days. You can plant partial shade–loving crops underneath the "grape tunnel." For growing grapes outside, it's essential that your grapevines be planted in a sunny position and away from any frost pockets. Outside or in, they require permanent support in the form of wires on a structure or fence (as for cordons, see p.169), and you can also prune grapes as a "standard," tied to one stake. This is perfect for edible leaf production (see p.165).

## CHOOSING GRAPE VARIETIES

Growing grapes successfully outdoors in cooler climates requires the appropriate varieties to survive the winter months and yield harvestable crops in the fall—unlike the varieties that are typically grown for wine in warm, dry, climates. Fortunately, small-scale vineyards are increasing in popularity, allowing you to see which varieties are successful in your area. Any grapes grown for wine can, of course, be eaten.

*Grapes ready for harvesting.*

## PRUNING

Grape pruning can easily become more complicated than for other fruit. Those growing undercover are best pruned as cordons, with one main leader tied to the polytunnel ceiling as it grows and fruiting spurs along the length. Every early winter, cut back the new growth on the leader by one third. Any side branches should be cut back to two buds, and in future years, cut back the branches growing off these to one bud. In the late spring, cut any dense growth that is blocking light to maturing grape bunches.

For outdoor grapes, follow the same process, but you can select four to six leaders to train either all as vertical cordons or all horizontally, using a cordon fence.

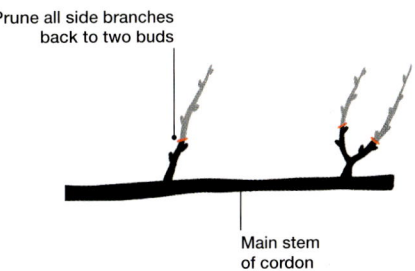

Prune all side branches back to two buds

Main stem of cordon

**Fruiting spurs**
*This close-up of a main stem of a grapevine shows how to prune each side branch to form a fruiting spur. The side branches should be spaced about 12in (30cm) apart.*

## FROST AND FLOWERS

Tree fruits and grapes have one common weakness: late frosts. When trees are in blossom, a hard frost can kill the flowers, which means you won't get fruit. Grapes are particularly susceptible when grown outdoors and will need to be protected by draping fleece over the plants if any frost threatens overnight. Pruning grapes so that they fruit 3ft (1m) or more above ground also helps protect from light ground frost.

# OTHER FRUIT TREES

I have covered the main fruit trees for a kitchen garden, but there are many other options available. Depending on your climate, some are suitable for outside, while others may need to be grown undercover.

The trees covered here are all hardy, but some need good summer weather for successful fruiting—one thing Wales isn't famous for, which is why I opt to grow many of these in a polytunnel.

Dwarf varieties reach maturity faster than more vigorous rootstocks and focus more energy on fruit production than on producing new leaves and stems. For any undercover growing, I will always select dwarf varieties in order to maintain a compact size rather than constantly battling a plant that wants to naturally grow into a huge tree.

## PEACH AND NECTARINE
These two beautiful and delicious fruits to grow are very similar, the main difference being that nectarines (*Prunus persica* var. *nectarina*) do not have the fuzz of a peach (*Prunus persica*) and when cooking will stay firmer too. Their blossom in early spring looks incredible. All varieties are self-fertile.

## APRICOT
A fruit tree with beautiful blossoms is the apricot (*Prunus armeniaca*). Its fruits are smaller than peaches and drier in texture, but I think they make the best jam out of all the tree fruits. All varieties are self-fertile.

## POMEGRANATE
People are often surprised to find that pomegranates (*Punica granatum*) can grow in the UK, provided that you choose a suitable variety and grow them undercover. They are hardy down to about 23°F (-5°C), so during very cold snaps, the tree needs to be wrapped in fleece. All varieties are self-fertile.

## MULBERRY
Unlike the tree fruits above, which are most suited to undercover growing in my garden, the mulberry (*Morus*) is a hardy fruit tree that's perfect for growing outside. The young leaves can be eaten after cooking (see p.165), and the fruits are refreshing, with a balance of sweetness and tartness. All varieties are self-fertile.

## QUINCE AND MEDLAR
Quinces (*Cydonia oblonga*) are fruits that have fallen out of popularity in recent years, perhaps because their fruits look a little bit like a hybrid between a knobbly apple and pear. Closely related to the quince and also in need of a good marketing team, medlar (*Mespilus germanica*) is another tree fruit to consider. Both fruits need to be cooked for eating, but they are famous for making incredible wine, jellies, jams, and marmalades. There are varieties and rootstocks available that suit smaller gardens and even patio growing.

## GREENGAGE
Greengages (a subspecies of *Prunus domestica*) are one of the most underrated fruits. They are just a green plum but have an incredible sweet flavor, and you won't ever forget the first time you try one—a perfect fruit for desserts and preserves. Most are self-fertile.

## CHERRY
Cherries (*Prunus avium*) are one of the true treats of summer. Please note that birds love cherries even more than we do, so grow dwarf cherries and protect them with netting if you want to enjoy any for yourself. Many modern varieties are self-fertile.

## FIG
Figs (*Ficus carica*) are a must, even if you just grow them in a large container, which will help restrict roots and thus encourage fruiting. They will thrive best if grown against a sunny boundary and protected with fleece during cold weather over the winter. Figs can also be grown undercover. As well as their fruit being edible, you can also cook and eat the young leaves; often they are used to wrap cheese.

*Harvesting my first batch of apricots from my undercover fruit forest.*

## PEPPERS AND NUTS

If you want to further explore other fruit-bearing trees to grow in a kitchen garden, I recommend looking at cobnuts (*Corylus avellana*, right), which are hazels bred specifically for nut production, and tree peppers (*Zanthoxylum* species), which come in Sichuan and Nepalese types. Cobnuts are an option for larger gardens and will suit partial shade. Don't expect a cobnut to provide you with an abundance of food, but growing your own nuts to enjoy over the fall is worth doing if you can. You can also coppice the cobnut for "hazel" sticks for supports for peas and beans. The pepper trees may seem like a gimmick, but they are very easy to grow and provide you with fragrant leaves as well as an abundance of peppercorn-like fruit, both of which are very useful in the kitchen.

# Annuals

# GROWING ANNUALS

The selection of annual vegetables, herbs, and flowers for the permaculture garden is huge. Each crop offers a particular characteristic, from unusual colors to disease resistance, and most importantly can provide different flavors.

Annuals tend to be sown and harvested within one growing season, but some crops, such as purple sprouting broccoli and spring cabbage, span two seasons. Unlike perennials, annuals are almost exclusively propagated by seed, and there tends to be a much greater range of characteristics within varieties of crops compared to perennials.

## TENDER LOVING CARE

The most important stage when growing annuals is getting them to a state of semi-maturity—when they have at least seven or eight true leaves. After this, they need far less tender loving care and, in most cases, can be left alone until harvesting. As a gardener, your role is to do everything you can to give each seed you sow the best possible start so the plant can look after itself.

*Midsummer in the kitchen garden; here, I am helping a loose runner bean plant back onto the support.*

*Saving seed from a dried pod of the stunning 'Rhondda Black' runner bean.*

## SEEDS

Selecting and obtaining seeds is a crucial part of a productive kitchen garden. There are many possible seed sources, including other gardeners, community seed banks, seed swaps, heritage seed companies, and larger seed suppliers. Every winter, I order seeds from different suppliers; where possible, I prioritize smaller suppliers, which are also where I go for the more unusual and rare varieties. All my recommended suppliers are listed on page 281, and I also have a list of my top variety choices (see pp.224–225).

### Seed storage and shelf life

The "sow by" date on the back of a seed packet is a germination guarantee that will meet the legal threshold success rate needed for commercially selling seed in that country. After that date, the viability of the seed will decrease over time, but even old seed can hold surprises, such as when Michigan gardener Luke Marion grew 85-year-old tomato seeds successfully, resurrecting a previously extinct variety.

Often when you purchase a seed packet, you only need to sow some of the seeds in a growing season. You can then store any leftover seeds for future growing seasons rather than having to buy new packets every year. There are many ways to store seeds, from a simple shoe box to a photo organizer. Ice-cream tubs and takeout plastic boxes work well and allow you to keep seeds airtight, which further increases their life-span. Whatever type of storage you choose doesn't matter nearly as much as where you keep it. For longevity, your seeds need to be in a cool, dry, dark place, such as the bottom shelf of a cupboard.

If you do have an old seed packet that is past its sow-by date, I suggest you do a test sowing of at least 10 seeds and note the results. There are a few crops that are particularly poor when it comes to viability, and I recommend sourcing fresh seeds annually for parsnips, sweet corn, leeks, and onions.

### Seed saving

Homegrown seeds, like homegrown food, are usually the best quality you can get, and over time, if you continue to save your own seeds, those varieties will better adapt to your climate and soil. The basics of seed saving are on pages 222–223, as well as why you should let some crops self-seed.

## HARVESTING

There are a few harvesting tips that can be applied to most crops. Early morning is the best time to harvest, when temperatures are cooler and the crops have a higher moisture content, contributing to an improved shelf life. When growing crops in rows or clumps, such as carrots or beets, harvest the biggest specimens first to allow the smaller ones to continue growing. For the best flavor, harvest at peak ripeness.

## THE VEGETABLE FAMILIES

There are seven main vegetable groupings in a kitchen garden: alliums, legumes, leafy, brassicas, roots, nightshades, and cucurbits. In this chapter, I go over each group, offering specific advice and a chart for each crop to help you get the most out of your garden.

### How to use the vegetable charts

Each vegetable has a chart to provide as much detailed information as possible that works in combination with the advice given about that specific family group.

**Sowing outside** Best sowing window to direct sow outside

**Sowing under cover** Best sowing window for starting in pots and modules in a protected environment

**Sowing depth** How deep the trench or hole should be

**Seeds per module** Multisowing information

**Plant spacing** Information for both individual plants and multisown clumps

**Harvest** The usual outdoor harvest window for this crop based on sowing window

# SOWING IN POTS AND MODULES

Sowing in pots, trays, and module trays (a tray of many cells) is vital for a productive garden. You can start off seedlings undercover earlier to plant when the weather improves and raise seedlings for succession planting (see p.218).

The process of filling modules (and pots) is the same for every seed; the only difference will be at what depth and how many seeds per module. I never use seed-starting mix when sowing my crops. Instead, I opt for a high-quality multipurpose peat-free mix or a homemade alternative (see p.55). The next stages after sowing in pots and modules are on pages 182–183.

## CHOOSING POTS AND TRAYS

There are so many types of pots, modules, and trays to choose from that sometimes it can be overwhelming. Over the years, I have whittled down my hodge-podge agglomeration to an efficient, tidy collection that covers all my needs for raising seedlings. I also don't wash pots and trays at the end of the season—it is a waste of time and effort.

### Pot options

Pots with a diameter of 2¾–3½in (7–9cm) are ideal for sowing larger seeds (like squash) or for raising lots of small seedlings (like lettuce) to then pot on. My primary use for these pots is for potting out smaller tomato seedlings (see p.206). There are also large 5–7in (13–17cm) diameter pots that can grow seedlings further; this is useful especially for allowing brassicas to continue maturing so that you can plant them once your tomatoes have been harvested.

### Module options

The most versatile size module to opt for is one with 1½ x 1½in (4 x 4cm) square cells. You can start anything from beets to Brussels sprouts in them. The cell size allows you to grow seedlings to a few true leaves, and they can then be transplanted or potted. Root trainers (module trays with long cells) are excellent for deep-rooting crops, such as runner and fava beans.

Trays that are not divided into cells can be used similarly to pots for thickly sowing seedlings that you will later prick out and pot on—usually into 1½in (4cm) modules. Smaller modules (1in/2–3cm) are useful for raising as many plants as possible under grow lights before potting them once they have a couple of true leaves.

## HOW TO SOW A MODULE TRAY

**1.**
Place your module tray on a potting bench (or on a piece of cardboard) and fill the modules with potting mix.

**2.**
Spread the potting mix evenly to fill all the cells.

**3.**
When the modules are full, press down the potting mix in each cell firmly with two or three fingers, then top it up with more potting mix, and do a final pat. This ensures that the root mass won't fall away from the roots when transplanting and reduces air space, which can hinder germination. Give the module tray a good watering —for about 5 seconds if using a watering can.

**4.**
Then, use your fingers to make a hole in each module at the approximate depth needed, depending on what you are sowing.

**5.**
Sow one seed or more in each hole.

**6.**
Cover with potting mix and use the palm and fingers of your hand to pat down the added mix, again ensuring that there are no air pockets. After labeling, water for another 5–10 seconds and place on your seedling shelves.

## Multisowing

Multisowing is a popular technique of starting multiple seeds in the same module and planting the seedlings in clumps—no thinning required. This works for a range of different crops and is a great way to save propagation space, potting mix, and water, not to mention time! My most common multisowings are peas (three or four seeds) and four or five seeds of radishes, beets, leeks, spring onions, annual herbs, and salads.

## ADAPTING YOUR SPACE
### Hanging shelf

If you have a polytunnel or greenhouse, a very simple way of increasing your shelving area for starting seed is by creating a hanging shelf. This can be made by creating a wooden frame, attaching some wire, and then tying this to the support bars of the polytunnel. The hanging shelf also doubles as a rodent-free propagation space, which is especially useful for keeping peas and beans protected.

### Heat mat and grow lights

For crops that need heat to germinate, such as warmth-loving fruiting crops (tomatoes and eggplants), especially early in the season, you will need to invest in a heat mat and grow lights. The heat mat provides the temperatures the seeds need to germinate, while the grow light prevents these seedlings from becoming leggy. An alternative is the top of a fridge, which is a warm place that can be used temporarily for getting the seedlings to emerge before moving them onto a warm, sunny inside windowsill.

## WATERING

Watering your newly sown module trays and young seedlings is simple. If the surface of the growing medium looks dry, use a finger to test it. If the top ½in (1cm) is dry and the seedlings haven't yet emerged, you will need to water. When the seedlings have emerged, water whenever the top ½–¾in (1–2cm) is dry. Overhead watering with a gentle sprayer is effective, but I would always do one pass and then another 10–15 minutes later. This is to make sure that the water goes down into the roots and doesn't just wet the surface. An alternative method is to place your module trays in a tray of water (see p.92).

## GENERAL CARE

For good airflow, make sure your polytunnel or mini-greenhouse is well ventilated during the day. If you ever see seedlings wilting but the modules are still damp, then this may be a result of damping off, which is caused by a lack of airflow and excessive watering. If you spot a couple of seedlings showing signs of damping off, move them to a warm, sheltered, sunny location immediately to encourage the soil to dry out. This may help, but in most cases, it is best to resow.

# SOWING DIRECT

Direct sowing is my favorite seed-starting method for strong plants. While module sowing is my primary method due to the restrictions of a short growing season, whenever I have the chance to direct sow, I always do that.

There are some crops that need to be directly sown, as transplanting may damage their roots: Carrots and parsnips are the most common. Directly sown seeds have the luxury of root space, unlike those in modules, allowing the roots to cover a much greater area and contributing to a more resilient plant. Some other crops, such as leeks and stemmed brassicas, can be directly sown in a "seed bed" to save on indoor space. A seed bed is a prepared area of ground (such as one section of a raised bed) that is sown early in the season to raise seedlings for transplanting. When the seedlings are removed, a crop can be planted in their place.

## PREPARING THE GROUND

Before direct sowing, some ground preparation may be needed. The ideal scenario is to form a tilth: a prepared area where the soil is nice and fluffy in texture and any large stones and twigs have been removed. The best tool for the job is a tarmac rake. Start by raking over the top 2–2¾in (5–7cm) of soil, using the flat edge of the rake. Then, tickle the teeth of the rake over the top 1in (2–3cm) so that it acts as a sieve, collecting the large pieces. Bring these all into a corner and use a spade to remove them. Give the surface one final rake over with the teeth to level it, turn the rake so the handle is vertical, and firmly press down on the surface with the flat side of the rake to remove air pockets.

## STICK AND STRING

Whenever you are direct sowing or transplanting, you will usually be doing so in straight lines. The easiest way to create a straight line for marking out is to get two straight sticks around 10in (25cm) long and tie a 6½ft (2m) length of string around 2in (5cm) from the top of both sticks. You now have an easily adjustable straight-line marker.

## SOWING IN ROWS

**1.**
Measure out your line with a piece of wood or stick and string (see box, left). Use a straight stick or handle to form a trench at the desired depth.

**2.**
Sow the seeds along the trench. Spacing does not need to be perfect, but try not to oversow, as it will take more of your time to thin than to sow carefully.

**3.**
Use your hands to push the ridges of soil on either side of the trench to cover the seeds and firmly pat down. Label the row clearly.

**4.**
Give the row a good watering or sow before heavy rain so nature can do that task for you.

## ONGOING WATERING AND THE PLANK METHOD

The "Bill Mollison" plank method is a very simple way to save time watering directly sown seeds by preventing the soil from drying out. After a row of seeds has been sown and watered, place a plank (such as one you would get from taking apart a pallet) over the row and leave it in place. After three or four days, start checking under the plank daily for signs of germination and remove it when you spot the first seedlings. During really hot, dry weather, you may still need to water under the plank. If you are not following the plank method, water whenever the top ½–¾in (1–2cm) of soil is dry until seedlings emerge and then whenever the top 1in (2–3cm) is dry for the following two or three weeks.

*Removing a plank to unveil a row of germinated leek seedlings.*

## BROADCAST SOWING

This method of direct sowing is applied to sowing cover crops or if you want to grow a polyculture mix of crops, such as salad greens or an edible flower and herb mix. Create a tilth as usual and then scatter seeds as evenly as possible over the surface. Lightly rake the seeds into the top ½–¾in (1–2cm), hold the rake vertically, pat down with the flat end of the rake, and then water.

### HUW'S TIP

It's important to know when it comes to sowing that on some occasions, even if you do everything in your power to give a seed the best possible chance of life, you are still working with nature. The only thing you can control is the actions you take, not whether the seedling wishes to germinate (or not).

# NEXT STEPS

By putting care into sowing, you should grow healthy seedlings. The next step is to give them more space to continue to mature by thinning, or by different forms of transplanting into a larger container or to their final growing position.

*Using a grip-cut tool to harvest thinnings as a microgreen to use in a salad.*

## THINNING

Thinning is the process of reducing the number of seedlings in a given space. For seedlings in modules or pots, you need to thin them if there are too many (for example, if you accidentally dropped two seeds into one hole). For direct-sown seedlings, you thin to ensure that there is enough space between each plant for it to mature without being constricted by its neighbors. Thinning is said to be best done with a pair of scissors or pruners so as not to damage the roots of the remaining plants. However, I've found that if you gently pull out seedlings as you thin, there won't be a problem. Choose whichever method suits you and always thin the smaller and weaker plants first.

## TRANSPLANTING
### Transplanting seedlings

The majority of your transplanting will be of smaller seedlings raised in 1½in (4cm) modules. In the bed where your crop is to mature, use a dibble, a trowel, or even your fingers to make a hole in the soil slightly deeper than the module size. Use a finger to pop the seedling out of the module and place the seedling in the hole. Firm around the seedling, making sure that the soil level of the bed matches that of the seedling, and water it. You can create an indentation in the soil so the seedling and soil immediately around it are slightly deeper; this creates a bowl effect, helping water go down to the roots in the early days.

*When handling young seedlings, such as when pricking out, hold them by a leaf to avoid crushing their stems.*

1. *Lifting a mature kale plant from outside.* 2. *Transplanted under cover, kale is more productive in the winter.*

## Transplanting larger plants

Water the pot thoroughly at least 10 minutes before transplanting to reduce root disturbance. Next, make a hole in the soil the size of the pot, grab the pot, place your fingers over the top with the stem between two fingers, turn the pot upside down, and firmly tap with your free hand on the base to release the roots. Place the roots in the hole, firm the soil around them, and water thoroughly. You can also make a deeper hole and add one or two generous handfuls of compost at the base—this is a must for hungry crops, such as tomatoes and squash.

## Transplanting bare-root seedlings

When it comes to transplanting stemmed brassicas and leeks, use a fork to gently lift up the roots and place in a bucket of water. Gently separate each seedling and use a dibble to make the planting holes, dropping each seedling to the desired depth. Water thoroughly and then fill in the hole around the stem.

## Potting on

Potting on is a form of transplanting where you move a seedling from a smaller pot or module into a larger one to give the roots extra space to grow. This is essential for keeping tender plants like tomatoes and peppers growing healthily while it is still too cold outside. Potting on involves filling a larger pot with a growing medium, making a hole the size of the seedling rootball, planting this in the hole, firming it, and finally watering it.

## Pricking out

Pricking out is a form of potting on, but for small seedlings that may only have their seedling leaves or first set of true leaves. Use a plant label or stick to gently scoop out some of the seedlings and, holding each by the leaf, gently pull the seedlings apart. Prepare pots or module trays exactly as you would for sowing, but use a pencil or stick to make a deeper hole to drop the roots and stem in (to just below the first leaves), then gently firm around each stem and water.

### HUW'S TIP

Whenever working with young seedlings, be it pricking out, potting on, or transplanting, always hold the seedling by the leaf rather than the stem. Holding by the stem can easily damage the plant, whereas even if a leaf is damaged, the overall success rate will be incredibly high. The success rate from a damaged stem of a tiny seedling is virtually nonexistent. For more developed seedlings, you can also gently hold around the rootball when transplanting or potting on.

### HARDENING OFF

Tender crops, such as squash, tomatoes, and bush beans, respond well to being hardened off before planting outside. This isn't necessary, but it does reduce transplant shock (when plants experience severe temperature change and are exposed to the elements of wind and direct light and take a few days to adjust, slowing growth). To harden off seedlings, bring them out from their home undercover (still in their pots and modules) and leave them outside during the day, placing them back undercover during the night. Do this every day for the five or six days leading up to transplanting. The reason I don't usually harden off unless it is the month following the last average frost date is that I can't be bothered, quite frankly, and the plants still grow fine once they've had a few days to settle. It is a balancing act: Do you want to sacrifice your time or sacrifice how quickly a plant takes to a new home?

### USING BIOCHAR

Adding a 10 percent mix of fine biochar (see pp.68–69) to your potting mix when pricking out or potting on will help encourage strong growth and healthy seedlings and, over the long term, will improve soil health in the ground where those seedlings will be planted. For transplanting, you can also add a couple of handfuls of a mix of 1 part biochar to 9 parts compost at the base of the hole beforehand.

# ALLIUMS

Alliums are the small but mighty onion family, well known for the incredible flavor they bring to the kitchen.

Leeks, onions, garlic, and shallots all thrive in full sun and enjoy rich ground with good soil moisture.

## GARLIC SCAPES

There are two categories of garlic: hardneck and softneck. Hardneck is more suitable for colder climates (think hardy hardneck) and produces a flower stalk known as a scape, which should be harvested before the flower opens. The scape can be eaten as a delicacy. Softneck garlic tends to store for longer and thrives in warmer climates. If you're in a colder climate, try growing softneck over the winter in a polytunnel or hoop bed.

## EAT THE LEAVES

Onions and shallots offer an extra harvest: their leaves. Pick one leaf per plant every so often in the growing season to use as you would a spring onion. At the main harvest, collect all the high-quality leaves, chop them into small sections, and freeze.

## LET LEEKS BLOOM

Leek flowers are giant chive flowers on stems that can reach almost 6ft (1.8m) and are loved by beneficial insects. The most bees I've ever counted on one leek blossom was 11, plus a couple of red admirals! To enjoy leek flowers, you will need to grow a hardy variety and leave some after the last harvest. The blooms can last a surprisingly long time over the summer.

## ONION SETS

Another way of growing onions is via sets, which are immature onions that when planted grow into mature onions. This gives you a faster sow-to-harvest window, opening up more succession planting options later in the season.

## STORING ALLIUMS

Store onions and garlic by drying them in a well-ventilated, dry location for a few weeks so the roots and leaves turn brown and papery. Once dry, place in jute or paper bags in a cool, dark, dry, and airy space to use throughout the winter. Leeks are best stored by blanching and freezing.

**LEEK**

| | |
|---|---|
| **Sowing outside** | Mid- to late spring (in a seed bed) |
| **Sowing under cover** | Late winter to mid-spring |
| **Sowing depth** | ½–¾in (1–2cm) |
| **Seeds per module** | 5 or 6 (thin to 4) |
| **Plant spacing** | Individual 8–10in (20–25cm); clumps 12in (30cm) |
| **Harvest** | Late fall to mid-spring (depending on variety) |

**SPRING ONION**

| | |
|---|---|
| **Sowing outside** | Mid-spring to early summer (early autumn for overwintering) |
| **Sowing under cover** | Late winter to early summer |
| **Sowing depth** | ½in (1cm) |
| **Seeds per module** | 5–7 |
| **Plant spacing** | Individual 1in (2–3cm); clumps 4–6in (10–15cm) |
| **Harvest** | Late spring to late fall |

## ONION

**Sowing outside** Early to mid-spring (sets and seeds)

**Sowing under cover** Late winter to early spring (sets and seeds)

**Sowing depth** ½in (1cm)

**Seeds per module** 4 or 5

**Plant spacing** Individual 6in (15cm); clumps 10in (25cm)

**Harvest** Midsummer (sets) late summer to early fall (seeds)

## ELEPHANT GARLIC

**Sowing outside** Late fall to early winter (cloves)

**Sowing under cover** N/A

**Sowing depth** 2in (5cm)

**Seeds per module** N/A

**Plant spacing** 10in (25cm)

**Harvest** Midsummer

## GARLIC

**Sowing outside** Late fall to early winter (cloves)

**Sowing under cover** N/A

**Sowing depth** 2in (5cm)

**Seeds per module** N/A

**Plant spacing** 6in (15cm)

**Harvest** Midsummer

## SHALLOT

**Sowing outside** Early to late spring (sets)

**Sowing under cover** N/A

**Sowing depth** 2in (5cm)

**Seeds per module** N/A

**Plant spacing** 6–8in (15–20cm)

**Harvest** Mid- to late summer

# LEGUMES

Legumes (peas and beans) are a wonderful group of crops that cover all layers within a garden, from sprawling bush beans to fence-topping climbers.

Peas and climbing beans are perfect for forming a border along the edge of a bed, growing up a fence, or twining up a trellis. If your garden is lacking structure, a few trellises with runner beans and peas dotted around will elevate the entire garden.

Legumes are often said to fix nitrogen in the soil, but this is only the case if the legumes are cut down as they begin flowering (which is what happens when you grow a legume cover crop, such as field beans—also delicious—or clover). Legumes prefer full sun, with rich, deep soils, but will crop in partial shade and sub-par soil.

## STORING LEGUMES

Peas and beans can be stored either by blanching and freezing fresh or by allowing them to dry in their pods, ideally on the plant. If conditions are wet, finish drying for 2–3 weeks on a tray indoors. Shell out the peas and beans and store in clean, dry, airtight containers to use for soups and stews.

## HUW'S TIP

Before assembling your climbing structures, check the final height of the crop you're growing to make sure the canes or posts will be tall enough.

*Get creative with the shape of your boxing ring to help it fit into different parts of your garden.*

## SUPPORT OPTIONS

There are numerous options when it comes to creating supports for growing legumes and other climbing crops. For canes, bamboo and hazel are the two most common options.

### A-frame

This structure of two rows of tall canes tied to each other at the top creates a "wall" of green growth and is an excellent choice for large gardens or to create a screen. It can be made shorter for medium-height peas. Ensure that each cane or pole is pressed deep into the ground to avoid collapse.

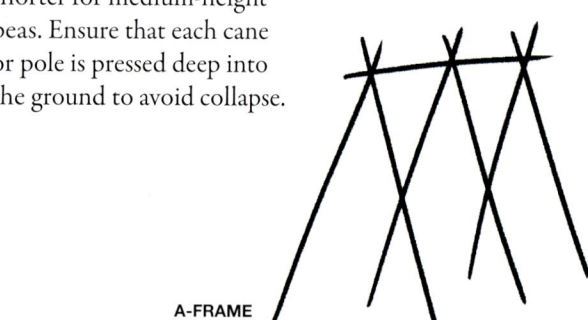

A-FRAME

### The fence

Install two sturdy posts and attach wire between them. Chicken wire and stock fencing are the two types I most often use. This support is ideal for peas, as their tendrils will wrap around the wire as they climb up. Alternative versions can be made with other netting materials, such as old electric fencing.

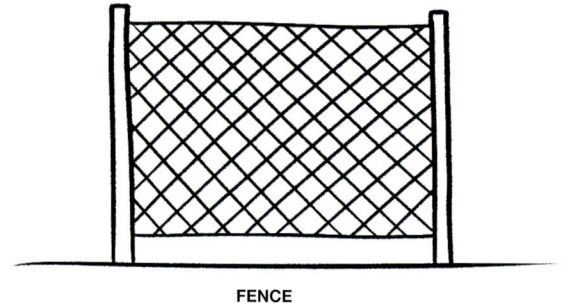

FENCE

## Boxing ring

For dwarf peas and fava beans, you can create a boxing-ring-style support where you add a post at all four corners of the group of plants and then run string around the perimeter, keeping the plants contained within. You can support the plants further by creating a criss-cross pattern with string perpendicular to the sides.

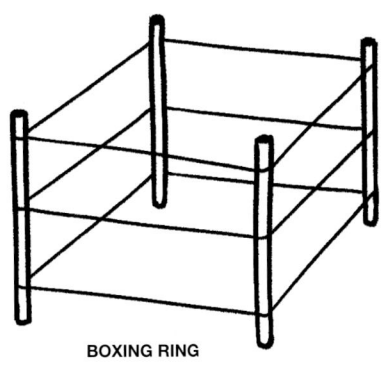

**BOXING RING**

## The roof

This clever way of growing climbing beans may take a little more effort to build, but it creates a wonderful seating area underneath or a place to grow leafy greens during the heat of summer without being in direct sunlight.

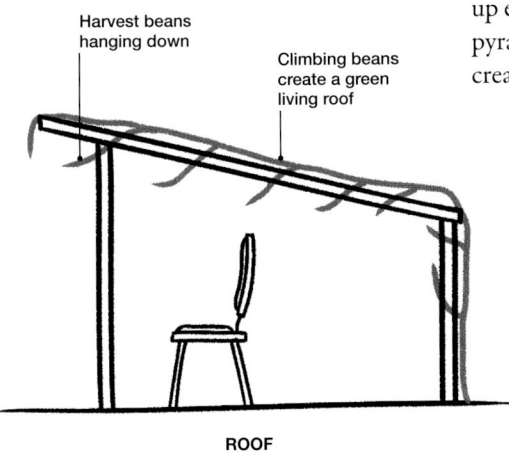

Harvest beans hanging down

Climbing beans create a green living roof

**ROOF**

## Wigwam

The wigwam is the perfect structure for the middle of a garden bed and works well for small spaces. Firmly press eight canes into the ground and tie them together at the top. Climbing beans will twist around the canes as they grow upward.

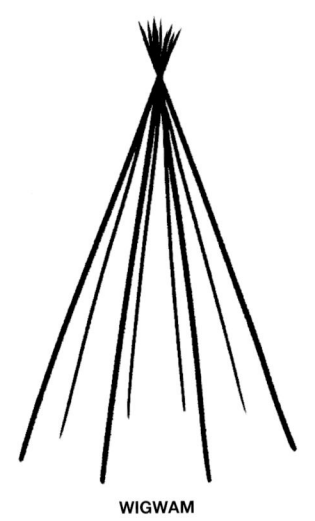

**WIGWAM**

## Pyramid

Four stakes or canes are pushed down into the ground to form a square and then tied together at the top similarly to a wigwam. Grow a climbing bean up each cane or tie string around the pyramid every 4–6in (10–15cm) to create a fantastic support for peas.

**PYRAMID**

## Cylinder

Using sheets of net-type wire allows you to tie the two long ends together to form a vertical cylinder. To keep it in place, thread three or four canes through the wire from the top and push firmly into the ground. Ideally, you want netting that allows you to put your hand through to reach any harvests on the inside. A shorter cylinder can be useful for dwarf peas and fava beans, or it can be made tall for climbing beans and peas.

**CYLINDER**

## Archway

An archway can bridge two beds, opening up more growing space for additional crops. By growing beans over the pathway, you can walk through the archway while harvesting. An archway also looks incredible and is the perfect space-saving solution for small gardens.

**ARCH**

## BEANS WITH A BUSHY HABIT

Bush beans, or dwarf beans, are one of my favorite crops to use for plugging gaps during the growing season and work well on the edge of a bed, allowing them to grow over the side rather than afffecting any other crops already planted. Find out more about space-saving techniques on pages 244–245. There are also dwarf varieties of runner beans that can be grown in the same way.

### EDIBLE LUPINS

**Sowing outside** Mid-spring to early summer

**Sowing under cover** Early spring to early summer

**Sowing depth** ¾in (2cm)

**Seeds per module** 1

**Plant spacing** 8–12in (20–30cm)

**Harvest** Early to mid-fall

### BUSH BEANS

**Sowing outside** Mid-spring to midsummer

**Sowing under cover** Early spring to midsummer

**Sowing depth** 1in (2–3cm)

**Seeds per module** 1

**Plant spacing** 8–12in (20–30cm)

**Harvest** Midsummer to mid-fall

### FAVA BEANS (BROAD BEANS AND FIELD BEANS)

**Sowing outside** Early to late spring

**Sowing under cover** Late winter to late spring

**Sowing depth** 2in (5cm)

**Seeds per module** 1

**Plant spacing** 12–14in (30–35cm)

**Harvest** Midsummer to mid-fall

## BEANS WITH A CLIMBING HABIT

Climbing beans include a vast range of varieties and are usually split between two groups: runner beans and climbing snap or green beans. Some varieties are grown specifically for large beans that can be dried and stored to cook over winter, while others are grown for the tender pods. Take this into account when selecting what to grow.

## CLIMBING BEANS (RUNNER AND SNAP BEANS)

**Sowing outside** Mid-spring to early summer

**Sowing under cover** Early spring to early summer

**Sowing depth** 2in (5cm)

**Seeds per module** 1

**Plant spacing** 8in (20cm)

**Harvest** Midsummer to mid-fall

## PEAS

**Sowing outside** Early spring to early summer

**Sowing under cover** Late winter to early summer

**Sowing depth** 1in (2–3cm)

**Seeds per module** 3

**Plant spacing** Individual 1½–2in (4–5cm); clumps 4in (10cm)

**Harvest** Midsummer to early fall

# LEAFY ANNUALS

Grow your own salad—but you don't just have to grow lettuce and spinach. Crops such as bok choy, which grows incredibly quickly, offer additional crunch and are a must for stir-fries.

Leafy greens are a group where the majority of crops are most commonly enjoyed raw. Provided that your garden has some kind of undercover protection and you opt for hardy varieties of greens, such as lettuce and spinach, you can enjoy year-round leaf production. This group thrives in full sun and partial shade, and I've even grown leafy greens successfully in "deep" shade. They need plenty of moisture but aren't as nutrient-hungry as other groups, so they can be grown in the less fertile areas of your garden. Leafy greens don't lend themselves to long-term storage and are best enjoyed fresh.

## SUMMER BLUES

The nemesis of many leafy greens is hot, dry weather, which can stress the plants and cause them to bolt (run to seed prematurely). This lowers the leaf quality and, in cases like lettuce, makes them inedible due to bitterness. To combat this, with the exception of chard, malabar spinach, and amaranth, which fare well during hot weather, it is best to plant leafy greens in partial shade from the start of June onward. Partial shade could be as simple as behind a south-facing A-frame of peas. The peas will take the brunt of the heat and sun, offering a cooler area for the leafy greens. Regular watering is the other essential to prevent leafy greens from bolting over the summer.

## SUCCESSION PLANTING

To guarantee consistent harvests of leafy greens over the growing season, you need to follow succession planting. This sowing technique is a little-and-often approach so you always have seedlings coming into maturity, which helps cover any cases of bolting. Sow a module tray with a selection of different leafy greens every two or three weeks from the early spring to the late summer. These seedlings can replace any leafy greens that are beginning to run to seed, be it prematurely or naturally, as well as plug any gaps in the garden. For more on succession planting different crops, see page 218.

## CUT-AND-COME AGAIN HARVESTING

A popular way of harvesting leafy greens is cut-and-come again. This is where a few of the biggest leaves are taken from each plant at a time, allowing the smaller ones to continue growing. This method means you can have a continuous little-but-often harvest from each plant for many weeks (for example, lettuce) or for many months (for example, chard).

## LETTUCE

| | |
|---|---|
| **Sowing outside** | Early spring to late summer |
| **Sowing under cover** | Late winter to late summer |
| **Sowing depth** | ½in (1cm) |
| **Seeds per module** | 4 or 5 |
| **Plant spacing** | Individual 4in (10cm); clumps 6–8in (15–20cm) |
| **Harvest** | Late spring to late fall |

## SPINACH

**Sowing outside** Mid-spring to late summer

**Sowing under cover** Late winter to late summer

**Sowing depth** ½–¾in (1–2cm)

**Seeds per module** 2 or 3

**Plant spacing** Individual 4in (10cm); clumps 6in (15cm)

**Harvest** Late spring to early winter (overwintering varieties in early spring)

## CHICORY, RADICCHIO, AND ENDIVE

**Sowing outside** Mid-spring to late summer

**Sowing under cover** Mid-spring to late summer

**Sowing depth** ½in (1cm)

**Seeds per module** 1

**Plant spacing** 6–8in (15–20cm)

**Harvest** Midsummer to late fall

## ARUGULA

**Sowing outside** Mid-spring to late summer

**Sowing under cover** Early spring to late summer

**Sowing depth** ½in (1cm)

**Seeds per module** 3 or 4

**Plant spacing** Individual 4in (10cm); clumps 6in (15cm)

**Harvest** Early summer to late fall

## MUSTARDS

**Sowing outside** Mid-spring to late summer

**Sowing under cover** Late winter to late summer

**Sowing depth** ½in (1cm)

**Seeds per module** 3 or 4

**Plant spacing** Individual 2–2¾in (5–7cm); clumps 4–6in (10–15cm)

**Harvest** Mid-spring to late fall

## PERPETUAL SPINACH AND CHARD

**Sowing outside** Early spring to early summer

**Sowing under cover** Late winter to early summer

**Sowing depth** ½–¾in (1–2cm)

**Seeds per module** 1

**Plant spacing** 8–12in (20–30cm)

**Harvest** Late spring to early winter (and early to late spring if overwintered)

## JAPANESE GREENS (MIZUNA, KOMATSUNA, AND OTHERS)

**Sowing outside** Mid-spring to late summer

**Sowing under cover** Early spring to late summer

**Sowing depth** 2in (5cm)

**Seeds per module** 1

**Plant spacing** 4–6in (10–15cm)

**Harvest** Late spring to late fall

## TREE SPINACH

**Sowing outside** Mid-spring to midsummer

**Sowing under cover** Mid-spring to late summer

**Sowing depth** ½in (1cm)

**Seeds per module** 1

**Plant spacing** 20in (50cm)

**Harvest** Early summer to late fall

## AZTEC BROCCOLI

**Sowing outside** Mid-spring to midsummer

**Sowing under cover** Mid-spring to late summer

**Sowing depth** ½in (1cm)

**Seeds per module** 1

**Plant spacing** 20in (50cm)

**Harvest** Early summer to late fall

## MALABAR SPINACH

**Sowing outside** Mid-to late spring

**Sowing under cover** Early to late spring

**Sowing depth** ¾in (2cm)

**Seeds per module** 1

**Plant spacing** 8–12in (20–30cm)

**Harvest** Midsummer to mid-fall

## AMARANTH (FOR LEAVES)

**Sowing outside** Late spring to midsummer

**Sowing under cover** Mid-spring to midsummer

**Sowing depth** ½in (1cm)

**Seeds per module** 3 or 4

**Plant spacing** Individual 10–12in (25–30cm); clumps 14–16in (35–40cm)

**Harvest** Early summer to mid-fall

# BRASSICAS

This is an incredible group of productive crops whose leaves and flowers offer a diversity of delicious flavors throughout the year.

## SOWING BRASSICAS DIRECT OR IN A MODULE

All brassicas can be sown either directly where they are to grow or in modules. For large brassicas (kale, cauliflower), you can propagate seedlings in a seed bed and then lift them bare-root and plant them out in their final spacings. These bare-roots respond well to being planted deeply (½in/1cm below the first set of leaves), which also leads to a stronger-stemmed plant. Be sure to firm the soil around the stems of large brassicas to prevent them from toppling over.

## NUTRITIONAL NEEDS

Brassicas enjoy rich soil, especially any sprouting or heading brassicas (rather than loose leaf), which are particularly hungry. A simple way to ensure large yields when planting out is to add one or two generous handfuls of homemade compost at the base of the transplant hole.

## STORING BRASSICAS

To store brassicas, such as cabbage and kale, either use fermentation techniques, such as kimchi and sauerkraut, or blanch and freeze, which is the best option for cauliflower.

## PESTS

Cabbage white caterpillars and pigeons are the two biggest brassica pests. The solution to both is to net your brassicas in a fine mesh that doesn't touch the leaves (cabbage white butterflies can lay their eggs through the mesh hole) or to grow them under a brassica cage.

## HUW'S TIP

Plant kale, cabbage, bok choy, Chinese cabbage, and purple sprouting broccoli plants in the early fall in the polytunnel for leaves over the winter and early crops (including flower shoots) during the hungry gap.

### BROCCOLI (PURPLE SPROUTING)

| | |
|---|---|
| **Sowing outside** | Early spring to early summer |
| **Sowing under cover** | Early spring to midsummer |
| **Sowing depth** | ½–¾in (1–2cm) |
| **Seeds per module** | 2 (thin to strongest) |
| **Plant spacing** | 14–16in (35–40cm) |
| **Harvest** | Midsummer to mid-fall (summer variety), late winter to late spring (early variety that overwinters) |

## BROCCOLI (CALABRESE AND TENDERSTEM)

**Sowing outside** Early spring to midsummer

**Sowing under cover** Early spring to midsummer

**Sowing depth** ½–¾in (1–2cm)

**Seeds per module** 2 (thin to strongest)

**Plant spacing** 14–16in (35–40cm)

**Harvest** Midsummer to mid-fall

## CAULIFLOWER

**Sowing outside** Mid-spring to midsummer

**Sowing under cover** Late winter to midsummer

**Sowing depth** ½–¾in (1–2cm)

**Seeds per module** 2 (thin to strongest)

**Plant spacing** 20–24in (50–60cm), wider for winter varieties

**Harvest** Midsummer to late winter (depending on variety)

## BRUSSELS SPROUTS

**Sowing outside** Early spring to early summer

**Sowing under cover** Late winter to early summer

**Sowing depth** ½–¾in (1–2cm)

**Seeds per module** 2 (thin to strongest)

**Plant spacing** 12in (30cm)

**Harvest** Late fall to midwinter

## BOK CHOY

**Sowing outside** Early spring to midsummer

**Sowing under cover** Early spring to late summer

**Sowing depth** ½in (1cm)

**Seeds per module** 2 (thin to strongest)

**Plant spacing** 8–10in (20–25cm)

**Harvest** Early summer to late fall

## CHINESE CABBAGE

**Sowing outside** Early spring to midsummer

**Sowing under cover** Early spring, or midsummer to early fall

**Sowing depth** ½in (1cm)

**Seeds per module** 2 (thin to strongest)

**Plant spacing** Smaller heads 12in (30cm); larger heads 16in (40cm)

**Harvest** Early summer to early winter

## KALE

**Sowing outside** Early spring to midsummer

**Sowing under cover** Late winter to early fall

**Sowing depth** ½–¾in (1–2cm)

**Seeds per module** 2 (thin to strongest)

**Plant spacing** 12–16in (35–40cm)

**Harvest** Midsummer to mid-spring

## CABBAGE (SPRING, SUMMER, AUTUMN, AND WINTER)

**Sowing outside** Spring cabbages in mid- to late summer; summer cabbages in late winter to early spring; fall cabbages in mid- to late spring; winter cabbages in late spring

**Sowing under cover** Early spring, or midsummer to early fall

**Sowing depth** ½–¾in (1–2cm)

**Seeds per module** 2 (thin to strongest)

**Plant spacing** Smaller variety 12in (30cm); larger variety 20in (50cm)

**Harvest** Spring cabbages in late winter to midsummer; summer cabbages in midsummer to early fall; fall cabbages in late summer to late winter; winter cabbages in late fall to early spring

# ROOT VEGETABLES

Roots consist of a wide range of crops that are grown for their large root or swollen stem. There are few things more satisfying than pulling out a large bunch of carrots from the ground or eating roasted golden beets and fennel.

To grow root crops successfully, you want a nice sunny position, deep soil, and good moisture. Being sturdy and low growing, roots are a great choice for areas of your garden more exposed to wind.

## CELERY, CELERIAC, AND ROOT BRASSICAS

Celery is technically a leafy green but is included in this category due to its similarity to celeriac, and because it is a crop that is in the ground for a long time. In cooler climates, both celery and celeriac need an early start to give the best chance of a good crop. To achieve this, begin seeds in smaller modules and use a heat mat and grow light to aid germination. Once the seedlings have a couple of true leaves, pot them on to larger modules to grow on further before transplanting in the late spring or early summer.

Kohlrabi, radishes, turnips, and rutabagas are technically brassicas, but I treat them as root vegetables due to their primary harvest being the root.

## LET SOME FLOWER

Leave behind a couple of carrots, parsnips, and fennel (if not growing the perennial herb) to flower the following year. They form umbelliferous flowers (in clusters with a flattish top), which are a magnet for beneficial insects, including hoverflies, lacewings, and ladybugs.

## STORING ROOT VEGETABLES

For carrots, beets, and winter radishes, lift and trim the greens, leaving a 1in (2–3cm) stem. Store in boxes filled with damp sawdust in a cool, dark place, such as the back of a garage or in a converted chest freezer for overwinter use (see p.116). Make sure the roots aren't touching. Parsnips, salsify, and rutabagas can be left in the ground over winter and harvested when needed; any left over can be blanched and frozen. To store turnips, fennel, and kohlrabi, blanch and freeze.

### CARROT

| | |
|---|---|
| **Sowing outside** | Mid-spring to midsummer |
| **Sowing under cover** | N/A |
| **Sowing depth** | ½–¾in (1–2cm) |
| **Seeds per module** | N/A |
| **Plant spacing** | 2in (5cm) |
| **Harvest** | Early summer to early winter |

## PARSNIP

**Sowing outside** Mid- to late spring

**Sowing under cover** N/A

**Sowing depth** ½in (1cm)

**Seeds per module** N/A

**Plant spacing** 4in (10cm)

**Harvest** Early winter to early spring

## RUTABAGA

**Sowing outside** Mid- to late spring

**Sowing under cover** Early to late spring

**Sowing depth** ½–¾in (1–2cm)

**Seeds per module** 1

**Plant spacing** 8–10in (20–25cm)

**Harvest** Late fall to late winter

## BEET

**Sowing outside** Mid-spring to midsummer

**Sowing under cover** Late winter to midsummer

**Sowing depth** ¾in (2cm)

**Seeds per module** 3 or 4

**Plant spacing** Individual 2½–2¾in (6–7cm); clumps 6in (15cm)

**Harvest** Midsummer to early winter

## CELERY

**Sowing outside** N/A

**Sowing under cover** Late winter to early spring

**Sowing depth** ½in (1cm)

**Seeds per module** 1

**Plant spacing** 12–16in (30–40cm)

**Harvest** Midsummer to early winter

## CELERIAC

**Sowing outside** N/A

**Sowing under cover** Late winter to early spring

**Sowing depth** ½in (1cm)

**Seeds per module** 1

**Plant spacing** 16in (40cm)

**Harvest** Mid-fall to early spring

## FLORENCE FENNEL

**Sowing outside** Mid-spring to midsummer

**Sowing under cover** Late winter to midsummer

**Sowing depth** ½–¾in (1–2cm)

**Seeds per module** 1

**Plant spacing** 8–10in (20–25cm)

**Harvest** Late summer to late fall

## RADISH

**Sowing outside** Early spring to late summer

**Sowing under cover** Late winter to late summer

**Sowing depth** ½–¾in (1–2cm)

**Seeds per module** 4 or 5

**Plant spacing** Individual 1in (2–3cm); clumps 4in (10cm)

**Harvest** Mid-spring to late fall

## WINTER RADISH

**Sowing outside** Mid- to late summer

**Sowing under cover** N/A

**Sowing depth** ½–¾in (1–2cm)

**Seeds per module** N/A

**Plant spacing** 2–2¾in (5–7cm)

**Harvest** Mid-fall to midwinter

## SALSIFY

**Sowing outside** Mid- to late spring

**Sowing under cover** N/A

**Sowing depth** ½–¾in (1–2cm)

**Seeds per module** N/A

**Plant spacing** 4in (10cm)

**Harvest** Late fall to late spring

## TURNIP

**Sowing outside** Mid-spring to late summer

**Sowing under cover** Early spring to late summer

**Sowing depth** ½in (1cm)

**Seeds per module** 4 or 5

**Plant spacing** Individual 2½–2¾in (6–7cm); clumps 6in (15cm)

**Harvest** Late spring to early winter

## KOHLRABI

**Sowing outside** Mid-spring to late summer

**Sowing under cover** Early spring to late summer

**Sowing depth** ½–¾in (1–2cm)

**Seeds per module** 1

**Plant spacing** 10–12in (25–30cm)

**Harvest** Early summer to late fall

# NIGHTSHADE FAMILY

The nightshade family contains what are arguably the two most popular kitchen garden crops: potatoes and tomatoes. It contains the spiciest crop too: chilies!

Due to the uniqueness of nightshades in comparison with each other, I have added specific growing information for each to ensure that you get the most out of them. All those listed are tender, so protection from frost (see pp.268–269) is vital.

## POTATOES

There are two core categories of potatoes: determinate (early and midseason) and indeterminate (most late season). Determinates tend to form smaller plants and produce tubers on one level, whereas indeterminates can produce potatoes on more than one level. Contrary to popular belief, the names *early* and *midseason* shouldn't be taken literally. Yes, they are often the first to plant and harvest compared to late season potatoes, but one of the best times to plant early varieties is in midsummer, yielding a crop before the first frost.

If you want good potato success, you need three things: high fertility, deep soil, and plenty of sun. You also want to make sure they never dry out. The easiest way to grow them is in rows in raised beds, adding plenty of organic matter to the base of each hole. You can also grow potatoes in 8–9 gallon (30–35 liter) tubs filled with compost or a 50:50 mix of well-rotted manure and topsoil.

*I will never tire of the excitement of a potato harvest.*

## BLIGHT

The biggest issue with potatoes and tomatoes is blight, which sadly is very common and can quickly destroy your harvest. Luckily, there are ways to prevent blight from causing carnage, which are covered in the healthy garden chapter (see p.266).

Potatoes (both in containers and beds) are one of the few annuals that I mulch generously with grass clippings, straw, leaves, or seaweed. Mulch ensures that there are good levels of moisture in the soil, which helps the plants thrive. Harvest by pulling up the plant and then rummaging through the soil for tubers. A fork helps make this more efficient. To store potatoes, dry them for a day laid out in the sun, turning over to their other side at midday, and then place in a jute bag and store in a cool, dark, dry, and airy location.

### Chitting potatoes

Chitting involves placing potatoes in egg boxes in a warm, bright place to encourage them to begin sprouting before planting them out. I find it's not necessary when growing potatoes, but if you are after the earliest undercover crops, chit four weeks before planting to give them a small head start.

## CHILIES AND SWEET PEPPERS

Peppers need to be started early under grow lights, as they have a long maturation period before they crop from late summer. In my climate, where sun is rare over the summer, I can only produce ripe peppers undercover. When plants are around 8in (20cm) tall, pinch off the top two sets of leaves to encourage bushiness. Peppers only need support if the harvest becomes unwieldy—in that case, tie the stem to a stake. Water peppers when the top 1in (2–3cm) of soil is dry. If you are after heat in mature fruits, stop watering your plants completely once half of the peppers have fully ripened and delay harvest. Store peppers by dehydrating them and then placing in an airtight container.

*Removing a tomato sucker to improve airflow.*

## TOMATOES

Like potatoes, there are also determinate and indeterminate tomatoes. The most common are indeterminate, also known as cordon, and these will continue growing and cropping up until the first frost. Determinate, or bush, tomatoes fruit in one flush and then die. Whatever type of tomato you grow, it needs very fertile soil and plenty of sun. Constant soil moisture is also vital, particularly when fruiting, as irregular watering can cause blossom-end rot and fruit cracking. For high-quality tomatoes, mulch and a soaker hose are your friends. Bush tomatoes are the easiest to grow, as they need no support or pruning. For grafting tomatoes, see p.129. To store tomatoes, make a tomato sauce or roast tomato chunks and freeze.

### Pruning and training cordon tomatoes

There are two ways you can grow cordon tomatoes: the neglect method or the pamper method. The pamper method involves growing the plant up a support, such as a stake or string attached to the top of a polytunnel or greenhouse. The plant is pruned rigorously, removing every sucker (side shoot emerging at a 45-degree angle above a stem leaf) to focus the energy on vertical growth and fruit production on the main stem. This works fantastically well but takes a lot of effort.

You can get equally good results, and often better, by doing minimal pruning and allowing some of the suckers on the tomato to grow—it is a complete myth that suckers don't produce fruit, and they can be supported by stakes or string. My preferred option is growing "neglect" plants in a cylindrical trellis. The more leaves, the more energy the plant can create via photosynthesis and, provided there is plenty of

organic matter in the soil, plants will also produce a strong root system. Simply remove any lower leaves in midsummer (below 16in/40cm) and any branches that may be growing too far away from the plant and clear the most congested growth.

Applying supplemental nutrition every two or three weeks via a liquid feed (amendment or worm tea, see pages 272–273) will really benefit health and production. In the late summer, I prune off any new tomato flowers so the plants focus on ripening fruits already set before frost.

### Outdoor growing

Tomatoes can be grown outdoors in cooler climates, but undercover will always produce better results. If you don't have the space for a polytunnel or greenhouse, grow bush tomatoes in a hoop bed or grow tested outdoor varieties that perform consistently in a similar climate to your garden.

### Cherry, salad, plum, and beefsteak tomatoes

One of the joys of tomatoes is just how many varieties there are. In fact, there are over 10,000 tomato varieties, with more joining the list every year. Every single tomato variety has its own unique characteristics, and the taste difference between each variety is noticeable. While tomato shapes are grouped into cherry, salad, and beefsteak, the real difference is between the individual varieties, and if you have space for 10 tomato plants, then grow 10 different varieties for an incredible choice.

## EGGPLANT

Eggplants need no special pruning or support apart from a stake. The best chance of success is growing them undercover; they need a long season, but patience is paid in dividends.

## SWEET CORN

While not a nightshade, sweet corn is a fruiting crop (like peppers, chilies, eggplants, and tomatoes). It is very simple to grow, but you must follow one rule: Grow a block/grid of at least 12, preferably 16, plants together. For sweet corn to properly develop cobs, wind pollination is essential, which is why you need to grow a bunch of plants in a small space to increase the chances of successful pollination.

## OKRA

Also known as ladies fingers, these heat-loving and tall-growing plants (up to 6ft/1.8m) provide mild-tasting edible pods that can be used in a wide variety of meals, such as stews and curries. They are best grown undercover. Harvest the pods when they are young and tender. In general, okra does not need support but may need staking if the plants are getting very tall and you are worried about knocking them over.

## POTATO

**Planting** Early spring to midsummer (for all varieties)

**Sowing under cover** N/A

**Planting depth** Determinate 4–6in (10–15cm); indeterminate 8in (20cm)

**Seeds per module** N/A

**Plant spacing** Determinate 10–12in (25–30cm); indeterminate 14–16in (35–40cm)

**Harvest** Midsummer to late fall

## CHILI AND SWEET PEPPER

**Sowing outside** N/A

**Sowing under cover** Mid- to late winter

**Sowing depth** ½in (1cm)

**Seeds per module** 1

**Plant spacing** 10–12in (25–30cm)

**Harvest** Late summer to mid-fall

## TOMATO

**Sowing outside** N/A

**Sowing under cover** Late winter to early spring

**Sowing depth** ½in (1cm)

**Seeds per module** 1

**Plant spacing** Determinate and indeterminate 20–24in (50–60cm); neglect method 3–4ft (1–1.2m)

**Harvest** Midsummer to mid-fall

*There is no shortage of variety to choose from when it comes to growing delicious tomatoes.*

## EGGPLANT

**Sowing outside** N/A

**Sowing under cover** Late winter

**Sowing depth** ½in (1cm)

**Seeds per module** 1

**Plant spacing** 20in (50cm)

**Harvest** Late summer to mid-fall

## SWEET POTATOES

If you like a challenge, I recommend trying sweet potatoes. While they can grow outside in a warm, sunny spot in cooler climates, your best option is to grow them as a ground cover in a polytunnel or hoop bed to mimic the warm, humid temperatures they originate from. Sweet potatoes are grown from "slips"—rooted shoots emerging from a sweet potato—and the plants can sprawl across the ground or be trained to grow up trellises. One variety to try is T65.

## SWEET CORN

**Sowing outside** N/A

**Sowing under cover** Mid- to late spring

**Sowing depth** ¾in (2cm)

**Seeds per module** 1

**Plant spacing** 14–16in (35–40cm)

**Harvest** Midsummer to early fall

## OKRA

**Sowing outside** N/A

**Sowing under cover** Mid- to late spring

**Sowing depth** ¾in (2cm)

**Seeds per module** 1

**Plant spacing** 20in (50cm)

**Harvest** Midsummer to mid-fall

# CUCURBITS

Cucurbits are a varied group of fruiting vegetables, including squash, melons, and cucumbers, that are an absolute staple of permaculture gardening.

The squash category is perfect for planting in underutilized land and produces a huge harvest with very little care and attention. Many winter squash varieties, which have tougher skins than summer squash, can be stored for a long time (some until midsummer the following year), which is particularly useful when it comes to the hungry gap (see pp.220–221). All cucurbits are tender, so be patient when planting out into a spot in full sun and harvest them before the last frost. Achocha, also known as the Bolivian cucumber, is an easy-to-grow crop undercover and provides fruits that can be eaten raw when small or stuffed and cooked when larger.

## SUPPORT

Most summer squash grow like a bush, but others are trailing or climbing. All trailing cucurbits, such as watermelons, can be trained up vertical supports, like legumes (see pp.186–187), to save space. You may need to tie on some of the branches, but this is a simple process that offers great results. Depending on the variety, any cucurbits growing vertically may need support as their fruit swell. This is to prevent gravity from bringing the whole plant crashing down. The best support for fruits is to create "nets" by tying old fabric to the trellis supports to act like a hammock for them to sit in. For any squash that you allow to trail on the ground, you can place straw under the fruit for tip-top condition, although there is no problem in letting them grow and ripen directly on the soil surface.

## FEEDING SQUASH PLANTS

Squash are some of the hungriest of all the crops. For the biggest harvests, dig a planting hole at least 12in (30cm) wide and 18in (45cm) deep and pack it with homemade compost or a 3:1 ratio of well-rotted manure and soil. Squash and melons need plenty of water, so mulch is recommended once plants have had four to six weeks of growth after planting out. You can also use a liquid feed every two or three weeks from midsummer. Cucumbers are also hungry and thirsty, but each will only need around half the fertility (a planting hole 6in/15cm wide and 8in/20cm deep, filled with goodness).

## MELONS

Melons are increasingly popular to grow undercover in temperate gardens thanks to heritage seed sourcing efforts. See the suppliers' list (p.281) for my go-to seed suppliers, some of which specialize in varieties most suitable for cooler climates.

## STORING SQUASH

Squash need a cool, dry place with good airflow. When harvesting, leave on at least 4in (10cm) of stalk, as this helps with longevity. The ideal temperature range is 50–59°F (10–15°C), but I've had many winter squash last to late spring on a cool windowsill indoors. Any squash with soft spots or other signs of rot should be composted immediately—a perfect treat for chickens!

**SUMMER SQUASH (ZUCCHINI, PATTY PAN, SPAGHETTI, AND OTHERS)**

| | |
|---|---|
| **Sowing outside** | Late spring to early summer |
| **Sowing under cover** | Mid-spring to early summer |
| **Sowing depth** | ½–¾in (1–2cm) |
| **Seeds per module** | 1 |
| **Plant spacing** | 28–32in (70–80cm) |
| **Harvest** | Midsummer to mid-autumn |

## WINTER SQUASH (PUMPKIN, GOURD, BUTTERNUT, AND OTHERS)

**Sowing outside** Late spring

**Sowing under cover** Mid- to late spring

**Sowing depth** ½–¾in (1–2cm)

**Seeds per module** 1

**Plant spacing** 3–5ft (1–1.5m)

**Harvest** Mid- to late autumn

## MELON (INCLUDING WATERMELON)

**Sowing outside** N/A

**Sowing under cover** Mid-spring

**Sowing depth** ½–¾in (1–2cm)

**Seeds per module** 1

**Plant spacing** Vertical growing 16–20in (40–50cm); trailing 3ft (1m)

**Harvest** Late summer to mid-autumn

## CUCUMBER

**Sowing outside** Late spring to early summer

**Sowing under cover** Early spring to early summer

**Sowing depth** ½–¾in (1–2cm)

**Seeds per module** 1

**Plant spacing** Vertical growing 12–16in (30–40cm); trailing 20in (50cm)

**Harvest** Midsummer to mid-autumn

## ACHOCHA

**Sowing outside** N/A

**Sowing under cover** Mid- to late spring

**Sowing depth** ½in (1cm)

**Seeds per module** 1

**Plant spacing** 3ft (1m)

**Harvest** Midsummer to mid-autumn

# HERBS

Annual herbs pack so much flavor into such a small space. They are easy to grow, are wonderful for plugging gaps, and can be grown undercover and outside, and their flowers are adored by beneficial insects.

Annual herbs are a great option for partial shade, particularly over summer. Parsley is an odd one out, as it is a biennial, but a hardy one, so overwinter it and enjoy fresh growth the following spring, then a magnificent flower display. I often plant dill and coriander around the garden for the flowers and then enjoy cooking with their fresh green seeds as an alternative harvest. For fresh annual herbs to use in winter, place leaves in ice-cube trays, fill with water, and then store in a freezer bag to take out and use when cooking.

## HUACATAY BLACK MINT

Also known as Peruvian black mint, this annual herb (below) from South America is an absolute must-grow. It can be used in the kitchen anywhere you would use coriander and has a hybrid coriander-mint taste with a zesty touch. It is easy to grow but needs heat to help with germination, so I start mine in mid-spring by using a heat mat and then, due to its tender nature, transplant after the risk of frost has passed.

### CORIANDER

**Sowing outside** Mid-spring to late summer

**Sowing under cover** Early spring to late summer

**Sowing depth** ½–¾in (1–2cm)

**Seeds per module** 4 or 5

**Plant spacing** Individual 4in (10cm); clumps 6–8in (15–20cm)

**Harvest** Late spring to mid-fall

## DILL

**Sowing outside** Mid-spring to late summer

**Sowing under cover** Early spring to late summer

**Sowing depth** ½–¾in (1–2cm)

**Seeds per module** 4 or 5

**Plant spacing** Individual 4in (10cm); clumps 6–8in (15–20cm)

**Harvest** Late spring to mid-fall

## CHERVIL

**Sowing outside** Mid-spring to midsummer

**Sowing under cover** N/A

**Sowing depth** ½–¾in (1–2cm)

**Seeds per module** N/A

**Plant spacing** 4in (10cm)

**Harvest** Midsummer to mid-fall

## PARSLEY

**Sowing outside** Mid-spring to early summer

**Sowing under cover** Early spring to midsummer

**Sowing depth** ½in (1cm)

**Seeds per module** 3–4

**Plant spacing** Individual 6in (15cm); clumps 10–12in (25–30cm)

**Harvest** Early summer through winter, and spring the following year

## BASIL

**Sowing outside** Late spring to midsummer

**Sowing under cover** Early to mid-spring (heat mat recommended) and late spring to midsummer

**Sowing depth** ½in (1cm)

**Seeds per module** 3–4

**Plant spacing** Individual 8in (20cm); clumps 14–16in (35–40cm)

**Harvest** Late spring to mid-fall

# FLOWERS

A permaculture kitchen garden aims to encourage maximum diversity in as many forms as possible. Annual flowers are essential to help form this diversity, with some covering all the bases: edible, beautiful, and pollinator-friendly.

The annual flowers on these pages are beautiful and useful and can be grown anywhere that is in full sun or light shade. The least "useful" of the list below are sweet peas, as they only offer aesthetic benefits, but it is a crime to not have at least one patch of sweet peas to cut and have on the kitchen table.

Perhaps growing a scented mix of sweet peas to offer an additional "yield" can better justify their role. Unlike the other flowers, African marigolds thrive in hot and drier conditions. The best location is to interplant them with peppers or with undercover tomatoes as a colorful border or groundcover.

## BORAGE

**Sowing outside** Mid-spring to early summer

**Sowing under cover** Early spring to early summer

**Sowing depth** ½–¾in (1–2cm)

**Seeds per module** 1

**Plant spacing** 10–12in (25–30cm)

**Flowering** Early summer to mid-fall (edible young leaves and flowers)

## CHINESE VIOLET CRESS

To get incredible edible flower displays from midwinter to late spring, Chinese violet cress needs to be overwintered. It will need protection from prolonged cold weather below 23°F (-5°C), but in most cases, it overwinters without fuss in zone 8 and warmer (see p.32). Alternatively, you can grow it in 8-gallon (30-liter) pots and bring these into a polytunnel or hoop bed over the winter for protection.

**Sowing outside** Late spring to midsummer

**Sowing under cover** Mid-spring to midsummer

**Sowing depth** ½in (1cm)

**Seeds per module** 1

**Plant spacing** 8–12in (20–30cm)

**Flowering** Midwinter to late spring (edible flowers), midsummer to late winter (leaves)

## SWEET PEAS

| | |
|---|---|
| **Sowing outside** N/A | |
| **Sowing under cover** Midwinter to early spring | |
| **Sowing depth** 1in (2–3cm) | |
| **Seeds per module** 3 | |
| **Plant spacing** Clumps 12in (30cm) | |
| **Flowering** Early to late summer (cut flowers, not edible) | |

### HUW'S TIP

As with perennial flowers, deadheading is a technique that can be applied to some annual flowers to promote long flowering seasons. Sweet peas, cosmos, zinnia, calendula, and African marigolds are the ones to focus on for deadheading.

## SUNFLOWER

**Sowing outside** Late spring to early summer

**Sowing under cover** Mid-spring to early summer

**Sowing depth** ½–¾in (1–2cm)

**Seeds per module** 1

**Plant spacing** Dwarf varieties 12in (30cm); tall varieties 16–20in (40–50cm)

**Flowering** Late summer to early fall (edible petals, cut flowers, and seeds)

## NASTURTIUM

**Sowing outside** Late spring to midsummer

**Sowing under cover** Mid-spring to midsummer

**Sowing depth** ½–¾in (1–2cm)

**Seeds per module** 1

**Plant spacing** 20in (50cm)

**Flowering** Midsummer to first frost (edible seeds, flowers, leaves, and stems)

## ZINNIA

**Sowing outside** Late spring to early summer

**Sowing under cover** Mid-spring to early summer

**Sowing depth** ½in (1cm)

**Seeds per module** 1

**Plant spacing** Dwarf varieties 12in (30cm); tall varieties 16in (40cm)

**Flowering** Midsummer to mid-fall (cut flowers, petals are edible but bitter)

## CALENDULA

**Sowing outside** Mid-spring to early summer

**Sowing under cover** Mid-spring to early summer

**Sowing depth** ½–¾in (1–2cm)

**Seeds per module** 1

**Plant spacing** 8–12in (20–30cm)

**Flowering** Midsummer to mid-fall (edible flowers and leaves)

## AFRICAN MARIGOLD

**Sowing outside** N/A

**Sowing under cover** Early to mid-spring (heat mat recommended)

**Sowing depth** ½in (1cm)

**Seeds per module** 1

**Plant spacing** 8–12in (20–30cm)

**Flowering** Early summer to mid-fall (edible petals)

## NIGELLA

**Sowing outside** Late spring to early summer

**Sowing under cover** Mid-spring to early summer

**Sowing depth** ½in (1cm)

**Seeds per module** 2 or 3

**Plant spacing** 12in (30cm)

**Flowering** Midsummer to early fall (some edible seed varieties available)

## GROWING FOXGLOVES

The foxglove (*Digitalis*) is a European wildflower with stunning flowering spikes (below), and it's a bumblebee magnet. As it is a biennial that likes to pop up around my garden (self-sown), each winter I will pot up the first season foxglove plants to then transplant at corners of raised beds or along the border as a featured plant. I allow a couple of the tower spikes to die back naturally, which will provide seeds for the next generation of foxgloves. Do not consume foxgloves: The flowers (and all parts of the plant) are extremely toxic.

## COSMOS

**Sowing outside** Late spring to early summer

**Sowing under cover** Mid-spring to early summer

**Sowing depth** ½–¾in (1–2cm)

**Seeds per module** 1

**Plant spacing** 4–6in (10–15cm)

**Flowering** Midsummer to mid-fall (some edible varieties available)

# BONUS HARVESTS

To show just how many additional harvests your annual crops provide, I have compiled a gallery of as many bonus yields as I could fit on these two pages.

I hope this offers you inspiration when it comes to looking at how you can incorporate these plants raw, straight from the garden into your meals, and that they are a fantastic source of conversation around the dinner table.

**Favorite bonus harvests**

**1.** Squash flowers and leaves

**2.** Brassica leaves

**3.** Brassica flowers

**4.** Beet leaves

**5.** Carrot leaves

**6.** Onion and shallot leaves

**7.** Leek flowers

**8.** Fennel fronds

**9.** Kale flower stems

**10.** Runner bean flowers

**11.** Pepper leaves (not all varieties are edible)

**12.** Rutabaga and turnip leaves

**13.** Radish pods and flowers

**14.** Pea shoots

**15.** Fava bean tops

**16.** Coriander and dill flowers and seeds

**17.** Calendula leaves

**18.** Cucurbit leaves (squash and cucumbers)

# SUCCESSION PLANTING

Succession planting has a simple goal: to grow two or more crops from the same ground over a growing season. So, when the first crop is harvested, a second crop is planted immediately in the same space.

This form of planting is the second most impactful factor for a highly productive garden, after having healthy soil. You could argue that growing undercover is more important than succession, but you would be missing out on a huge amount of undercover potential if you didn't plant in succession.

Examples of succession planting could be leeks following potatoes, chard following bok choy, and kale following fava beans. It also works for when you have an overwintered crop, as you can plan for what will go in its place once it is harvested. One example could be harvesting overwintered garlic at the end of June and then transplanting climbing beans. But what about crop rotation? In a permaculture garden, crop rotation isn't necessary; this is covered in the next chapter (see pp.228–255).

Succession planting is a term that is also applied to growing vegetables in a little-but-often manner to extend the harvest period of that crop and reduce gluts.

## SUCCESSION PLANTING GUIDE

Here is a guide on what to sow in modules in mid- and late summer for succession planting outside for gardens with a first average frost date of mid-fall.

If you are new to gardening, the easiest way to start succession planting is to sow a selection of the crops listed below every couple of weeks in module trays, and use these seedlings to fill any spaces that emerge over the late summer and early fall.

**Sow in midsummer**

Beets

Bok choy

Bush beans

Carrots, quick-growing (forcing varieties direct outside)

Cauliflower, winter-type

Chard

Coriander and dill

Cover crops (see pp.74–76)

Fennel

Kale

Kohlrabi

Salad leaves

Spring onions

Turnips

**Sow in late summer**

Bok choy*

Chicory

Chinese cabbage*

Cover crops (see pp.74–76)

Fava beans for shoots

Kale

Mustard and oriental salad greens (mizuna, etc.)

Peas for shoots

Radish

Radish, winter-type (direct outside)

Salad leaves*

Spring cabbage*

Turnips

* Sow in first two weeks of late summer

# POLYTUNNEL TIMINGS

By combining succession planting with the earlier and longer harvests polytunnels provide, you are many steps closer to being able to provide all of your vegetable needs year-round.

The final task is ensuring that you have enough to overcome the hungry gap (see pp.220–221). The timings for sowing, planting, and harvesting in the growing information given for crops in this chapter refer to growing outside (with the undercover sowing times given separately). There are a few "exception" plants, such as peppers, eggplants, and tomatoes, where the best results are only possible in cooler areas if they are grown to maturity undercover. In warmer temperate areas, however, the sowing and harvesting timings would be nearly identical whether you are growing on undercover or outside.

## EARLIER CROPS

For annuals that are usually grown outside, polytunnels (and hoop beds) can significantly extend the harvesting window. For starters, you can plant and sow directly at least four to six weeks earlier in a polytunnel than you would outside.

**Example: early potatoes**

|  | Early/mid-late spring | Early/mid-/late summer | Early/mid-/late fall | Early/mid-/late winter |
|---|---|---|---|---|
| Plant in polytunnel |  |  |  | ▨▨▨ |
| Harvest in polytunnel | ▨▨▨ |  |  |  |
| Plant outdoors | ▨▨ |  |  |  |
| Harvest outdoors |  | ▨▨▨ |  |  |

## LATER CROPS

A polytunnel or hoop bed gives you a longer harvest window after the first frost, offering protection so that crops can be harvested deep into winter, where outside they would struggle with the wet and freeze–thaw conditions. This is particularly useful for leafy greens, such as bok choy, which have some frost resistance but quickly lose quality after some hard frosts, and for many root vegetables that aren't as tough as parsnips. Here is an example of two carrot crops sown at the same time, but the hoop bed offers a far greater span of harvest opportunity.

**Example: carrots**

|  | Early/mid-/late spring | Early/mid-/late summer | Early/mid-/late fall | Early/mid-/late winter |
|---|---|---|---|---|
| Sow in hoop bed |  | ▨ |  |  |
| Harvest in hoop bed | ▨ |  | ▨▨▨▨▨▨ | ▨▨▨▨ |
| Sow outdoors |  | ▨ |  |  |
| Harvest outdoors |  |  | ▨▨▨▨ |  |

# HUNGRY GAP

The hungry gap is the leanest period of the year when the winter vegetables have finished, but the summer crops are still maturing. This is typically mid-spring to early summer.

I've learned that the hungry gap only exists due to a lack of planning, and even though it is often the leanest time of year, it doesn't mean it can't be the most abundant. To make a hungry gap a period of abundance, gardeners must embrace a diversity of growing approaches that all contribute to the harvests. Here are four possible approaches in your kitchen garden:

- **Overwintering**—Grow hardy crops that can survive the winter outdoors and then come into harvest during the hungry gap.
- **Long-term storage**—Grow crops that you can freeze, dehydrate, ferment, or simply store in a cool, dry, dark place, where they will keep until deep into the hungry gap.
- **Hot beds**—These provide a frost-free growing environment even in the depths of winter, greatly increasing the range of harvestable crops over the spring and early summer (see pp.60–61). With a hot bed, not only is salad self-sufficiency made easy; you can be harvesting cauliflower, carrots, zucchini, dwarf peas, beets, and spring onions from the late spring onward if sown in midwinter. The hardest decision to make is what to prioritize growing. My approach is to use the hot bed to bridge the leanest period you foresee over the hungry gap.
- **Polytunnel**—For hardy crops that need a little extra protection from the cold and wet of winter, a polytunnel can greatly extend their harvest period, allowing you to then preserve them at the end of the winter in time for the hungry gap as well as enjoy some early sowings (see p.219).

## PICKLING AND DEHYDRATION

As well as freezing and storing produce in cool, dark, dry spaces, I also use pickling and dehydration to extend the shelf life of my crops. Quick pickles are a great way to extend a crop for four to six weeks by storing in the fridge. Dehydrated crops can last up to six months at room temperature if completely dehydrated and kept in an airtight jar in a cool place, and much longer if vacuum-sealed. You could grow an early crop of radishes in a hot bed to then quick pickle and enjoy, opening space for the next crop in the hot bed as soon as possible and giving you a supply of radishes for weeks to come.

## FERMENTATION

Fermentation consists of a range of techniques that allow you to preserve and enhance homegrown flavors, including over the hungry gap. You can make fruit vinegars, wines, krauts, kimchis, fermented hot sauces, kombuchas, and much more from your crops. Some may only extend shelf life for a month or so, while others, if processed correctly, can provide you with flavor for years to come. To start your fermentation journey, obtain a copy of *The Art of Fermentation*, written by Sandor Katz.

### HUW'S TIP

There are many perennials that are harvested over the hungry gap, including the majority of the herbs (see pp.140–145), rhubarb (see p.138), asparagus (see p.139), and the perennial brassicas (see pp.132–133).

## BONUS APPROACH: FORAGING

Supplement your garden harvests with wild foods. Two primary wild foods I enjoy are nettles in the mid- to late spring as a spinach alternative and wild garlic, which I harvest and process to enjoy for months to come.

## CROPS FOR THE HUNGRY GAP

With careful planning, here is a quick breakdown of the 18 annual crops (not including the individual salads and herbs) that can be stored and harvested over the hungry gap.

| CROPS | GROWING TIPS | HARVESTING AND STORING |
|---|---|---|
| Bok choy | Start this incredible fast-growing crop in modules in early spring | Harvest undercover from mid-spring and from late spring outdoors (see p.196) |
| Cabbage, Chinese | Sow in modules undercover early and grow on undercover or plant out | Harvest from late spring onward (see p.196) |
| Cabbage, spring | Overwinter outside | Harvest leaves throughout spring and then heads in early summer (see p.196) |
| Carrots and beets | Overwinter undercover | Do a final harvest in early spring to process and freeze (see pp.198–199) |
| Garlic | Plant bulbs in mid- to late fall | Harvest "green garlic" from mid-spring: This is the stalk and undeveloped bulb, which is completely edible |
| Herbs | Dill and coriander can be sown in modules in later winter | Harvest undercover from mid-spring (see pp.210–211) |
| Kale flower stems and purple sprouting broccoli | Overwinter outside | Enjoy the tender sweet flower shoots until late spring (see pages 194 and 196) |
| Leeks | Overwinter outside | Harvest late-bolting varieties until late spring, then blanch and freeze the rest to access over the rest of the hungry gap (see p.184) |
| Onions | Select storage varieties | Harvest and store for up to 12 months in a cool, dry, dark place. Check regularly and remove any soft onions to maintain the quality of the batch. Alternatively, freeze chopped onions in late winter to use (see p.185) |
| Potatoes, early | Start off early undercover | Harvest from mid-spring (see p.206) |
| Radish | Sow undercover in late winter | Harvest undercover sowings from early spring and from mid-spring for outside (see p.202) |
| Salad leaves | Start off early undercover; includes anything from spinach to pea shoots (see pp.216–217) | Harvest from mid-spring |
| Squash, winter | Choose long-lasting varieties, such as 'Crown Prince' | Harvest and store in a cool, dark, dry place (see p.209), where they can last until summer the following year |
| Rutabaga and parsnips | Leave outside over winter | Harvest in early spring to process and freeze (see p.199) |
| Turnip | Start in modules in later winter | Harvest outside from late spring onward (see p.203) |

# SEED SAVING

Saving your own seeds is highly rewarding, and over time, your crops will better adapt to your soil and climate if you use the best specimens to save seed from. It also builds resilience and self-sufficiency, not to mention cost savings.

**BEGINNER SEED SAVING**

There are three rules of seed saving:
**1.** Save seeds from your healthiest, most productive specimens.
**2.** Dry the seeds properly to avoid rotting.
**3.** Label everything, from the seed crops to the seed packets.
To get started, choose beginner-friendly crops that are mostly self-pollinating: beans, peas, tomatoes, and lettuce. You can also save some tubers and bulbs as well as herb seeds.

**Beans and peas**

These are the easiest! Let a few pods naturally dry (turn brown and crispy) on the plant and pick out the peas and beans. Then, place a baking sheet on a sunny indoor windowsill and lay out the peas and beans so they're not touching. Let them dry for a further three or four weeks, turning occasionally, and store in labeled envelopes.

**Tomatoes**

Allow a tomato to ripen and then scoop out the seeds. Place a few teaspoons' worth in a glass jar half filled with spring or unchlorinated water. Leave at room temperature for three to five days, mixing daily. Then, remove floating seeds and pour the remaining seed mixture through a fine sieve. Rinse well with water. Spread the seeds on parchment paper to dry in a warm, dry spot for around five days; store in a labeled envelope.

**Lettuce**

You only need one lettuce plant to save a lot of seeds. Let it flower and allow the flower heads to turn "fluffy." Then, cut the flower stem and let it dry on a tray in a cool, dry place, such as a north-facing indoor windowsill, for another three to four weeks. Firmly shake the dried flower head into a bucket, banging it against the side to release the seeds. The seeds will be "dirty," as other bits of the lettuce plant will be present, but that is only a small issue when it comes to storing and sowing.

**Tubers and bulbs**

Potatoes and perennial tubers are easy to save "seed" from, as you just take a few tubers from the harvest to store in a cool, dry, dark place over the winter and plant them again in the spring. The same applies to garlic: Plant the individual cloves in the late fall from the bulbs you harvested in the summer.

*Harvesting peas for seeds from dried pods. These will be stored in an airtight jar, ready for sowing the following spring.*

A female squash flower (left) and male squash flower (right).

### Herb seeds

Herbs, such as coriander, dill, caraway, and parsley, are easy to save seeds from: You just let a few plants flower and collect seeds after they have dried on the plant. If it is at the end of the growing season and the seeds aren't quite dry, hang them in a polytunnel and shake off the dry seeds into labeled envelopes three or four weeks later.

### NEXT STEPS

Saving seeds from crops that need cross-pollination is slightly more advanced. Cross-pollination means that a flower needs pollen from the flower of another plant of the same species for pollination to occur and seeds to develop. Kale is the same species as cabbage (*Brassica oleracea*), meaning that if they both flower, there will be cross-pollination, which will create hybrid seeds that have a mixture of characteristics. Carrots can cross-pollinate with the wild carrot, resulting in imperfect seeds.

To keep seed varieties pure, professional seed savers place insect-proof mesh over kale or carrots just before flowering to ensure there is no "contamination." Then, for the plants within to cross-pollinate, they introduce fly maggots to pupate, turn into flies, and pollinate. Once the flowers have gone, the mesh is removed, and the seed is saved when mature. Biennial crops that flower in the second year, such as kale, leeks, carrots, and beets, may need protection over the winter in cold climates.

The good news is that if you're saving seeds just for yourself, you needn't be as strict as professional seed savers, as you aren't selling seeds of named varieties. Provided you only allow one species of a crop to flower (or if you are allowing two to flower, keep them as far apart as possible), you will almost always get good results. If all seeds disappeared from this world and I had to do it all myself, I would much rather have a little cross-pollination than no seeds at all.

### Saving seeds from squash

Squash that cross-pollinate create seeds that, if grown, can result in bitter fruit. To avoid this, you can hand-pollinate squash using flowers of the same variety, early in the morning when the flowers open. When the female flower first develops and before it opens, tie a mesh bag over it to prevent any chance of pollination. Take a male flower, use a paintbrush to get as much pollen from the stamen as possible, then brush the pollen on the stigma of the female flower in the mesh bag as its petals first open. Once complete, gently tie or tape the flower shut to keep any bees from visiting and loosely tie colored string on the flower stem to mark that as the fruit to save seeds from.

### HUW'S TIP

**Seed saving should only be done on open-pollinated crops. These aren't hybrids, meaning the saved seeds will grow true to type. It is not advised to save seeds from F1 and other hybrids sold commercially. They have two different parents, selected for two characteristics to show in the first generation (F1). While the first generation will show uniform results, any seeds from F1 crops when sown can vary widely in their characteristics and are much less reliable than seeds from open-pollinated crops.**

## LANDRACE VARIETIES

If you have some space and love seed saving, why not take it a step further and develop your own landrace variety? This is a genetically diverse variety (diversity is strength) developed to be as resilient as possible for a given area. To do this, plant a mix of varieties of the same crop (such as fava beans or beets) together in a small space, allowing them to cross-pollinate, and save the seeds. Over the next few seasons, select the specimens showing the characteristics you want (removing those you don't want before flowering). Characteristics to select for could be good pest tolerance, a more compact growth habit, a higher yield, or a different color, harvesting window, or flavor. In five to ten years, you will have your own unique landrace variety that will be uniform in growth and fully adapted to your space. See resources (p.280) if this interests you.

# FAVORITE VARIETIES

These are my favorite annual and biennial main crop varieties in my kitchen garden. For each, the first named variety is my staple choice, for productivity, resilience, and taste; the second has a characteristic that makes it a showstopper, be it flavor, color, growing habit, or resilience.

## Alliums

**Leek** 'Bandit', 'Hilari'

**Spring onion** 'Parade', 'North Holland Blood Red'

**Onion** 'Sturon', 'Lilia'

**Garlic** 'Germidour', 'Carcassonne Wight'

## Legumes

**Bush beans** 'Tendergreen', 'Amethyst'

**Broad beans** 'Aquadulce Claudia', 'Crimson Flowered'

**Climbing snap beans** 'Cobra', 'Borlotti'

**Runner beans** 'Scarlet Emperor', 'Greek Gigantes'

**Peas** 'Ambassador', 'Llanover'

**Snow peas** 'Oregon Sugar Pod', 'Golden Sweet'

## Leafy annuals

**Lettuce** 'Bronze Arrowhead', Celtuce

**Chicory** 'Palla Rossa', Cicoria di Chiavari

**Spinach** 'Giant Winter', strawberry spinach

**Chard** 'Fordhook Giant', 'Peppermint'

**Mustard** 'Dragon Tongue', 'Wasabi'

**Amaranth** 'Velvet Curtains', 'Loves Lies Bleeding'

## Brassicas

**Sprouting broccoli** 'Tenderstem', 'Claret'

**Cauliflower** 'All the Year Round', 'Di Sicilia Violetto'

**Brussels sprouts** 'Groninger', 'Red Rubine'

**Bok choy** 'Joi Choi', 'Santoh'

**Kale** 'Dwarf Green Curled', 'Nero Di Toscana'

**Chinese cabbage** 'Yuki', 'Hilton'

**Spring cabbage** 'Durham Early', 'Wintergreen'

**Summer cabbage** 'Golden Acre', 'Greyhound'

**Winter cabbage** 'Ironhead', 'Saint Michael of Verona'

*'Tigerella' is one of the best-tasting tomato varieties out there.*

*The famous 'Tenderstem' broccoli is a delicious must-grow.*

## Roots

**Carrot** 'Resistafly', 'Purple Dragon'

**Rutabaga** 'Tweed', Gilfeathers' turnip-swede

**Parsnip** 'Tender and True', 'White Gem'

**Beet** 'Boltardy', 'Golden Detroit'

**Celery** 'Victoria', 'Giant Red'

**Florence Fennel** 'Rondo', 'Colossal'

**Radish** 'Poloneza', rat-tail

**Winter radish** daikon, 'Black Spanish Round'

**Turnip** 'Golden Ball', 'Milan Purple Top'

## Nightshade family

**"Early" potato** 'Charlotte', 'Swift'

**"Late-season" potato** 'Maris Piper', 'Sarpo Mira'

**Chili pepper** 'Padron', 'Lemon Drop'

**Sweet pepper** 'Kaibi Round, 'Sweet Spiralus'

**Tomato** (Huw's top 5 varieties)—'Tigerella', 'Green Zebra', 'Black Russian', 'Honeycomb', 'Lulu'

**Eggplant** 'Black Beauty', 'White Dourga'

**Sweet corn** 'Golden Bantam', 'Glass Gem'

## Cucurbits

**Summer squash** 'Verde Di Italia', 'Tromboncino'

**Winter squash** 'Winter Luxury' pumpkin, 'Jumbo Pink Banana'

**Cucumber** 'Marketmore', 'Passandra'

**Melon** 'Sivan', 'Minnesota Midget'

## Herbs

**Coriander** 'Leisure', 'Confetti'

**Parsley** 'Italian Giant', 'Hamburg'

**Basil** 'British', 'Lettuce Leaf'

## Flowers

**Sweet peas** traditional mixes, 'Suzy Z'

**Sunflower** 'Sunspot', 'Velvet Queen'

**Zinnia** 'Zinderella Lilac', 'Queen Lime'

**Calendula** 'Gypsy Festival', 'Orange Flash'

**Cosmos** garden mix, 'Apricot Lemonade'

**Nasturtium** 'Climbing Mixed', 'Ladybird Rose'

*'Resistafly' allows you to grow carrots without the need for protective measures against root fly.*

*A mini sweet-pea medley for the dining table.*

# Polyculture

# EXPLAINING POLYCULTURE

Now that we've covered all individual aspects of a permaculture garden, from principles to plants, this chapter explores ways of connecting these pieces together to create functional and productive spaces.

Polyculture is where many plants are grown mixed together. It's the opposite of monoculture blocks of single plants. You can visualize this by picturing a meadow in comparison to a field of wheat. Polyculture can work at any scale—from a plant pot to a whole field. I hope that these next few pages fill you with ideas and inspiration that you can adapt and apply to your own space. If you plan to do major projects, it is worth understanding your soil, particularly pH and structure (see pp.46–49), to ensure success. Polycultures can also be wholly annuals, wholly perennials, or a medley of both.

## POLYCULTURE THINKING

When creating any form of planting, whether it's a small pot on your balcony or a huge mixed border, use these nine polyculture questions as your starting point for deciding about each plant. This will help you group together productive, beautiful, and resilient polyculture plantings. In a nutshell, you become your own garden designer.

1. **Plant height and spread** How big is each plant at maturity?
2. **Flowering times** Do you want to save the seeds?
3. **Harvest period** When will this crop and then be cleared?
4. **Nutritional needs** Is it hungry or not?
5. **Root space** Are the roots deep or shallow?
6. **Light levels** Is it sun-loving, or would it work in shade?
7. **Water levels** Is it thirsty, or can it do well in dry areas?
8. **Color** What colors are the leaves and flowers?
9. **Pest and disease pressures** Is it known to attract or ward off particular issues?

## COMPANION PLANTING

This is an approach to planting that looks at how particular plants can benefit one another, such as growing basil under tomatoes to help deter pests. The issue with companion planting is that many planting combinations have no scientific backing and may be vague or focus on lesser crops that support a primary crop. I've found that because a combination works for one person, people think it will work for everyone, and the pairing becomes an absolute combination. Very often, correlation doesn't equal causation, especially in an already healthy garden.

While I have every confidence that there are fantastic companion plantings, with many yet to be proven, my approach is to pair plants in a way that makes intuitive and logical sense. For example, I would never grow potatoes under cordon tomatoes, as they are both a blight risk and very demanding of nutrients, and the potatoes would be harvested before the tomatoes ripen, so the tomato roots would be disturbed. However, cordon tomatoes, which have a tall stem, could be grown with plants underneath that won't cause damage when harvested, such as herbs and flowers.

There are some really lovely ideas in companion planting, but like crop rotation (see p.259), I feel it hinders the creativity and productivity of a garden if followed to the letter.

## "With polyculture, you have the freedom to choose to plant in both regular and irregular patterns."

*A polyculture abundance in my kitchen garden, consisting of a plethora of different flowers, herbs, and vegetables in a small space.*

# FRUIT TREE GUILD

One of the most common polyculture techniques seen in permaculture is fruit tree guilds. A guild is a group of plants that are grown together for mutual benefit.

A fruit tree guild is made up of plants grown under a fruit tree, which offer specific characteristics, such as attracting beneficial insects, visual polyculture (see pp.248–251), fertility for the tree, and additional edible harvests. For small spaces, guilds are a lovely alternative to food forests (see pp.36–37), and you have the option of incorporating both perennials and annuals as well as making the guilds as simple or as diverse as you wish, provided that you work with the space you have.

The main rule to follow for guilds is to make sure that the stem of the tree is kept clear to ensure good airflow (for reducing disease risk). If any of your lower plants grow large, this can be easily managed by cutting back vigorous growth by the stem with a pair of shears. Use the nine polyculture questions (see p.228) alongside the lists of recommended plants below to help you create your own guilds, but I have included a few examples as a starting point.

## RECOMMENDED GUILD PLANTS TO START WITH

| Perennial herbs and flowers | Annual herbs and flowers | Soft fruit |
| --- | --- | --- |
| Bergamot | Amaranth | Alpine strawberries |
| Chives | Borage | Currants |
| Echinacea | Calendula | Gooseberries |
| Mint | Coriander | Rhubarb |
| Poppy | Cosmos | Summer strawberries |
| Rose | Dill | **Additional plants** |
| Salvia | Dwarf sunflower | Comfrey |
| Spring bulbs | Nasturtium | Globe artichoke |
| Thyme | Parsley | Nettle |
| | Phacelia | Sorrel |
| | Zinnia | |

**A SIMPLE FRUIT TREE GUILD**

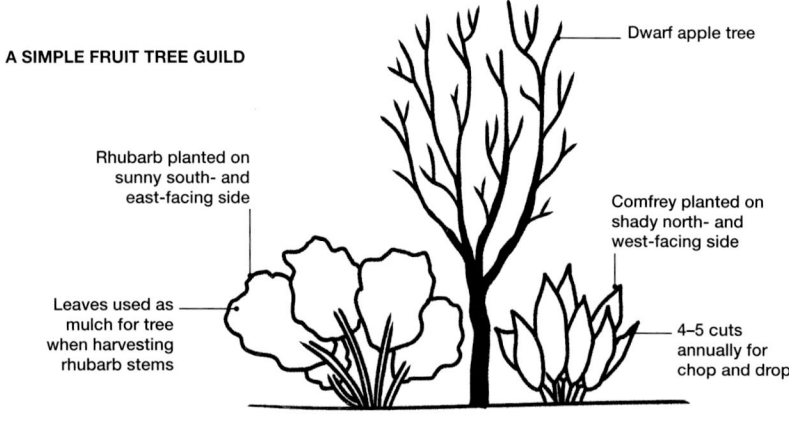

Dwarf apple tree

Rhubarb planted on sunny south- and east-facing side

Comfrey planted on shady north- and west-facing side

Leaves used as mulch for tree when harvesting rhubarb stems

4–5 cuts annually for chop and drop

**Plants that help each other**
*A very simple guild consisting of rhubarb on the southern side and comfrey on the northern. Both plants help keep a clear stem for the tree by outcompeting any weeds, and comfrey along with rhubarb leaves can be chopped and dropped to add fertility.*

*Planting up a fruit tree guild in spring, including comfrey, strawberries, and bulbous nettle.*

**FRUIT TREE GUILD OVERHEAD VIEW**

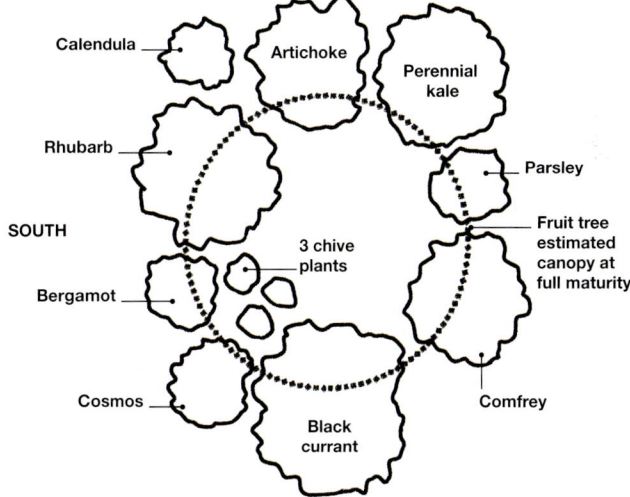

Calendula

Artichoke

Perennial kale

Rhubarb

Parsley

**SOUTH**

3 chive plants

Fruit tree estimated canopy at full maturity

Bergamot

Cosmos

Comfrey

Black currant

### Example guild planting scheme around an apple

*Remember to take into consideration the eventual size of the canopy if you're planting around younger trees.*

### HUW'S TIP

If you are going for a fully perennial guild, you can use edging made of metal or plastic to prevent grass from encroaching and mulch with a 2–3in (5–7cm) layer of wood chips to promote fungally dominated soil and reduce weeds.

*A mature fruit tree guild under an apple, including amaranth, snap bush bean, calendula, strawberry, rudbeckia, and bulbous nettle.*

# THE HERB GARDEN

A dedicated herb garden can offer a wonderful corner of colors and aromas. An herb garden can be as small as a planted-up pallet collar bed or consist of multiple beds.

You could combine all of your herbs in a random manner for a lovely organic look or group herbs into categories, such as herbs for teas, herbs for salads, and herbs for roasting. When laying out a herb garden, focus on the positioning of your perennial herbs first. For annual herbs, you have the flexibility of growing them wherever there is space as well as incorporating them within your annual vegetable beds.

*The herb garden at my plot consists of metal beds for easy harvesting and to keep some herbs, such as mint, from spreading.*

Some perennial herbs, such as lemon verbena and black currant sage, are rather tender and can be killed in cold winters. If you wish to grow these in the ground or in beds, place them on the edge so it is easier to lift the plants in the late fall to keep them protected undercover until they can be planted back in their original place the following spring.

### The firepit herb garden

I believe every garden, if possible, should have a firepit or grill to enjoy in the evenings and to cook your incredible homegrown food. When cooking on a grill, having access to fresh herbs elevates the whole experience for making rubs, sauces, and dips, not to mention refreshing cold drinks.

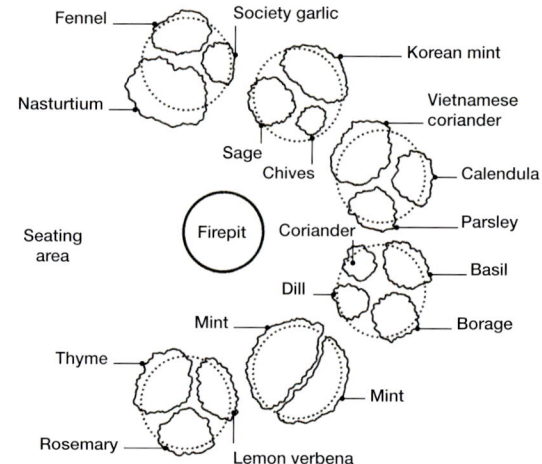

### Container herb garden by a firepit

*Here, half whiskey barrels house an herb garden to harvest for cooking on the fire, and some edible flowers have been added, which can be used for garnishing.*

### HUW'S TIP

A simple way to enhance your herb garden is to select some annual edible flowers (see pp.212–215) that can quickly fill any small spaces and add splashes of color among the herbs.

# THE FRUIT GARDEN

A dedicated fruit garden is a lovely way of creating a natural yet productive growing area for medium to large spaces.

**FIVE STEPS TO DESIGN YOUR OWN FRUIT GARDEN**
Growing all of your fruit in one place makes it easier to look after the trees, protecting them from birds and squirrels (see p.264). Bear this in mind when spacing your fruit plants, ensuring that it is as easy as possible to protect them. High-risk fruits, such as blueberries and red currants, could be planted in lobe patterns or at the ends of the soft fruit garden for ease of netting.

**1. Position your fruit trees** The most permanent feature of any fruit garden will be the fruit trees. You will need to decide which rootstock you will be using (see p.161), and it is better to space the fruit trees with more distance than usual to allow enough light and space for the soft fruit understory.

**2. Create the plan** Apply the nine polyculture questions (see p.228) to the key fruits you will be growing in addition to trees, focusing on the tallest to shortest (general height order: trailing berries, raspberries, jostaberries, currants, blueberries, gooseberries, rhubarb, strawberries) to find where they best fit around the fruit trees. Do this as a rough outline.

**3. Include additional plants** If you wish to add more plants, such as comfrey, herbs, or perennial flowers, put these in the smaller gaps between fruit crops or at the edges. You could use a guild approach for the area around each tree (see pp.230–231).

**4. Decide on varieties and nurseries** Once you have the rough pattern of your fruit garden, you'll want to iron out the details (design from pattern to details, see p.20). These may include which varieties you wish to grow, which will help you decide on final spacings. Explore nurseries and local groups to make sure the trees can be sourced.

**5. Observe and interact** Once your garden is planted, observe how the plants establish. You may need to step in and adjust the design by removing/repositioning plants as they mature, but it will be mostly mulching, protecting, and harvesting.

**HUW'S TIP**
As blueberries have a different soil pH requirement than the rest of the crops, they may be best grown together in amended soil or in their own bed next to the fruit garden.

**A fruit garden for a large area**
*An example backyard fruit garden featuring 16 different trees and soft fruits, with additional comfrey and perennial herbs to increase soil and plant health.*

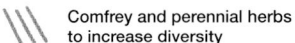
Comfrey and perennial herbs to increase diversity

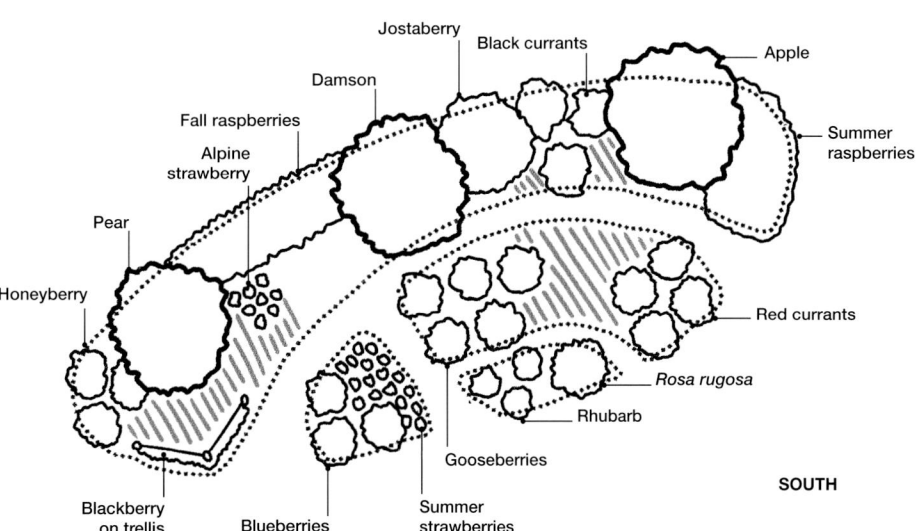

Jostaberry

Black currants

Apple

Damson

Fall raspberries

Summer raspberries

Alpine strawberry

Pear

Honeyberry

Red currants

Rosa rugosa

Rhubarb

Gooseberries

Blackberry on trellis

Blueberries

Summer strawberries

SOUTH

# PERENNIAL EDIBLE BORDERS

All gardens have some form of boundary, and a boundary is always an opportunity for planting a border. An edible border is productive as well as visually pleasing.

For small to medium-sized gardens, perennial borders along the boundaries are a lovely way to surround the more productive inner areas of the garden by adding color, structure, softening, and more food!

## ASPECT

**East- and west-facing boundaries** The tallest plants should be grown at the back to make it easier to maintain and harvest if you can only access the border from one side (your neighbor may not appreciate you hopping over into their garden!).

**North-facing boundaries** Plants of similar heights should be grown together to minimize additional shading. Prioritize leafy perennial vegetables and herbs.

**South-facing boundaries** These are highly valuable growing areas, and the approach to planting differs from other aspects. With the greatest sun exposure and warmest temperatures, south-facing boundaries are perfect for productive sun-loving annual crops, like tomatoes and beans, or for growing fruit trees. Place the tallest at the back so they don't shade those in front. If your garden doesn't have a direct south-facing border, treat your southeast- or southwest-facing boundary as south.

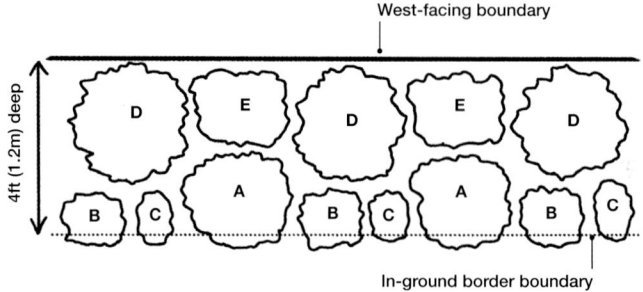

**West-facing border plan**
*This diagram is an example of a west-facing perennial border planted up with edible and supportive nonedible perennials.*

A Comfrey
B Thyme
C Chives
D Globe artichoke
E Verbena

## VISUALS AND COLOR

Due to the positioning of borders as the last line of sight in the garden, I aim to make them as visually pleasing as possible by mixing textures and colors, such as mashua planted under globe artichokes. You can learn more about the art of visual polyculture in a permaculture garden on pages 248–251.

## "WILD" BORDERS

One of my favorite aspects of working with perennials is being able to create borders that appear wild to an untrained eye yet are full of food and color. A wild border is a great way to experiment with polyculture plantings and can feature flowers, herbs, fruit, and vegetables. Over time, you can adjust the border by removing any plants that might be struggling and replacing them with an alternative. The only real consideration should be plant spacings and making sure you don't grow something that could easily take over the whole bed, such as mint. I would also suggest doing an initial mulch of wood chips, and then the only mulching could be as simple as chopping and dropping vegetative growth within the border.

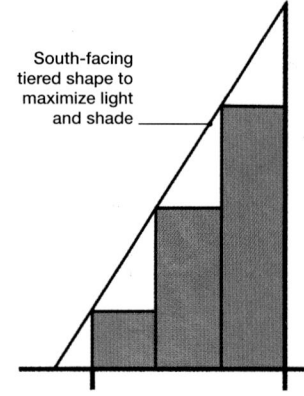

**South-facing boundary**
*A simple formula for planting up sunny boundaries is to arrange plant heights in thirds, with the tallest at the back.*

South-facing tiered shape to maximize light and shade

*Planting up a perennial edible border; here I'm planting catnip for herbal teas.*

*The same border less than two months later. Note that I allowed squash to grow into the border too.*

## KEEPING THINGS SIMPLE

Don't feel you have to squeeze in as many different plants as possible when it comes to borders. Often, less is more for impressive displays and simplicity of maintenance. A good rule of thumb is to pick three to five key edible plants and to space them in a regular or irregular pattern along the length.

### Low-maintenance edible perennials for east- and west-facing borders

| |
|---|
| Alpine and summer strawberries |
| Black currants |
| Globe artichoke |
| Jerusalem artichokes |
| Leafy perennial vegetables |
| Mashua |
| Oca |
| Perennial brassicas |
| Rhubarb |
| *Rosa rugosa* |

### Low-maintenance herbs for perennial borders

| |
|---|
| Catnip |
| Chives |
| Fennel |
| Korean mint |
| Rosemary |
| Thyme |

### Great nonedible perennials

| |
|---|
| Bulbs |
| Comfrey (Bocking 14 variety) |
| *Verbena bonariensis* |

## ANNUAL EDIBLE BORDERS

All the approaches mentioned here can be applied to annuals, which may make more sense in certain situations. You may live in rented accommodations and only be allowed to grow annuals in the ground, for example, or perhaps your garden is particularly small and you are aiming to eat as much from the garden as possible. Utilize succession planting (see p.218) in annual borders for the maximum visual impact and yield.

# CHICKEN FOOD FOREST

This multifunctional space provides protection, entertainment, and supplemental nutrition for the chickens while offering seasonal forageable yields for you to enjoy alongside compost to use for your garden beds.

Chickens naturally scratch the surface of the ground, looking for bugs, seeds, and sprouts to eat. They particularly enjoy scratching in loose ground—which is why chickens and mulch do not pair well! However, if you put chickens in the right location, you can use their natural behavior in a way that makes compost, as outlined on pages 78–79.

Chickens enjoying foraging for grubs and sprouts among a thick hay mulch under currant bushes.

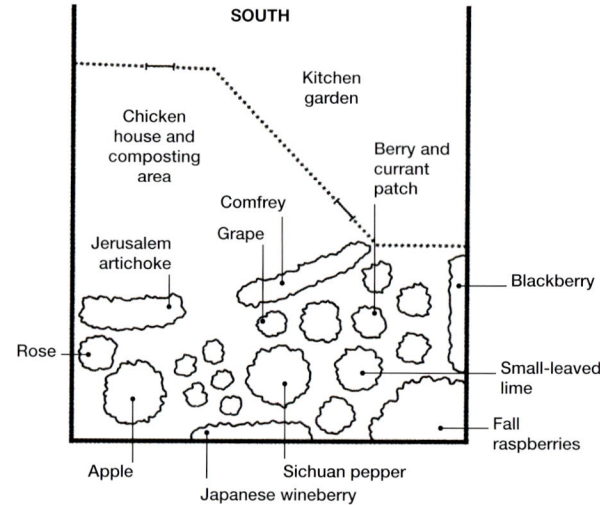

**CHICKEN FOOD FOREST**

SOUTH

Kitchen garden

Chicken house and composting area

Comfrey

Grape

Berry and currant patch

Jerusalem artichoke

Blackberry

Rose

Small-leaved lime

Fall raspberries

Apple

Sichuan pepper

Japanese wineberry

*An example of stacking functions (see p.27), this area can grow many different crops for the kitchen while also making compost.*

A chicken food forest provides the gardener with additional nutrition, while the chickens enjoy anything left over, such as missed berries falling to the ground. The planting consists of mostly perennial vegetables and fruits, which are protected either with small fences or large rocks placed around their root system. The chickens will do an excellent job of keeping any weeds down, control pests by hunting bugs, and, of course, provide fertility to the plants via their manure. It has a dedicated compost production area, usually close to the coop or on a boundary that borders the garden so you can throw any compost materials over the fence into the system.

The best plants to include in a chicken food forest are tree fruits and large soft fruits, such as currants and gooseberries, trailing berries around the boundaries, roses, and Jerusalem artichokes. Comfrey is also easy to integrate, and you can build wire boxes that allow you to grow annual crops between the perennials, should you wish. Above is an example diagram of a chicken food forest at the end of a suburban garden.

# INTEGRATING DUCKS IN THE GARDEN

If your context allows, integrating ducks within your garden should always be a consideration. Ducks are expert slug busters as well as egg providers.

Unlike chickens, which will quickly scratch up your whole garden, ducks leave a much lighter footprint. If you grow in raised beds with sides, ducks are much happier walking around rather than over them. Happy ducks need water (you can create a pond out of an old bathtub) and grass in which to forage for snails, slugs, and other creatures. In larger spaces, an orchard with soft fruit is ideal for ducks, but even in small spaces, you can be clever with design to have beneficial, happy ducks.

## DUCKS AND COMPOST

Making compost with ducks doesn't follow the same approach as with chickens because ducks don't scratch in the same way. Instead, the best method is to create a deep mulch system where you pile up organic matter, such as straw, sawdust, grass, garden waste, and leaves, in a concentrated area. The simplest way to do this is to create a small fenced run adjacent to their house. This should be fox-proof, and it is where you feed them breakfast and supper, so they spend some time there each morning and evening. Their manure will incorporate with the mulch and over time will build up a generous layer of compost. At the end of the growing season, scrape back the mulch and use the compost underneath to mulch your beds.

## THE FORTIFIED GARDEN

The goal of a fortified garden is for the ducks to act as a line of defense against slugs for as much of the perimeter as possible to prevent slugs from targeting the annual crops. Here, there are two defined areas: the duck run, which encompasses dwarf and semi-dwarf fruit trees and soft fruit, and the vegetable garden. The ducks can easily be let into the vegetable garden area to conduct slug busts on a regular basis, but they don't have a free-for-all around your vegetables. They have a small area inside the duck run to protect them from foxes in the mornings and evenings, which is a deep-mulch system for creating compost (see left). This design, with three to five ducks, should produce enough compost (if enough mulch material is brought in, such as wood chips and clippings) for the entire plot to be self-sufficient in compost.

*The "quack pack," as my friend and fellow gardener Adam Jones likes to call them, here in action among my beds.*

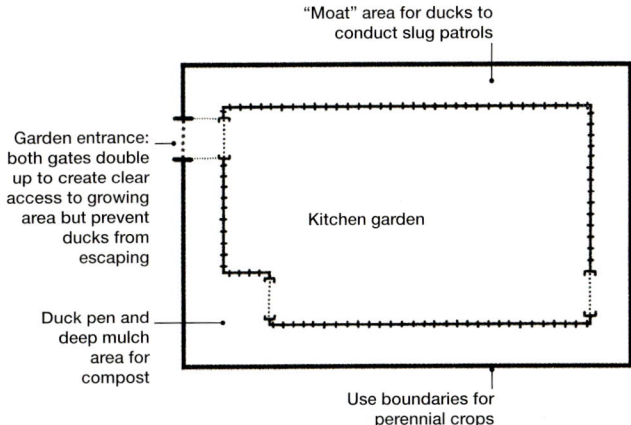

"Moat" area for ducks to conduct slug patrols

Garden entrance: both gates double up to create clear access to growing area but prevent ducks from escaping

Kitchen garden

Duck pen and deep mulch area for compost

Use boundaries for perennial crops

**A fortified kitchen garden for a half-size allotment plot**
*Perennials are grown inside the duck run around the perimeter to maximize productivity.*

# THE FORAGER'S GARDEN

This space will provide year-round supplemental nutrition from foraging what's available, but the core benefit will be boosting the biodiversity around your garden.

The forager's garden is a partially managed food forest and would be classed as zone 4 (see pp.42–43). Unlike in a kitchen garden or orchard, it's vital that you don't get too attached to any of the crops you plant in a forager's garden. This area of the garden is about working with nature and allowing nature to select what thrives and what dies. All you do is lay the foundation and make sure vegetation is managed enough for you to walk through the garden. Apart from that, you want to be as hands-off as possible for this mini-ecosystem to thrive.

After planting, the only management will be chop and drop (see p.62) for clearing weeds as well as occasional pruning to tame any plants that begin to get out of control (the prunings

*Harvesting crab apples from a hedgerow on my parents' smallholding.*

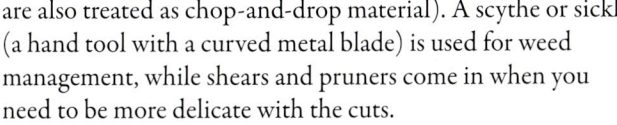
*Wild blackberries (above) and elderflower (right) are two wild food icons of the foraging world.*

are also treated as chop-and-drop material). A scythe or sickle (a hand tool with a curved metal blade) is used for weed management, while shears and pruners come in when you need to be more delicate with the cuts.

By chopping and dropping, you get to select what stays and what goes. Should there be a patch of nettles, perhaps you leave it to harvest it as greens and keep some for butterfly and ladybug populations. If you come across a plant that is not thriving, cut it down to make space and allow the dropped material to decompose and help nourish a new plant.

## NATIVE SPECIES

A successful forager's garden requires plants that look after themselves. You will have the best success with emphasis on native species (see p.26). For me, this could include hazel (nuts), hawthorn (leaves and berries), elder (berries and flowers), blackthorn (berries), crab apples, wild rose, blackberries, raspberries, good King Henry, mint, and wild garlic. After native plants, the next stage would be low-maintenance hardy perennials, such as apples, currants, gooseberries, Jerusalem artichokes, a range of perennial herbs, and leafy perennial vegetables.

## THE FORAGER'S BED

If you have only a small garden, a really fun project is to create a forager's bed, which is a perfect way to use up old or almost empty seed packets. Over the spring sowing season, put any old and spare herb, vegetable, and edible flower seeds in a glass jar. Then, in the late spring/early summer, broadcast sow these into an empty bed and water thoroughly (see p.181).

Within a few days, the first seedlings will appear, and within a month, the bed will be covered in a carpet of green. At this stage, you'll want to randomly remove around one-third of the plants to reduce the competition a little or focus on thinning baby greens for an edible harvest. Then, once or twice a week, visit the bed and harvest anything that is ready at that stage. As time progresses, the act of harvesting will further clear space to allow bigger plants, such as stemmed brassicas or even tomatoes, to grow on and mature.

# LINEAR FOOD FOREST

A linear food forest is a productive row of perennial edible plants that is 6½–13ft (2–4m) wide and as long as you want. You can access it from both sides, making management and harvesting simple.

The structure of the linear food forest is created by planting fruit trees (and/or nut trees) at a set distance, and then the shrub layer, between the primary fruit trees, consisting mainly of soft fruits, but you can include very dwarfing fruit trees and roses. The next layer is the herbaceous one, on either side of the primary tree and shrub layers, which consists of perennial vegetables. The ground-cover layer is mainly bulbs and perennial herbs. There will be some crossover (herb fennel grows tall and would be better suited in herbaceous, for example), but the main goal is to arrange the planting in height order and know what dies back each winter versus what remains above ground.

## GRASS AS GROUND COVER

With food forests there is often this romantic vision that the ground is covered in mint, wild garlic, and strawberries. The reality is that strawberries need quite a bit of management to prevent them from being swamped by grasses and wildflowers, and mint, although it does spread, has the downside of dying back each winter, which gives time for native plants to grow and smother the mint crown. Heavy mulching around your ground cover helps reduce this, as well as chop and drop, but sometimes the easiest ground cover is a natural one of grasses and wildflowers. These benefit from being cut every summer to keep the whole garden from turning into a wild space.

## CHOOSING AND MAINTAINING FRUIT TREES

It takes a minimum of five fruit trees to make an orchard, so select five or more if you want a linear food forest orchard. Choose suitable rootstock sizes so you can scale this accurately to your context: A 33ft (10m) length would fit five M27 apple trees, while 65ft (20m) would fit the same number of M26 apples. You could make a very short linear food forest with just three fruit or nut trees. The fruit trees and soft fruits are pruned each winter to maintain shape and encourage heavy cropping, and winter is also the time to mulch with wood chips or even well-rotted manure. Summer mulching is done with grass cut from the paths surrounding the linear food forest and chop and dropping (see p.62) between the plants.

*Planting a new linear food forest; here, I'm adding a wild garlic plant.*

*A mature linear food forest at Tap o' Noth Permaculture Farm in Scotland, where I first discovered this technique.*

**PLANTING SCHEME FOR A LINEAR FOOD FOREST**

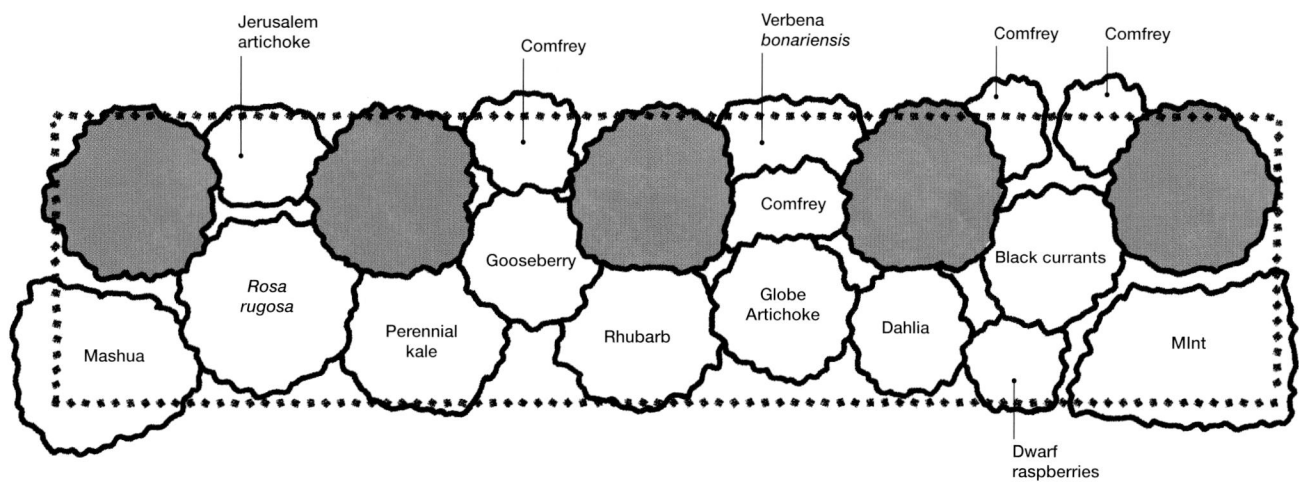

Jerusalem artichoke · Comfrey · Verbena *bonariensis* · Comfrey · Comfrey · Comfrey · *Rosa rugosa* · Gooseberry · Globe Artichoke · Black currants · Mashua · Perennial kale · Rhubarb · Dahlia · Mint · Dwarf raspberries

*This suggested scheme is for a 33 x 8ft (10 x 2.5m) linear food forest, starting with the M27 apple trees in place, forming the key structure, and then planting up the surrounding space.*

**KEY**

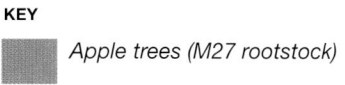

*Apple trees (M27 rootstock)*

## ORIENTATION

The orientation of your linear food forest can depend on multiple factors, and these three points will help you decide what will be most suitable for your goals:

**1. Windbreak** Which direction is the prevailing wind coming from, and could a linear food forest act as protection for the rest of the garden?
**2. Topography** Are you on a slope? If so, planting on contours along the slope (rather than up or down) will evenly capture water moving downhill and make it easier for you to navigate along the row when harvesting and maintaining.
**3. Climate** North to south ensures more even sunlight distribution throughout the day, but east to west will create a long south-facing edge, which can be used as a microclimate.

For getting the most out of a north-to-south linear food forest, you can increase spacings between the fruit trees to open up more light over the spring and summer when the sun is lower or plant the herbaceous crops on the east side (to enjoy the cooler mornings) and soft fruit on the west for the warmer afternoons. For a west-to-east linear food forest, position sun-loving crops on the south and leafy crops on the north of the fruit trees to maximize efficiency with available light.

If you have limited choices when it comes to positioning, such as a long but narrow garden, it is important to know that both north to south and east to west will work but may not be optimum in your situation.

## INTEGRATING CHICKENS AND DUCKS

Poultry can be carefully included to benefit linear food forests. Chickens could be introduced in the early summer for a short period to clear a bit of the undergrowth and to clean up in the late fall. Ducks could go in for a few hours every couple of weeks to keep down slugs. To contain poultry within a set area, invest in high-quality electric fencing, which gives you the flexibility to be able to create temporary "paddocks" for poultry throughout your garden.

# THEMED BEDS

A bed within your garden can be treated as its own mini-garden, incorporating multiple vegetables alongside herbs and flowers.

A true themed bed contains crops and edible flowers grown at a scale where harvests are substantial (32 sq ft/3 sq m of growing space and larger), and the crops are annually dominated. Themed beds are an idea I first saw by Vera Greutink, a permaculture gardener based in the Netherlands.

## UNDERCOVER, OUTDOORS, OR BOTH?

Themed beds are not restricted to being only inside or outside. One of the best themes I've come across for a family kitchen garden is a pizza bed: tomatoes, basil, and any other crops you would like as a topping, such as bell peppers, eggplant, sweet corn, onions, and spinach. For this to be possible in my climate, I would need to have this bed in a polytunnel. It is important when creating your own theme that it is something that excites you, and in some cases, you could integrate a cold frame or a small hinged hoop tunnel within an outside themed bed to extend the range of crops you can grow.

## THE HUNGRY GAP BED

This themed bed is designed to provide a steady supply of harvests from mid-spring to early summer. The ideal size is 10 x 4ft (3 x 1.2m) (see pp.276–277). You can include spring cabbage, purple sprouting broccoli, leek, kale, rhubarb (perennial), chives (perennial), field beans (over the winter), and green garlic. Any gaps that emerge from harvesting are plugged with early spring sowings of salad leaves, annual herbs, and radishes.

## THE COLORFUL SALAD BED

One single raised bed about 10 x 4ft (3 x 1.2m) can provide a family of four with the majority of their salad needs from the mid-spring to late fall. By growing a range of varieties of the following vegetables, focusing on different colors and textures, you will always be able to quickly gather a stunning salad in just a few minutes. Choose from nasturtium, borage, calendula, spring onions, chives, bok choy, lettuce, radish, oriental greens, chard and kale (grow both as baby leaf), snow peas, and sugar snap peas.

## OTHER THEMED BED IDEAS

**Flower medley** Grow a mix of annual edible flowers and some perennials, such as dahlias, roses, and chives, alongside crops that provide edible flowers, such as zucchini, runner beans, fava beans, arugula, and radishes.

**Pollinator bed** Grow a mix of perennial and annual flowers, such as Korean mint, bergamot, zinnia, calendula, yarrow, and cosmos, to attract beneficial insects to your garden.

**Weird and wonderful** Set aside a space to grow weird and wonderful varieties of vegetable crops that can serve as excellent conversation starters around the dinner table, like many of the perennial tubers. It could also be a place for growing old vegetable varieties that have fallen out of fashion but deserve love, such as salsify.

*Clockwise from right: a harvest from a pizza-themed bed; an edible flower medley; and deadheading calendua growing in my pollinator bed.*

# MAXIMIZING IN-BED POLYCULTURE

Within a kitchen garden, there are almost unlimited opportunities to increase polyculture, and one of my favorite areas is within the annual vegetable beds, although perennials can also make an appearance.

If done correctly, increasing polyculture in your vegetable beds should have minimal impact on the yield of your staple crops yet significantly boost the beauty and resilience of your space and, of course, provide a greater variety of harvests.

## POLYCULTURE TECHNIQUES IN ANNUAL BEDS
Here are some of my favorite techniques to use in your vegetable beds to boost polyculture.

### Oversowing
We gardeners have a tendency to sow and grow many more seedlings than we need. I see this as a strength, as it builds in resilience: We have back-ups in case of damage, and anything left over can be used to increase the polyculture of the garden. There is no such thing as a completely full garden: There are always opportunities, and your job is to seek them out!

### Plugging gaps
There are always going to be gaps around the garden, and as you harvest, more gaps will emerge. Gaps need plugging—we don't want bare soil, so ensuring that living plants occupy the ground for as long as possible is essential for healthy soil. The approach I take is to be a plant matchmaker. I look at the range of spare seedlings I have and choose which I think would be the most appropriate to grow in each gap, taking into account how the already-present crops will grow over the coming weeks.

Small gaps are suitable for tall or upright-growing crops, such as leeks, dill, and kale. Larger gaps may suit leafy greens, root vegetables, or even cauliflowers. Alternatively, you could make a mini growing frame for a spire of peas. It is important that you approach gap plugging creatively, and using the principles from visual polyculture (see p.248–251) will further help. You can also direct sow as a way of plugging gaps (see pp.180–181).

### Patching
This is a form of gap plugging as a response to failures or replacing underperforming plants. For example, if you've transplanted multisown clumps of beets and one of those clumps dies for no apparent reason, but you have no spare clumps, plant something else in its place. Another example is if you are growing a group of crops, such as sweet corn, and after a few weeks, one of the plants just doesn't seem to be growing, you could remove this weak plant; first, it is a potential pest or disease risk, and second, you can transplant something else in its place to grow and harvest.

### Interplanting
This is where you plant crops (usually two) alongside each other in a repeating or closed pattern. Carrots sown in rows with onions is a popular example. The goal is for the scent of the onions to deter and confuse carrot root flies (see p.265). Another option for these crops would be to grow onions in a bubble pattern and direct sow clumps of carrots within each bubble. I interplant parsley or coriander between my runner beans at the base of the trellises. The coriander works particularly well on the north side of a wigwam, as it will enjoy the shade and not bolt as quickly. Interplanting can include squeezing in a fast-growing crop that is harvested before the main crops matures and takes over the whole available space. I find bok choy to be an excellent interplanting option when planting out my winter and spring cabbages. An easy one to try in the spring is a row of radishes between your potatoes.

## Diagonal planting

Another pattern for interplanting that can also be done as a way of increasing the yield of one crop in the same area is by planting in diagonal rows rather than grids. If all the plants are going to grow to approximately the same size, a diagonal pattern allows you to space each row more closely together, fitting more plants within the same footprint.

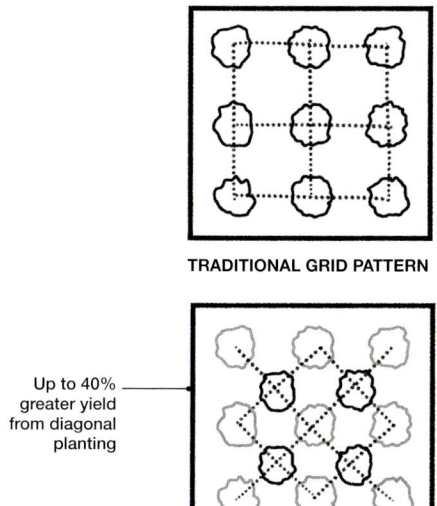

**TRADITIONAL GRID PATTERN**

Up to 40% greater yield from diagonal planting

**DIAGONAL PATTERN**

*Planting in diagonals maximizes the total space of your beds. You can grow similar-sized plants together using this approach.*

## Underplanting

This form of interplanting emphasizes using the "empty" ground that comes about when tall crops begin to mature. Tomatoes and kale are a perfect example. When you plant them into their final spacing, you don't want to plant other crops that may compete and hinder their progress initially, but once a tomato plant is over 3ft (1m) tall, there is space underneath to plant low-growing crops that grow in partial shade. Even if you are already growing such plants as basil and African marigolds or calendula alongside tomatoes, underplanting is about the space underneath the plant, so you can add more basil, plus calendula, nasturtiums, slow-to-bolt salad and coriander varieties, and carrots.

## Corner planting

The corners of your raised beds offer a unique opportunity to plant a crop that you can encourage to grow over the side of the bed. Ideally, choose a plant that can tolerate drier conditions, as the corner is the first area to dry out. I like to use corners to either add a splash of color or some height. Every winter, I will keep back a parsnip or a group of leeks in the corner of a bed to allow them to flower later that year. This is one of the easiest ways to maximize polyculture with no extra effort. These annual crops make great corner plantings: nasturtium, calendula, dwarf cosmos, tumbling tomato, bush snap beans, and annual herbs.

*Tying up a flowering parsnip to a stake to keep it in place. These umbelliferous flowers are adored by beneficial insects.*

## INTEGRATING PERENNIALS

Perennials can also make an appearance to maximize in-bed polyculture. When integrating perennials within your annual beds, it's vital to think carefully about placement and question whether perhaps it is better to dedicate a whole bed to perennials rather than mixing them in with annuals. This is because perennials are permanent (or at least for a few growing seasons), and they don't have the same compost needs as annual beds.

For ease of management and planning, it's usually best and simplest to grow annuals and perennials in separate beds or to keep perennials at the ends or corners of beds. Various herbs and tubers make fantastic corner plantings, such as thyme, chives, oca, and Chinese artichokes. When adding perennials, consider their growth habit, water and fertility needs, and how they will visually affect the space. I find perennial herbs (such as lemon verbena) and flowers to be the easiest to add to annual beds, but you can even include a dwarf fruit tree if you wish at one end, plant a guild surrounding it, and then grow annual crops in the rest of the bed.

**PERENNIAL AND ANNUAL BED**

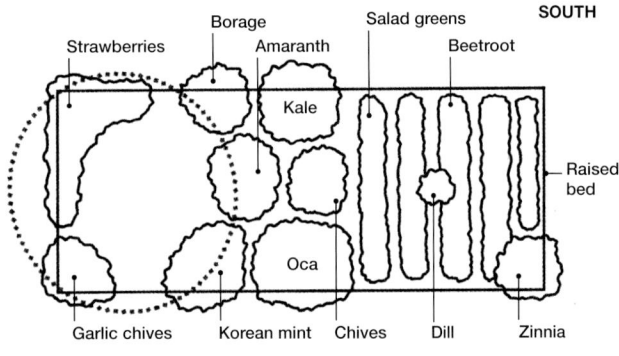

This plan shows a hybrid raised bed of perennials and annuals for maximum diversity without sacrificing yield.

## Transitioning a bed from annual to perennial

As I have been progressing toward a more perennially dominated style of kitchen garden, there are some beds in the transition phase, as they are heading toward being fully perennial. This is because some perennials need a growing season or two to mature, while others get underway immediately. Asparagus, for example, in the first year of planting could work as your salad bed, and then the following year, you could plant strawberries; the spears will grow through the strawberry layer. Both plants occupy different dimensional spaces, which is key to a successful interplant, with both crops performing well.

## Using perennial tubers

While incorporating most perennials requires a degree of caution, the exception is perennial tubers due to how they are harvested. I treat a lot of my perennial tubers as annuals because if I harvest all their tubers, there is no plant left in the ground. Oca, for example, which will rot in the ground if left over a harsh wet winter, is essentially grown exactly like you would a potato: Harvest, store, and plant out again in the spring.

## BIODIVERSITY ISLANDS

The plants that act as beneficial insect magnets (see p.261) can be used to add biodiversity islands. In raised beds, this could be an end section planted up with a medley of flowers, opting for a natural planting style rather than following a set pattern. Biodiversity islands among annual vegetables are suitable for nonspreading perennials, such as Korean mint, bergamot, and achilleas. A rule of thumb I like to follow each year is to section out around 10 percent of my growing space throughout my garden exclusively for biodiversity. Creating pots for beneficials can count toward this 10 percent coverage (see p.256).

*A lemon verbena (perennial) growing among a sea of annual plants, including coriander to the right, squash to the left, and pink cosmos.*

# VISUAL POLYCULTURE

While a kitchen garden rich in different crops will naturally look beautiful, there are a few simple techniques to turn your garden into a feast for the eyes and a place where you will want to spend as much time as you can.

## CONTRAST

Creating contrast, where you have strikingly different elements in close association, provides wonderful, visually stimulating interest. Here are the three core areas of contrast that can be applied to a kitchen garden setting.

### Textural contrast

Growing crops with contrasting leaf textures close to each other, such as beets, oca, and fennel, creates a powerful visual aesthetic. Another example is intercropping onions and carrots, both of which have very different leaf shapes.

### Color contrast

There are two types of color contrast: complementary (using opposite colors from the color wheel) and analogous (using colors next to each other on the color wheel). An example of complementary planting would be growing yellow calendula in front of violet-shaded kale, while analogous planting could be growing red, red-orange, and orange nasturtiums together.

### Size/growth habit contrast

Another opportunity to add stimulating contrast to your garden is making use of the wide range of plant sizes and growing habits available. For example, if you have a salad bed, placing a wigwam in the middle for climbing beans to grow up adds visual interest. Planting tumbling tomatoes along the edge of the salad bed will contribute to the aesthetic appeal.

The more layers a garden has, the more visual interest it can provide. Be mindful of striking a balance between visuals and productivity—layering height on the horizontal allows for this, with the shortest crops in the front and the tallest behind, being careful that the tall will not shade the short.

## COLOR WHEEL

A color wheel (below) shows colors in relation to each other, with contrasting colors opposite each other and analogous ones next to each other. Referring to this wheel can help you add elements of color contrast throughout your garden when creating your planting plan. Perhaps the most eye-popping color contrast of them all is red and green. Fortunately, a few crops naturally create this contrast without needing to be next to another plant. The four most common are runner beans, red chilies, tomatoes, and red chard.

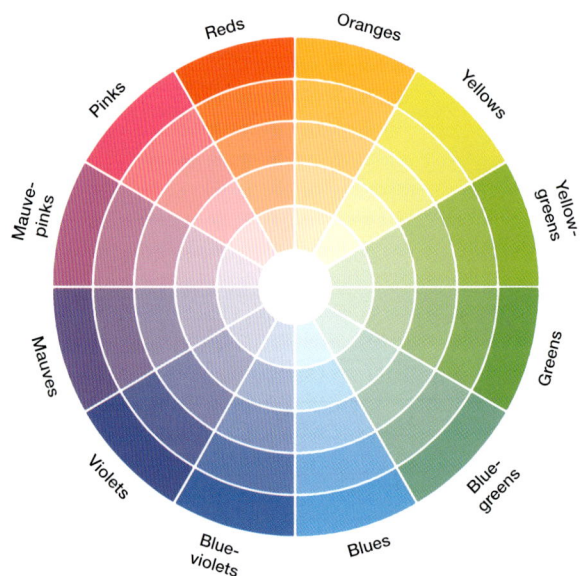

Clockwise from left: a squash flower amid flowering coriander; dill flowers and amaranth; a vertical trellis of runner beans, adding visual interest; complementary blue borage and orange calendula; and mauves and yellow-greens of **Verbena bonariensis** and runner beans.

## HARMONIOUS PLANTING

While contrast is stimulating, harmony is relaxing. Pockets of harmony in the garden form calming corners, which could be located at the ends of key views (see box, opposite) as a warm invitation. Harmony is created by growing a block of either analogous-colored plants or matching leaf textures. Pastel color schemes (like a border of cosmos, or heritage sweet peas) are excellent for creating harmonious displays. Growing delicate-leaved plants together, such as dill, confetti coriander, and chamomile, can also evoke a sense of calm.

## IMPACT PLANTS

Many gardeners have a go-to crop to visually lift any overly green corners of the garden. As well as using pots for pollinators that can be moved around (see p.255), my go-to is amaranth, specifically *Amaranthus cruentus*. This is one of the most stunning plants I know: It adds not only height and color interest but a wonderful texture in the form of its seed heads. Two other highly recommended plants for impact are sunflowers (especially dwarf ) and nasturtiums.

*Enjoying fennel seeds as a garden snack.*

## VIEWS

What are your favorite views of your garden? For me, the view from the tool shed and across the garden to the greenhouse is one of my favorites (below). Knowing your best-loved views will help you implement aspects of visual polyculture in your planting plans. Use red arrows on your garden plan to highlight the key views. When planning visual polyculture, be guided by what combinations excite you the most. If one aspect isn't a success, you can always change it next year.

## VARIETIES

Gardeners have access to more weird and wonderful varieties of crops than ever before: black tomatoes, purple peas, golden beets, and yellow carrots, to name a few. The Internet has made it easy to obtain seeds of stunning varieties that would never exist in the local garden center. Take a look at the suppliers list (see p.281) for recommended seed merchants that offer unusual varieties that will turn heads at harvest time.

# POLYCULTURE POTS

Large pots can be treated as their own self-contained garden in the same way that you can treat garden beds. Ideally, you want pots with a minimum diameter of 16in (40cm) in order to fit a variety of plants.

I would recommend growing only annuals when it comes to polyculture pots, and if you have a balcony and can only grow in pots and containers, perennials should occupy their own.

A simple height order from tallest at the back to lowest at the front is the main design rule for planting up pots. You can space things a little closer than you would in a garden bed, but don't feel tempted to pack in loads of plants really tightly, as they will all end up suppressing the growth of each other, and you will have poor yields as a result.

The limitations of a pot offer a great opportunity to be clever with space. A pot has a very high boundary to growing area ratio, and you can use this to your advantage by encouraging plants to spill over the sides. You can create a small trellis on the north side of the pot for peas and beans to climb up but have this trellis coming out at a slight angle away from the pot. This opens up more space at the lower levels, allowing you a greater choice of crops to grow.

Some annuals are not suited to polyculture pots, as they grow too large or are very hungry and need as much root space as possible. These include wide brassicas, such as cauliflower, as well as potatoes, squash, and non-tumbling tomatoes. The annuals listed below are a good starting point to design your own polyculture pots.

## ANNUALS CROPS FOR POLYCULTURE POTS

| Tall | Medium | Low |
|---|---|---|
| Climbing beans | Borage | Beets |
| Cucumber (trained) | Bulb fennel | Carrot |
| Kale | Calendula | Coriander |
| Peas | Dill | Bush snap beans |
| Sunflower | Leeks | Leafy greens and salads |
| | Perpetual spinach | Nasturtium |
| | Zinnia | Parsley |
| | | Radish |
| | | Spring onion |
| | | Tumbling tomatoes |

*After harvesting new potatoes from tubs, place the soil back in and plant up with other edible crops to make the most of growing food in smaller areas.*

A wild mixed annual planting in a metal container
(above) and a pot for beneficial insects with rudbeckia
as the centerpiece (right).

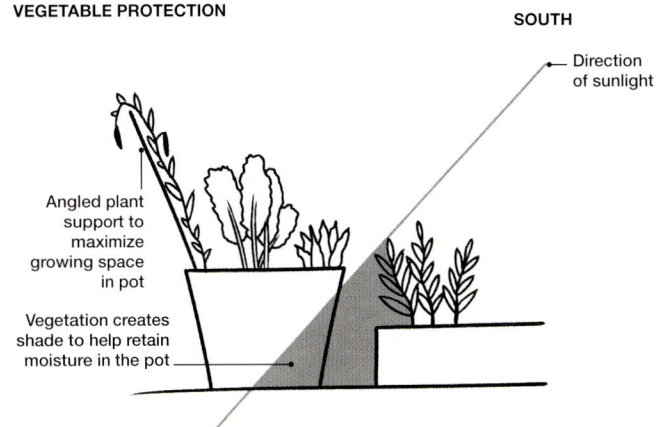

Direction of sunlight

Angled plant support to maximize growing space in pot

Vegetation creates shade to help retain moisture in the pot

*In summer, shade from vegetation is a "yield" that can be used to reduce watering needs.*

## WATERING AND MAINTENANCE

Pots can dry out quickly, particularly if a whole side of the pot is exposed to the sun. One way to mitigate this is to place pots behind low vegetation, which will cast shadow on the side of the pot and reduce evaporation. Mulch is your friend when it comes to growing in pots. Finding shade for your pot, coupled with a 2in (5cm) mulch of grass clippings or semi-decomposed fall leaves, will help keep as much moisture as possible within the pot and keep your plants healthy and stress-free.

I also highly recommend setting up a drip irrigation system if you have more than a handful of pots, to make watering as simple as possible (see pp.92–93). Soil health within a pot is a limiting factor due to there being a very small mass. As a result, pots benefit the most from regular applications of liquid nutritional and biological amendments (see pp.272–273).

## HUW'S TIP

Look out for dwarfing varieties of crops, such as patio runner beans or snap peas, to further extend design possibilities.

## POTS FOR BENEFICIALS

Pots make great mini-islands for biodiversity, and if you choose something like a potato tub, its portability allows you to move the pot to different locations in the garden. Plant up three to five potato tubs with a mix of beneficial insect magnet plants each year, and if you spot a rather green section of the garden, you can move one of the pots to add a pop of color and, of course, encourage beneficial insects into that area.

# A healthy garden

# A STRATEGY FOR HEALTH

Pests have natural predators, including the gardener, while diseases do not and need a preventative approach focusing on microbial diversity. Polyculture helps increase resilience and reduce pest and disease outbreaks.

A permaculture garden needs pests. It's a bold statement and can raise a few eyebrows. Pests are needed for two core reasons: to highlight unhealthy plants and to encourage a strong predator population. Every gardener will also need to deal with diseases.

## HIGHLIGHTING UNHEALTHY PLANTS

Plants are like humans—the healthier they are, the less likely they are to be affected by ailments—but they are not invincible. For example, it's possible for annual vegetable crops to ward off aphids, flea beetles, or caterpillars if they're healthy enough, yet weak plants can eventually succumb to the attack. The process of building soil health in your garden will increase the health and resilience of your plants. Diseases (and pests) are discouraged by growing in polyculture to reduce how easily they spread and by a diversity of microbiology in the soil and on the plant. This is mainly created through healthy soil and by adding microbially rich amendments (see pp.272–273).

## PREDATOR POPULATION

Avoiding chemical pesticides is nonnegotiable, so the alternative is to recruit beneficial insects to act as natural biological control. Predator insects and/or their larvae are one of the core natural services a gardener can use in their quest for an abundant garden. For example, only the larvae of hoverflies eat aphids, not hoverflies themselves, but ladybirds and their larvae both eat aphids. My approach is to plant in a way that encourages the adult forms of these predator insects to the garden (see p.260). The most valuable predators are the larvae of common pollinator insects, such as hoverflies, parasitic wasps, and lacewings. Ladybugs, which indirectly pollinate plants by moving from flower to flower, searching for aphids, have larvae that, at their peak of growth, consume more aphids daily than their adult counterparts. Other beneficial insects, such as ground beetles and spiders, don't pollinate but greatly help with pest control.

Whenever I spot an issue, such as aphids on the tips of roses, I will closely monitor the situation and take action if I feel that the attack is getting out of hand (for more about intervening with specific pests, see pp.262–265). In around 20 percent of scenarios, I will end up taking direct action, but I find that patience often leads to balance. Nature exists in a state of dynamic equilibrium, so whenever there is too much of an imbalance, nature works to self-regulate. A garden can make use of this natural tendency toward equilibrium, but because it is a managed system with intended yields, the gardener will need to take action when necessary.

### Attracting beneficial predators

The strategy for recruiting beneficial predators to your garden is simple: Make your garden a home for wildlife, not just a holiday destination. How is this achieved? Polyculture. When a pest or disease comes across a monoculture consisting of what they like to eat or infect, it's easy for them to damage or destroy all of the crop. In a polyculture, by splitting your crops into smaller groups and planting other crops in and around them, perhaps adding a few flowers and herbs here and there, you create a situation that makes it much harder for a pest or disease to take over because there are living barriers in the way.

To quote a saying that also applies to polycultures: Don't put all your eggs in one basket. One simple way of applying this is to grow one crop in two different parts of your garden. Polyculture reduces risk, improves crop health, and encourages beneficial insects. Polyculture can also give you more time for nature to sort out balance if you do get a pest issue rather than it spreading quickly before predators get a chance to take action. For more detail on polyculture, see pages 228–255.

## BIRDS IN THE GARDEN

Birds are in the unique situation of straddling both the pest and beneficial predator categories, showing how important context is. A blackbird in your strawberry patch is a pest, but when it is eating a snail, it is a friend.

My garden is a patchwork quilt of different perennials and annuals that form a resilient ecosystem.

## RESILIENT AND RESISTANT PLANT VARIETIES

One strategy in a garden to further reduce certain pest and disease issues is to opt for resistant varieties. There is an increasing range of vegetable varieties that show good resilience to common diseases, such as blight-resistant potatoes or clubroot-resistant cabbages. Resistant varieties for pests include carrot varieties that are carrot fly resistant, such as 'Flyaway' and 'Resistafly'. While the vast majority of these resistant varieties are modern hybrids, their taste is still far superior to any shop-bought counterparts. I will always prioritize growing heritage and open-pollinated varieties, but if a modern variety enables the gardener to have a maggot-free carrot or a blight-free outdoor tomato crop versus constant failure, I would opt for success every time.

## WHAT ABOUT CROP ROTATION?

In a nutshell, crop rotation is when crops are grown in plant groups, such as all the roots together, and moved to a new location the following year. They don't return to the same place for another two or three growing seasons. This popular organic gardening technique was originally developed for field-scale growing as a way to reduce a build-up of soil-borne pests and diseases as well as nutrient imbalances.

I haven't followed crop rotation for around 10 years. It is not a pattern that exists in nature. More crucially, when you grow crops in blocks of families, you are creating a form of dynamic monoculture (monoculture that moves location annually). Growing all of your brassicas in one section of the garden, for example, forms a monoculture of brassicas, resulting in an increased risk of all the diseases and pests associated with brassicas causing significant damage.

Provided that you follow succession planting (see p.218), integrate some polyculture planting, and add organic matter to the ground annually, crop rotation is not needed. In the most extreme cases of soil-borne issues, such as cabbage root fly, then just grow your cabbage in a new location the following year. I haven't even mentioned how limiting crop rotation is for planning where to grow your annual crops each year.

259

## BENEFICIAL INSECT MAGNETS

The right flowers will attract beneficial insects to your garden like moths to a flame. Common practice is to plant the perimeters of a garden with these magnets, but I would strongly encourage you to place them throughout the garden. A simple method is to dedicate a few corners or ends of your garden beds for planting as "pollinator islands," enticing beneficial insects to journey through your crops, providing better coverage and protection against pests. You can also plant "pollinator pots," which you can use as mobile magnets for areas that may be lacking flowers. The perimeters of a garden are a great place to let wild/native plants for beneficial insects grow, such as a patch of nettles, which are the food source for a range of butterfly caterpillars and are popular hunting grounds for ladybugs.

The flowers of the following plants are the most powerful beneficial insect magnets. I have divided them into my top annuals, biennials, and perennials to help with deciding what to grow and where.

Aim to integrate as many different umbelliferous flowers as possible within your garden. The umbrella-like flowers of such plants as carrot, dill, and parsley offer easy-to-access nectar and pollen for numerous beneficial insects. Joshua Sparkes, a farmer experimenting with natural farming techniques in North Devon, UK, adds one aromatic herb in every vegetable bed to encourage beneficial insects, and dill is one of his popular choices.

> "A study in the 1960s found that more than 300 insect species visited carrot flowers—if that doesn't make you grow umbellifers, I don't know what will!"

## A THRIVING GARDEN CHECKLIST

If you aim to check off as much of this checklist as possible every growing season, you will be well on your way to having a thriving and resilient garden.

- Continue to actively work on improving long-term soil health.
- Mix annual herbs and flowers with your vegetable plantings.
- Allow some of your vegetable crops to flower.
- Grow staple crops in more than one location when possible.
- Leave a patch of nettles and wild grasses to grow.
- Let your perennial herbs flower.
- Succession plant whenever possible (see p.218).

| Annuals | Biennials | Perennials |
|---|---|---|
| Borage | Bulb fennel | Angelica |
| Calendula | Carrot | Bergamot |
| Coriander | Foxglove | Catnip |
| Cosmos | Leek | Chives and garlic chives |
| Dill | Parsley | Echinacea |
| Marigold | Parsnip | Herb fennel |
| Nasturtium | | Mint |
| Phacelia | | Oxeye daisy |
| Sunflower | | *Verbena bonariensis* |
| Zinnia | | Yarrow |

*Clockwise from top left: Bumblebees, butterflies, honeybees, and hoverflies are the most common pollinators in my kitchen garden.*

# PEST SOLUTIONS

There will be times when pest trouble will get out of hand, and you will need to take action. I have tried and tested many natural solutions over the years, and here I share the ones that have consistently made the biggest difference.

## SLUGS AND SNAILS

Perhaps the most famous permaculture quote of all time is "You don't have a snail (or slug) problem, you have a duck deficiency!" which is often attributed to Bill Mollison. One of the big challenges, particularly in the damp, humid climate of the UK, is that there isn't a native predator (apart from frogs) that targets slugs efficiently. While some birds and opossums target them, they are more opportunistic eaters, and there are many things more palatable than a slug. The Khaki Campbell and Indian Runner ducks are the most effective slug and snail predators that a gardener can use. If your kitchen garden is surrounded by a duck run (see p.237), in a similar fashion to a moat, you will be well on your way to a low-slug growing experience.

### Slug hunting

The next most effective option is to do slug hunts in the evening from an hour after dusk, when slugs become most active. This takes time and is easier done with another person, but I have not yet found a better way to prevent seedlings from disappearing overnight. From my experience, doing a slug hunt every third night stablizes slug damage.

### Nematodes

The next option is to purchase slug nematodes. This is a living biological amendment that is highly effective, providing protection for up to six weeks. Nematodes are microscopic worm-like organisms that have a diverse range of roles. Some nematodes exclusively target slugs without affecting any other

## THINK LIKE A SLUG

To help successful slug hunts, or if you can't go out on one of the evenings, put down items that they will hide under during the day. The Victorians used rhubarb leaves for this (right, and p.138), but sheets of cardboard (far right), planks, large containers, paving stones, and tarpaulins all work. The day before, lay these down around the garden, and the following morning, turn them over to pick off all the slugs.

*By hanging mesh shelving from a polytunnel, I can raise seedlings without worry of slug damage or rodent attacks.*

life, which is exactly what the nematodes available to purchase (Nemaslug) offer. Ideally apply Nemaslug every six to eight weeks, starting in mid-March through to mid-fall.

There are recipes out there claiming that you can make your own slug nematodes, but this is incredibly unpredictable, and considering how complex a process it is to create effective concentrations of active nematodes, the investment is worth the security of knowing that it will work.

### Seedling size

Small seedlings are far more vulnerable to slug and snail damage (or overnight decimation) compared to larger seedlings. If you suffer from slug issues, direct sowing may be a greater challenge for this reason. I've found that by starting seedlings in modules and growing them until they have four or five true leaves, they will fare much better than being put out right after the first set of true leaves has appeared. To have even more resilient seedlings, pot them into 2¾in (7cm) or 5in (1 liter) pots on shelving. I would prioritize your staple crops for this technique rather than using up all the shelving space for spinach seedlings!

### Slug pellets

Organic gardening–approved ferric phosphate slug pellets (a compound of phosphorous, oxygen, and iron) can be used as a last resort for the most severe slug damage. Pet- and wildlife-friendly, they can be applied very sparsely around plants.

## BIRDS

The only true way to protect crops from birds is to cover crops with netting. You can grow soft fruits in a fruit cage (see p.126). Many kits are available to gardeners for frames and netting for raised beds (see p.276). You can also add visual repellents, such as hanging up CDs, which spin and reflect light.

*For smaller raised beds and pots, covering strawberries (and other soft fruits) with organza bags prevents birds from eating them.*

## APHIDS, BLACKFLY, AND WHITEFLY

These sap-sucking insects target the most tender growing tips of both annuals and perennials. Blackfly are a common sight on the tops of fava beans and seem to appear overnight! To prevent blackfly, pinch off the growing tip when the fava beans start flowering. In any other case, when you spot these insects, a strong jet of water is an effective way to knock them off. You can also make a natural soap spray (see p.273) for the most severe cases, which does not affect beneficial insects. Spray any affected areas generously, including the underside of the leaves, and repeat if the problem persists.

## CABBAGE WHITE CATERPILLARS

There are two types of cabbage white caterpillars: the large and the small white. Typically, the large white caterpillars (yellow and black) cause the biggest nuisance, but small whites are much harder to identify due to being completely green. Look for yellow eggs on brassica leaves and pick off any caterpillars you find. If you have chickens, they will be most happy! The other option is to grow brassicas under butterfly-proof netting —but make sure that the leaves don't touch the netting, as the butterflies can still lay eggs!

## RABBITS

If you have rabbits, the only effective option is to create a rabbit-proof boundary around your garden. You will need strong rabbit-proof wire, as rabbits can gnaw through weaker chicken wire. A typical fence is no match, as they can burrow underneath. Depending on what tools you have at your disposal and the type of soil you have, there are two options to prevent burrowing. The first is to bury the rabbit wire 12in (30cm) deep vertically into the ground. The easier option is to fold a 1ft (30cm) lip of wire at the base of the fence, extending away from the garden, and cover it with a light layer of soil. Rabbits want to dig up against the boundary and will meet wire—they won't know to start digging from over a foot away.

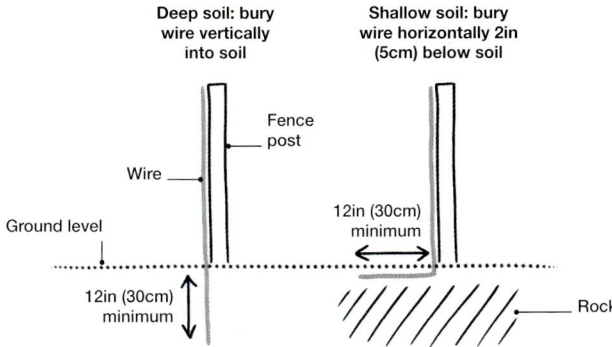

**Rabbit-proofing a fence**
*Wire needs to be buried vertically or horizontally to make a barrier to digging.*

## CARROT ROOT FLY

Carrot root flies typically fly less than 2ft (60cm) from the ground. The simplest option is to grow carrots in taller raised beds. If this isn't possible, either grow under insect-proof mesh or choose varieties resistant to carrot root fly.

## CABBAGE ROOT FLY

Cabbage root flies are one of the most damaging pests, but there are some simple ways to prevent them. If I begin to have issues with them, I am more cautious in the following growing seasons. The adult flies lay eggs in the soil by the base of the brassica stem; the larvae eat the roots. One popular organic technique is to purchase or make collars (6in/15cm diameter) to go around the base of your stemmed brassicas. I have found rubber to be the best material for homemade collars. Mulching is another option, as it is harder for the adults to access the soil. There are also nematodes to buy that target cabbage root fly.

## FLEA BEETLES

Flea beetles target brassica seedlings and are particularly bad during dry weather. They create lots of little holes in the leaves of the seedlings, severely affecting their growth due to reduced photosynthesis. In most cases, the seedlings can get through this stage, but direct sown brassicas are most vulnerable in the late spring to early summer, so start in modules to prevent issues.

## LEEK MOTH

These affect onions, garlic, and leeks. The caterpillars tunnel through and eat foliage, stems, and bulbs; affected leeks rot quickly. The only effective solution for leek moths is to grow these alliums under a permanent insect-proof mesh.

## GETTING A BALANCE

In harder-to-eradicate cases, such as leek moth and cabbage root fly, focusing on polyculture and recruiting beneficial insects are what I've found to be the best ways of greatly reducing damage without having to cover most of my garden in netting and mesh, which is rather unsightly. It's important for me to have the right predators to allow nature to always work toward that balance between predator and prey.

# DISEASE SOLUTIONS

Some disease is unavoidable and isn't always a death sentence. Rust often appears on my leeks in the fall but has gone by the winter. Blight, on the other hand, is a disease I do not wish to see, as once you have it, very little can be done.

Diseases are often harder to eradicate through active control, unlike many pests, so prevention is the best strategy. Keep going with regular applications of biological amendments to help outpopulate the pathogens (see pp.272–273), and of course, improve soil health (see pp.46–81) and grow crops in polycultures wherever possible (see pp.228–255).

## BLIGHT

Blight is the worst garden disease, a fungus-like organism that affects tomatoes and potatoes. There are two types. Early blight causes small brown spots on leaves, starting on the oldest of the leaves. The best strategy is to remove any affected leaves, and in most cases, although the plant may weaken, you can still get a good crop. Late blight is far more severe, causing dark brown rot lesions in stems and leaves and then rotting the potato tubers and tomato fruits. Outdoor tomatoes are at an increased risk of late blight compared to undercover, so choose resistant varieties where possible. Undercover tomatoes need plenty of air flow around each plant to prevent stagnant conditions.

## RUST

This disease causes rust-like spots on alliums and legumes, which can reduce photosynthesis and, as a result, vigor. In some cases, rust can take hold and severely affect a harvest, such as garlic. I've found that growing a handful of different garlic varieties in two or three spots around the garden always brings me success. If you grow garlic faster by using hoop beds, you can harvest earlier, before rust can get underway.

## POWDERY MILDEW

Powdery mildew has a white, powdery appearance on leaves and affects peas, some root vegetables, and some cucurbits. Like rust, it reduces photosynthesis and, therefore, vigor of plants. When you first spot powdery mildew, you should cut off any affected leaves and apply LAB (see p.273) every few days. There is an increasing number of resistant varieties available.

## DOWNY MILDEW

This disease affects peas, lettuces, brassicas, and cucurbits, causing leaf discoloration, with the underside of leaves showing gray or purple mold. Remove any affected leaves, and for undercover situations, avoid watering in the evening, as extended moisture on leaves can increase the risk of infection.

## CLUBROOT

This disease affects brassicas, causing stunted growth and distorting the roots. It is a serious soil-borne disease, meaning it can stay in your soil for many years. Growing brassicas in a different location annually is a way to prevent buildup, and you need to keep working on soil health. If you do have clubroot-affected soils, opt for resistant varieties or grow your brassica seedlings in larger pots (5–7in/1–2 liter size) of compost to a semi-mature stage before planting so they get a head start.

## WHAT TO DO WITH DISEASED MATERIALS?

There is a hot debate about whether you should or shouldn't compost diseased materials. My approach is to compost almost all diseased materials. This is because the composting process—even cold composting—can deal with the majority of pathogens and spores. Powdery mildew, for example, overwinters either on living plant tissue or on fallen leaves. Composting solves this, but the key is to bury any diseased material into a compost bin rather than let it sit on the top. For clubroot and blight, burn the affected/infected parts of the plant—such as the roots for clubroot—and compost the rest.

# FROST PROTECTION

Frost impacts tender plants by causing the water inside plant cells to freeze, expanding and thus damaging the cell wall. These plants, and others, need frost protection.

The last and first frosts mark the growing window of each year. The average last and first frosts are the greatest influence in terms of my timing for sowing and transplanting. The downside of being an "average" is that the goalposts change each season: Your last frost could occur a few weeks earlier or later than the average, resulting in the need for a "buffer" zone to ensure that you and your plants don't miss your window.

Tender plants, which will be killed or severely damaged by frost, are not the only crops to look out for. The blossoms of fruit trees, such as apples, are also tender—a late frost can severely affect orchard production for an entire growing season. The benefit of trees being on a stem is that the blossoms will be better protected from ground frosts.

Young plants tend to be less frost-resilient than mature ones, and repeat freezing and thawing can damage even hardy plants, which is partly why a hardy crop like beets overwintered undercover versus outdoors retains much better quality.

## THE 39-DEGREE RULE
The first step to protect your plants from frost is by keeping an eye on the weather forecast around your average frost dates. Whenever an evening temperature is forecast to be 39°F (4°C) or below, I make sure all of my tender annuals are protected; I close the hoop beds, place biodegradable fleece over plantings, and bring peppers indoors, for example. To get an approximate snapshot for the next couple of weeks, I use the website AccuWeather, which works worldwide.

## TUCK UP AND CLOSE THE DOOR
The two most common frost-protection techniques involve shutting any ventilation of undercover growing structures and placing a layer of insulation over any outdoor crops. Biodegradable fleece is the best insulation option, with some offering protection down to 23°F (-5°C). This fleece can also be wrapped around small fruit trees to protect their blossoms, but take care to prevent the fleece from ripping.

Early season plantings will benefit from a permanent layer of lightweight fleece for the first three or four weeks to raise the ambient temperature. Use hoops to create temporary low-profile hoop houses to drape fleece over and weigh down either side with stones, bricks, or logs.

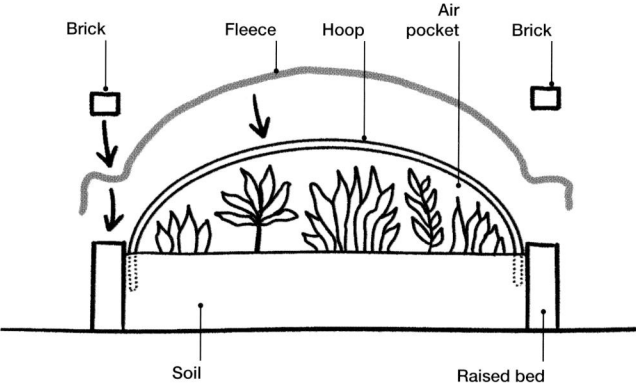

**Lightweight fleece covering**
*For maximum insulation, aim to have only a small space between leaf and fleece, creating a small pocket of warmer air.*

The last frosts of the season tend to be light, but in the event of a very hard frost, such as 25 or 27°F (-3 or -4°C), double up polytunnel protection by also adding fleece over plants and double up fleece on outdoor crops. You may need to add some supports to prevent the heavier application of fleece from pressing down on your plants, especially with the added weight of morning dew. It is always better to overprotect in case temperatures drop further than forecast.

## HARDENING OFF

Hardening off (see p.183) helps reduce the shock of outdoor conditions for tender crops raised in the comfort of a polytunnel or on a sunny indoor windowsill. While a frost is going to damage a squash plant whether it is hardened off or not, a hardened squash will fare much better during cold nights and under frost protection.

## THE POWER OF PATIENCE

Although this is very difficult for gardeners (especially me) to do at the start of a new growing season, the simplest way to reduce the chances of frost damage is to not put yourself in a risky situation in the first place. Patience holds so much power when it comes to panic-free gardening, and late sowings always have a tendency to catch up! Of course you will need to start off your tomatoes before your last frost, but maybe hold back on the squash?

## FIRST FROST

As your average first frost date approaches, keep an eye on the forecast. It is up to you to make the decision of whether you want to protect your tender crops. If not, do a final harvest the day prior to a forecast frost to ensure that the edible part of the crop does not get damaged. I will only protect crops from a first frost if there is an expected early frost, but from October onward, I am happy to let nature take its course.

## HOT BEDS

Do not forget to make use of hot beds (see pp.60–61) to enjoy early sowings in a frost-free environment as well as to create a place to keep tender seedlings warm on cold nights. If you are in colder growing zones, such as 4 or 5 (see p.32), when making a hot bed, use a row of straw bales as the walls to insulate the bed and maintain consistent heat output, even if temperatures fall to -4˚F (-20˚C).

*Hardy winter crops don't need protecting from the first frosts, unlike more tender plants, saving you time and providing harvests over winter.*

# Practical information

# RECIPES FOR AMENDMENTS

On these pages are recipes for all the liquid amendments mentioned in the book. Dilute them as recommended before use.

These amendments all need to be diluted with water before application. If possible, use rainwater. If you only have access to mains water, which contains chlorine that will kill biological life, you can let a vessel of mains water sit for 24 hours for the chlorine to naturally dissipate. These liquid amendments can all be applied by a watering can. Lactic acid bacteria (LAB) can be added to the soil via a watering can or for the purpose of mitigating disease issues.

For applying LAB to leaves, you can use a hand-held or pressure sprayer. This is also a good method for nutritional amendments, such as the diluted concentrate or worm tea, as plant leaves can take up nutrients faster than the roots.

## WEED FEED

The simplest amendment of them all. Throw together a bunch of weeds, including grass, dock, thistle, nettle, and dandelion in a bucket, roughly chop up, top up with water, and then cover with a lid. An optional extra is to add a handful of leaf mold to the top of the bucket to encourage diverse biology to help decomposition. Leave it for two weeks and then start using the liquid on your plants. A multi-ingredient approach will ensure a diverse spectrum of nutrients. You can use the same approach for just a single plant input if you want specific nutrients, such as grass for a nitrogen-rich feed. This technique also works for a homemade comfrey feed for your fruiting crops. As you use the liquid, top it up with additional plant matter and water for a continuous supply.

**Type of amendment** Nutritional

**Dilution ratio** 1:20

**When to use** Every 2–3 weeks, particularly during flowering and fruiting

**Storage** 1+ year

## CONCENTRATE

Pack an empty barrel, dustbin, or large bucket with comfrey, dock, or nettle leaves. Place a few heavy stones on top of the leaves to act as weights and loosely place a lid over the top. After around six months, the plant matter will have broken down into a thick, dark syrup-like concentrate (above) that you can use as a liquid feed. The benefit of this over a weed feed is that there won't be bad odors.

**Type of amendment** Nutritional

**Dilution ratio** 1:50

**When to use** Every 2–3 weeks, particularly during flowering and fruiting

**Storage** 1 year (glass jar with lid)

## WORM TEA

The worm tea collected from a worm bin (above) makes for an excellent liquid amendment. A worm bin can provide a steady supply throughout the year.

**Type of amendment** Nutritional (some biological benefits)

**Dilution ratio** 1:10

**When to use** Every 2–3 weeks, particularly during flowering and fruiting

**Storage** Use immediately after tapping the worm bin

## MAKING SOAP SPRAY

Soap spray isn't an amendment but a treatment for aphids. Here is how to make it. Use 100 percent natural dishwashing liquid mixed with water at a ratio of about ¼fl oz (5–10ml) of dishwashing liquid to ¼ gallon (1 liter) of water. Place it in a spray bottle and generously spray affected areas.

## JADAM MICROBIAL SOLUTION (JMS)

This is an excellent amendment to improve the biology and structure of poor soils and to kick-start soil life for a new growing season. Make it where you are to use it; for example, if it is for your polytunnel beds, keep the bucket in your polytunnel. This is to encourage the correct microbes that suit the temperature of the growing location. In a jute bag, large cotton sock, or a stocking leg, add two well-boiled potatoes and mash together. The starch of the potatoes is what will feed the microbes. Then, add a handful of leaf mold from under a deciduous tree (this is to inoculate the solution with native biological life). Place the bag or sock into a bucket of 20–40 gallons (70–150 liters) of rainwater. Rub and squish the sock contents in the water until the water clouds. Loosely place a lid on top and leave for two to four days. Once you see a mass of white foam/bubbles on the surface, often forming a ring, the amendment is ready to be used. Mix in a teaspoon of sea salt to add some mineral supplementation. Note that a warmer ambient temperature is required to make JMS, so during the cooler weather in the early spring, outdoor creations of JMS may take several more days for the foam to appear.

**Type of amendment** Biological

**Dilution ratio** 1:20 for planted areas, 1:10 for bare ground

**When to use** Early spring through to mid-fall

**Storage** Use within 12–24 hours

## LACTIC ACID BACTERIA (LAB)

LAB is used to speed up composting and improve soil health and can be applied to plant leaves to prevent disease issues and help defend against outbreaks. Place unwashed organic white basmati rice in a sieve over bowl A and pour 1 pint (500ml) of water over it. Get bowl B and place the sieve on this empty bowl. Pour the rice water from bowl A over the rice, so bowl B catches the water. Keep moving the sieve between bowls, pouring the water over the rice and using the bowls to capture it, doing this around 15 times, until the water is very cloudy. Use the rice for cooking. Place the cloudy rice water in a glass jar, put a paper towel over the top, secured with a band, and leave in an ambient place undercover away from direct light for three to five days. Once a scum has formed and the water smells like old water from a vase of flowers, pour this into a larger jar with organic whole milk. The rice water should be around 1:5 ratio with the milk. Use the paper towel lid again for this larger jar and leave at room temperature out of direct sunlight for around five days, by which time the "curds" and "whey" will have separated. Compost the curds on the top, and the resulting liquid left over is a highly concentrated liquid of lactic acid bacteria.

**Type of amendment** Biological

**Dilution ratio** 1:1000

**When to use** Throughout the growing season to keep plants and soil healthy; weekly on plants showing the first signs of disease

**Storage** 2 months in a fridge

# HOW TO MAKE A HOT BED WITH COLD FRAME

To make a hot bed, you need to make an outer frame and fill it with hot compost and a growing medium before placing the cold frame on top to retain the heat. For more about the materials to use to fill a hot bed, see page 61.

### You will need

Letters correspond to lengths of wood, as shown on the diagram opposite. Use wood 1in (2.5cm) thick; it will help retain heat and last longer.

### For the cold frame

1 plank 45x4in (115x10cm) for F+G

2 planks 43x4in (110x10cm) for H+I

2 planks 45x8in (115x20cm) for C+D

2 planks 47x8in (120x20cm) for A+B

1 plank 47x4in (120x10cm) for E

4 pegs: 2 12in (30cm) (J); 2 ¾x8in (2x20cm) (K), made from 2x2in (5x5cm) wood

2in (4–5cm) stainless steel screws

2 galvanized U-nails (staples)

### For each light

2 51in (130cm) lengths of 2x2in (5x5cm) wood

2 20in (50cm) lengths of 2x2in (5x5cm) wood

1 plank 16x2in (40x5cm)

2 thin planks 24x2in (60x5cm)

2 thin planks 43x2in (110x5cm)

1 sheet of 32x79in (80x200cm) polytunnel plastic

3in (8cm) stainless steel screws

2in (5cm) stainless steel screws

### For the outer frame

Pallets, fence panels, and posts, or other lengths of scrap wood to create a 60x60in (150x150cm) box

3in (8cm) stainless steel screws

Cardboard

### Tools

Bungee cord

Saw

Drill

Screwdriver

Hammer

Scissors or utility knife

**LIGHT AND COLD FRAME**

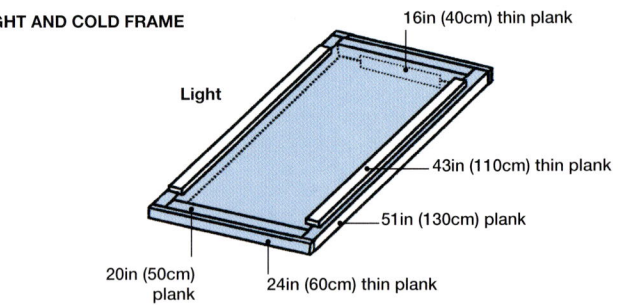

Light

16in (40cm) thin plank

43in (110cm) thin plank

51in (130cm) plank

20in (50cm) plank

24in (60cm) thin plank

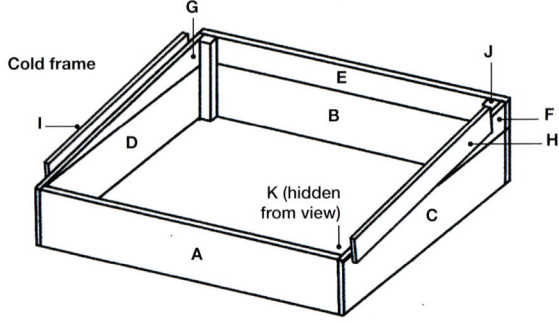

Cold frame

G

J

E

B

I

D

F

H

K (hidden from view)

C

A

## BUILDING A COLD FRAME

**1.** Cut the plank for F and G diagonally to create two triangles.
**2.** Create the base of the growing frame by screwing the two 8in (20cm) pegs (K) to either end of plank A, and the two taller 12in (30cm) pegs (J) to either end of plank B.
**3.** Attach each end of planks C and D to the pegs you screwed to planks A and B to make a rectangular frame.
**4.** Screw each end of plank E to one of the 12in (30cm) taller pegs at the back.
**5.** Screw the short edge of each triangular piece of wood, F and G, to the taller 12in (30cm) pegs. Measure 4in (10cm) in from the narrowest end of each and attach a screw down into the plank below to secure.
**6.** Screw planks H and I to the sloping sides at the same slant and with a 2in (5cm) lip above, 1in (2.5cm) in from either end.
**7.** Hammer in a U-nail just in from the top end at the midpoint of plank C to form an eye for the bungee cord. Hammer in another U-nail in the corresponding position on the outside of plank D.

## MAKING THE LIGHTS

**1.** Attach the two 20in (50cm) 2x2in (5x5cm) lengths to both ends of the two 51in (130cm) 2x2in (5x5cm) lengths using the 3in (8cm) screws to make a rectangle.
**2.** Screw the smaller 16in (40cm) plank onto the inside of one of the 20in (50cm) 2x2in (5x5cm) sections so that half of its width protrudes, using the 2in (5cm) screws. This acts as a lip to keep the light from sliding down the growing frame.
**3.** With the lip on the underside, lay the polytunnel plastic on top so there is an equal overhang of plastic at each end.
**4.** Place the thin 24in (60cm) plank at the very top of the plastic sheet (the lip end), pull the plastic sheet around it and roll it up and around four or five times toward you. Then, screw the plank flush with the outer edge of the 20in (50cm) 2x2in (5x5cm), using 2in (5cm) screws at equal spacings.

**5.** Place the second thin 24in (60cm) plank at the other end of the plastic sheet and roll it up, as before. The plastic will tighten as you move toward the 20in (50cm) 2x2in (5x5cm), but give it an extra turn or two so the sheet is as taut as possible. Now, screw the plank to the outer edge of the 20in (50cm) 2x2in (5x5cm) using 2in (5cm) screws at equal spacings.
**6.** To keep the long sides of the plastic in place, screw two 43in (110cm) planks along the top of both the 51in (130cm) planks (lip is still underneath), using 2in (5cm) screws at equal spacings. Trim off the excess plastic.
**7.** Repeat the process for the second light.
**8.** Place both lights directly on top of the cold frame. They should fit snugly.

## MAKING THE OUTER FRAME AND ADDING FILLING

**1.** Use pallets, fence panels, or other lengths of wood to create a 60x60in (150x150cm) frame, leaving one side open. Driving in fence posts and attaching each side is usually the simplest way to make a strong structure.
**2.** Place a thick layer of cardboard at the base to act as bottom insulation.
**3.** Start to fill the frame with the material. Alternate between the green and brown materials for every forkful or bucketful.
**4.** After a layer of mixed materials around 6in (15cm) deep is added, water with a couple of watering cans (about 3–6 gallons/20–30 liters) and walk over or firmly pat down the material. Reducing air spaces helps create low-and-slow heat generation.
**5.** Once the material has reached your target height, add a 6in (15cm) layer of growing medium on top. This could be a mix of topsoil and compost and is what you will direct sow in. Water thoroughly once more.
**6.** Wait two days for temperatures to settle before placing the cold frame on top and sowing.

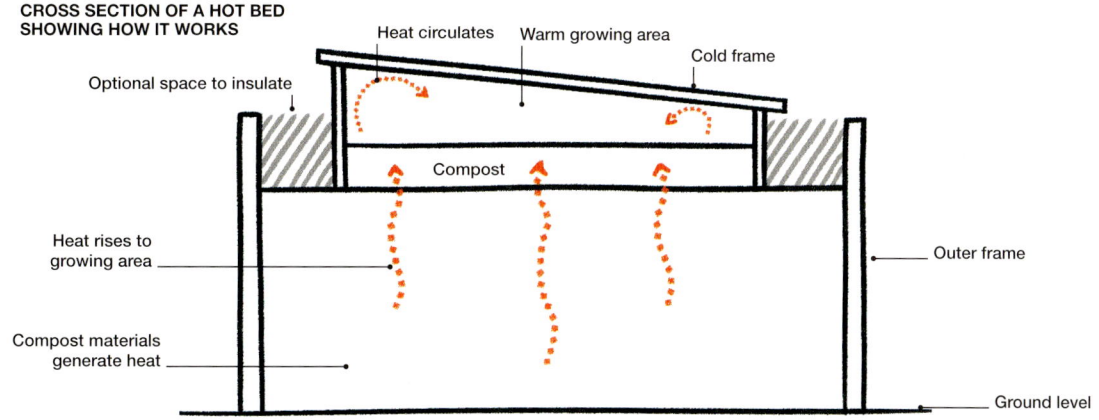

CROSS SECTION OF A HOT BED SHOWING HOW IT WORKS

Heat circulates — Warm growing area — Cold frame — Optional space to insulate — Compost — Outer frame — Heat rises to growing area — Compost materials generate heat — Ground level

# HOW TO BUILD A RAISED BED WITH HINGED HOOP

Hoop beds are essentially raised beds with a "hoop house," a mini-polytunnel, on top. They are filled in the same way as any raised beds.

The method shared here is to make a 10ft (3m) x 4ft (1.2m) hoop bed, which perfectly fits my raised beds, but you can adjust the width and length to suit your beds if you already have some assembled. First, you need to build a simple but durable wooden raised bed, which the hoop element will attach to.

## BUILDING A RAISED BED

This is my go-to way of building wooden raised beds for growing vegetables, flowers, and herbs. This is a guideline to help you have more flexibility when searching for wooden boards and screws.

### You will need

2 118in (300cm) lengths of wooden board 1¼–2in (3–5cm) thick

2 47in (120cm) lengths of wooden board, 1¼–2in (3–5cm) thick

12 3–4in (8–10cm) wood screws

### Tools

Electric drill

2¾in (7cm) drill bit suited to your screw diameter

Screwdriver drill bit

**1.** First, prepare your workspace. Choose a flat, stable surface to assemble your raised bed. Ensure that you have all the tools and materials ready.
**2.** Position the 47in (120cm) boards between the ends of the two 118in (300cm) boards to form a rectangular shape. Ensure that the shorter boards are sandwiched inside the longer boards, aligning their edges evenly.

**3.** Using your 2¾in (7cm) drill bit, drill three evenly spaced pilot holes at each end of the 118in (300cm) boards, into the ends of the 47in (120cm) boards. These pilot holes will help prevent the wood from splitting when screws are inserted and will ensure a strong join.
**4.** Switch to the screwdriver drill bit. Insert the 3–4in (8–10cm) screws, one through each drilled hole in the 118in (300cm) boards, securing them to the ends of the 47in (120cm) boards. Make sure the corners are flush and square.
**5.** Move to the other end of the bed and repeat the process with the other 47in board. Once complete, you have a raised bed frame ready to move to its final position. For different options to fill the raised bed, see pages 108–109.

**RAISED BED**

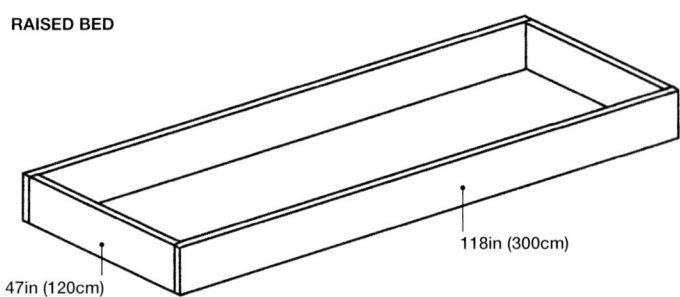

47in (120cm)

118in (300cm)

## MAKING AND ATTACHING A HOOP

### You will need

3 118in (300cm) lengths of 2x3in (5x8cm) timber

2 47in (120cm) lengths of 2x3in (5x8cm) timber

2 24in (60cm) lengths of 2x3in (5x8cm) timber

2 118in (300cm) lengths of 1x2in (2.5cm x 5cm) roofing batten

8 118in (300cm) lengths of 1in-thick (25mm) MDPE pipe

3 stainless steel door hinges

16ft (5m) x 11½ft (3.5m) UV plastic sheeting

3in (8cm) stainless steel screws

1½in (4cm) stainless steel screws

95in (240cm) total length of thin wood strips (any lengths)

Nails (longer than the wood strips)

### Tools

Hammer

Wood saw

Tape measure

Pencil

Drill

1in (25mm) drill bit

1. Assemble all the materials and tools, cutting timber to the correct size if necessary. Check to make sure the frame will fit flush with the raised bed and adjust lengths if needed.
2. Make the frame by laying the two 118in (300cm) timbers and the two 47in (120cm) timbers on a flat surface to form a rectangle. With the wider sides of the wood facing upward, use 3in (8cm) screws to join the corners together securely.
3. Stand the two 24in (60cm) timbers vertically at the mid-point of each narrow end of the rectangle. With the wider side of the wood facing outward, use 3in screws to attach each firmly to the frame, directly on top in the center. To complete the frame, screw the third 118in (300cm) length of timber to the two uprights and ensure that it is flush with the top.
4. Use 1½in (4cm) screws to fix the two hinges, one at 39in (100cm) and the other at 79in (2m), along the long side of the hoop structure. Now, attach the hinges to the long side of the raised bed.

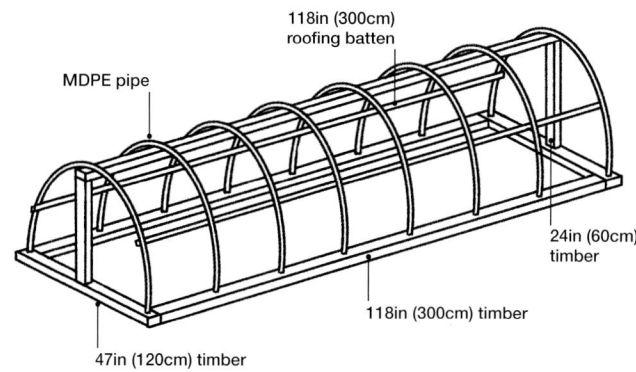

118in (300cm) roofing batten

MDPE pipe

24in (60cm) timber

118in (300cm) timber

47in (120cm) timber

5. Before fitting the lengths of pipe for the hoops, make eight holes along each 118in (300cm) side of the frame, using the 1in (25mm) drill bit. Drill a hole approx 2in (5cm) from each end and then space the remaining six holes around 17in (42cm) apart.
6. Insert the eight 118in (300cm) lengths of pipe into the holes and bend over the frame to create a hoop. The first hoop may need to be trimmed to the ideal length so that it bends nicely over the wooden frame, and you can cut the other seven hoops to the same length as needed to create hoops over the frames. Screw through the top of the frame and the pipe to hold the hoops firmly in place.
7. Now, attach each 118in (300cm) length of roofing batten halfway up each hooped side to strengthen the frame. Ensure that the batten is on the inside of the hoops and runs lengthwise, then attach it by screwing through the pipes.
8. To attach the plastic cover, first lay the sheet over the hoop frame, ensuring that all sides are equal. Next, nail each of the thin wood strips to the plastic along both sides and around both ends so it's securely attached all the way around the base of the frame. You can also roll the thin wood strips a few times around the plastic to help pull the plastic taut, and it will reduce the chance of the plastic tearing when you nail the wooden strips in place. It may be easier to work with a partner as you move around the hoop house, pulling the plastic taut as you go.

# RESOURCES

## BOOKS

*The Plant Lover's Backyard Forest Garden: Trees, Fruit and Veg in Small Spaces*, Pippa Chapman (2022)

*The Fermentation Kitchen*, Sam Cooper (2024)

*How to Grow Perennial Vegetables,* Martin Crawford (2012)

*Creating a Forest Garden*, Martin Crawford (2010)

*Hotbeds: How to Grow Early Crops Using an Age-Old Technique,* Jack First (2013)

*The Living Soil Handbook*, Jesse Frost (2021)

*From What Is to What If: Unleashing the Power of Imagination to Create the Future We Want*, Rob Hopkins (2019)

*Landrace Gardening: Food Security through Biodiversity and Promiscuous Pollination*, Joseph Lofthouse (2021)

*The Regenerative Grower's Guide to Garden Amendments*, Nigel Palmer (2020)

*The Woodchip Handbook*, Ben Raskin (2021)

*The Self-Sufficiency Garden: Feed Your Family and Save Money,* Huw Richards and Sam Cooper (2024)

*The Vegetable Grower's Handbook: Unearth Your Garden's Full Potential*, Huw Richards (2022)

*Small Is Beautiful: Economics as If People Mattered,* E. F. Schumacher (1973)

*JADAM Organic Farming*, Youngsang Cho (2016)

*The Earth Care Manual: A Permaculture Handbook for Britain and Other Temperate Climates*, Patrick Whitefield (2016)

## MAPPING AND PLANNING
Satellite imagery earth.google.com
Position of the sun suncalc.org
Hardiness and frost dates plantmaps.com

## USEFUL AND INTERESTING WEBSITES
Marcher Apple Network marcherapple.net
Permaculture Association permaculture.org.uk
Plants for a Future pfaf.org

## YOUTUBE CHANNELS
Andrew Millison
David the Good
Edible Acres
Freedom Forest Life
Discover Permaculture with Geoff Lawton
Happen Films
Liz Zorab – Byther Farm
Niall Gardens
Self Sufficient Me
Tap o' Noth Permaculture – a Food Forest Farm

# SUPPLIERS

**COMPOST**
Dalefoot compost
Melcourt compost

**POLYTUNNELS AND GREENHOUSES**
First Tunnels
The Greenhouse People
Polycrub

**VERY USEFUL HORTICULTURE BRANDS**
Containerwise
EverEdge
Gardena
Gardening Naturally
Mulch Organic
Vego Garden
Wormcity

**SEEDS**
Alma Proust
Chiltern Seeds
Kings Seeds
Premier Seeds Direct
Real Seeds
She Grows Veg
Tamar Organic
Vital Seeds
Wales Seed Hub

**PLANTS**
David Austin Roses
Farmyard Nurseries
Frank P. Matthews
Incredible Vegetables
Sarah Raven
Seven Acres Permaculture Plant Nursery
Urban Herbs

# INDEX

Main crop entries are indicated with **bold** page numbers.

# ACKNOWLEDGMENTS

**AUTHOR ACKNOWLEDGMENTS**

First and foremost, I wish to thank my publishers, DK, for supporting me in creating a book on permaculture, and for trusting me and my passion for this way of producing food. As a result, it has been my most enjoyable project yet, and I feel very grateful for that. I particularly want to thank my managing editor, Ruth, for listening to my many perspectives and opinions on things and being a real advocate for this book concept; to my design team, Glenda and Christine, for making this book beautiful; and to my editor, Lucy, for being so patient, thorough, and all-out brilliant!

A big part of this book is, of course, the photography, and I had the utter pleasure of spending one day a month for over two years working again with the incredibly talented Jason Ingram. I would also like to thank my close friend and colleague (and fellow author) Sam Cooper, who has been my sounding board, brainstorming partner, and thought provoker through much of this process. Finally, none of this would exist without the amazing people who decide to spend their precious time watching my videos—I am deeply honored by your support.

**PUBLISHER ACKNOWLEDGMENTS**

DK would like to thank Jo Whittingham for sample copyedits, Newman and Eastwood Ltd for styling, John Tullock for consulting on the US edition, Kathy Steer for proofreading, Ruth Ellis for indexing, Steve Crozier for repro, Dan Crisp for assistance with illustrations, and Izzy Poulson and Noor Ali for design assistance.